Buy and Hold Is Dead

Buy and Hold Is Dead

How to Make Money and Control Risk in Any Market

THOMAS H. KEE

WILEY

John Wiley & Sons, Inc.

Published by John Wiley & Sons, Inc., Hoboken, New Jersey.
Published simultaneously in Canada.

For general information on our other products and services or for technical support,
please contact our Customer Care Department within the United States at
(800) 762-2974, outside the United States at (317) 572-3993 or fax (317) 572-4002.

Wiley also publishes its books in a variety of electronic formats. Some content that
appears in print may not be available in electronic books. For more information about
Wiley products, visit our web site at www.wiley.com.

Library of Congress Cataloging-in-Publication Data:

Kee, Thomas H.
  Buy and hold is dead : how to make money and control risk in any market /
Thomas H. Kee.
      p.   cm.
  Includes index.
  ISBN 978-0-470-45841-9 (cloth)
  1. Portfolio management.   2. Risk management.   3. Investments.   I. Title.
  HG4529.5.K44 2010
  332.6–dc22

                                                          2009021632

Printed in the United States of America.

10 9 8 7 6 5 4 3 2 1

To Christie, who always helps me
find my Comfort Zone.

Contents

Preface

The Comfort Zone
A Lifestyle for Today's Investor

Managing risk is something most investors are not used to. Money managers and brokers tell us to just add more, stay invested at all times, and they tell us we will make money over time if we do. During the past 10 years, we have learned that advice cannot be trusted. In fact, all major averages are negative over a ten-year span. Buy and hold investors have gotten nowhere, but behind. Not only has "buy and hold" failed, but given the current and future economic environment, this pattern is likely to continue for many years. For now, buy and hold is dead.

This book will detail the current and future economic conditions facing the world using a demand-side analysis. This is a proprietary study. Although it is revealing of cyclical trends and therefore an integral tool to actionable policies, most investors will gather one universal truth. We all must control our risk because the economic weakness is not over.

Professional traders and investors do this every day. They specialize in risk control. Using rule-based trading strategies, they can limit their losses and maximize their returns regardless of market direction or economic conditions.

Unfortunately, most normal investors have not been able to accomplish the same. Most do not have time. Instead, they rely on managers who are in the business of collecting fees and staying invested at all times. Not only does that create a conflict of interest, but that old-school approach has cost the investing public trillions of dollars in recent years.

Managing Risk Is Not a Choice, It Is a Requirement

Everyone needs to manage risk, but that presents obvious problems to normal investors. With a conscious understanding of the limitations normal investors have, I have developed a strategy that anyone can use to gain an edge over institutional investors. I am going to reveal rule-based strategies that can be used today to help manage risk and realize opportunity without sacrificing time or lifestyle. Normal investors will no longer sit at the mercy of their mutual fund or money managers, and take blow after blow from the market. Instead, by leveraging the nimble reflexivity of non-institutional investors, I have produced a strategy that gives normal investors an edge. The playing field has changed, and from this point forward, smaller investors have the upper hand.

However, no one said investing was easy. It is tough sometimes. Thankfully, most of the time it is much harder than it has to be. We have all been brainwashed by big brokerage firms, and it is time that someone stood up and was heard. In fact, most people should be screaming at the top of their lungs. Brokerage firms care more about generating fees than they care about your wealth. Once we all realize that, we will all take the time to learn how to do it ourselves. I am going to lay out the plan, give you specific strategies, and point you in the right direction, but you need to want to move forward. Stop being a pawn in the game immediately and stay ahead of the curve from now on.

This book is a catalyst to financial independence. You cannot rely on your money manager to protect your wealth. This is a responsibility we all must assume for ourselves. The collapse of 2008 has proven that already. Therefore, the next step is to move forward with wealth preservation in mind. That is the reason I have written this book. I want you to know that you can do better than your money managers and make money in a volatile market, and I am going to show you how to do it.

The market, by which I mean the U.S. stock market, offers everyone unique opportunities to make money *all the time regardless of market conditions.* All we need to do is recognize them. Rationally, sometimes that is easier said than done. However, that overused phrase doesn't apply all the time, either. In fact, I dispel many similar myths in this book, and I will point you in a direction so that you can embrace the volatile conditions of today, and the oscillating market cycles of tomorrow, with ease. I will introduce you to the Investment Rate model, which is a combination of tools that will help you protect your wealth and realize opportunities for the rest of your life. If you are reading this book as a result of your distress given the market declines of 2008, after my strategies are revealed you may consider the pain of 2008 to be a most valuable blessing. From here, you will find the way to a better lifestyle, something that can be embraced forever. The lasting impact of my strategies will change the way you approach your investments in the market, in real estate, or in private business by allowing you to grow without exposing yourself to the risk of loss such as you may have experienced in 2008.

Rule-Based Strategies Are Integral

For you the investor, it is time to start moving forward. However, forward is not one-directional. Opportunities surface when the market goes up, and when the market goes down. Your prospects are only limited by your own obstacles. Fortunately, those impediments can be overcome, and showing you how is my mission. I am going to offer strategies that work in both up and down markets, that adjust by themselves, and that keep you on the right side of the curve at all times. More important, though, I am also going to reveal a refined approach to market strategy that removes your personal limitations and allows you to take advantage of opportunities whenever they arise. Included here is a model for wealth management, and risk control, too.

This book should be of interest to all investors, whether in the stock market, real estate, or personal business. The investment strategies I offer in this book have kept my clients on the right path through thick and thin, and they can do the same for you. My clients include government officials, businessmen, doctors, lawyers, professors, hedge fund managers, investment advisors, independent investors, managers, retirees, and employees from all industries, from many parts of the world.

My clients have found solace in my process. I make current and ongoing investment decisions easier. This goes a long way in down markets, but the process works when the market trends higher as well. The quantum of solace that I am able to offer to my clients reverberates through their lives. It transcends mere investing and it betters lifestyles. I will provide that same leadership to you. It will impact your quality of life as well.

Do you hesitate to proceed, unwilling to embark on a complex discussion of economic and investment theory? If so, I understand. Therefore, I will also keep it simple. In that way you will have a clear understanding of current and future economic trends. Knowing the direction of the market in advance will aid you with your investment decisions going forward. Most important, you will end with a complete understanding of the proactive investment strategy best suited for you. Everyone can do this. Proactive strategies incorporate risk controls that protect your investments from loss, provide opportunities at all times, and are the direct catalyst to profitability and the preservation of your wealth. These strategies work regardless of market direction and in any economic environment, and I'll explain how. You just need to take the first step by reading this book. From there, everything else will fall into place.

The Ultimate Goal

My ultimate objective is to bring you to the comfort zone. This is a place where your investments no longer negatively affect your emotional state.

This is where market woes no longer stifle your personal life. This is a place where you will be comfortable with yourself, your decisions, and your direction. Ultimately, this will help you live a better life, and that should be your personal goal. This can be achieved when you become secure with your decisions and comfortable with your investment choices. Therefore, my goal is to provide you with that opportunity.

To reach the comfort zone, you will need to embrace change. You will need to extract and employ the innovative ideas and strategies that I will teach you. However, not all of these have been accepted by the mainstream investment community yet. I assume that they will be at some point, but to many my approach will be different than anything they have found before. This may not be easy for you, but important decisions never are. Without a doubt, the market has already told us that we need to make these decisions, and this book makes them much easier. Aspiring to reach the comfort zone is in itself a life-changing decision. Thanks to the declines in 2008, you might also recognize the need to change your investment strategy for the first time too.

Warren Bennis, founding Chairman of the Leadership Institute at the University of Southern California, has noted, "Innovation by definition will not be accepted at first. It takes repeated attempts, endless demonstrations, and monotonous rehearsals before innovation can be accepted and internalized...." I believe that the disciplined approach associated with the strategies I offer is the cornerstone of investment success. The results of my innovative approach have been extremely rewarding to my clients already.

Peter Drucker may have said it best. This renowned author and professor explained, "Innovation is ... the act that endows resources with a new capacity to create wealth." That is exactly what I do. Through this book I will empower your current resources to create wealth going forward and make money in a volatile market.

Think Outside of the Box

Are you still unsure about employing concepts that are not yet widely accepted? Consider then the fame of Deepak Chopra, named recently as one of the top 100 icons of the current era, according to *Time* magazine.

Deepak Chopra is considered an innovator and a leader in the field of mind-body medicine. He has transformed the meaning of health by incorporating the best of Western medicine with natural healing traditions from the East. In essence, he has changed the art of healing with innovations that were strongly resisted when first introduced in the West, but which are now widely accepted by educated persons across the globe.

Deepak Chopra teaches a system of healing and preventive medicine that dates back 5,000 years. Originating in India, Ayurvedic medicine is now popular in many social circles because it helps balance mind, body, and soul. It is the science of life.

The popularity of this science is based on its ultimate objective. His Perfect Health Course can help free people from disease, aging, and death. This sounds like a far-reaching goal, but he has already indisputably proven that it works. Our elite are believers in his system right now, and the masses are starting to recognize its healing power every day. The root of this power lies within ourselves. In fact, in order to liberate ourselves from sickness or pain, we need to tap into our awareness and bring our lives into balance.

Changing people's minds about long-held beliefs was necessary for Deepak Chopra to gain Western acceptance of his teaching. I aspire to a similar goal in the field of investment strategy.

In fact, some of these same principles apply to our investments. The Perfect Health of our portfolios also lies within. Emotional balance is required. Liberating ourselves from the sickness and disease that flare up regularly in our portfolios is critical. Poor investment strategies often cause our investments to decline and that in turn troubles our minds and burdens our lifestyle. These losses hurt our pocketbook, and that affects our psychological approach toward new investments in a meaningful way. Eventually, that could also have a negative impact upon investment performance. Understandably, that happened to many people in 2008. It may have happened to you. In this book I will teach you to deal comfortably with the occasional losses that even the best portfolios will suffer. In some cases, I will show you how to avoid these altogether too. This is my goal. I will take you to the comfort zone, and that path starts with recognition.

The Comfort Zone Lies Ahead

You will not be alone. Thus far, many investors have already taken the steps to get there. Many elite investors have been using my system for a long time. My work is regularly published through various media channels, I have been featured in *Barron's,* I write an article for MarketWatch every month, and I was nicknamed the Grim Reaper by Erin Burnett on CNBC for predicting the demise of our stock market in the middle of 2007. Reuters provides my Economic and Market Analysis to its institutional clients every day, and I operate a website that serves my broad audience. These and other Tier 1 clients have already realized the value of my simple, yet effective approach and they have embraced my strategies.

Now my path leads to you. In the chapters that follow, you too will learn how to understand current economic and stock market cycles, how to anticipate future economic and stock market cycles, and how to position yourself so that your investments never become a burden again. You will gain a comprehensive understanding of the proactive trading strategies that I use regularly. One or more of these strategies will be immediately actionable for you, too. They integrate both risk control and opportunity in a methodical, structured, and easy-to-follow design that can be used at all times. They will empower you to invest successfully, no matter what the economy or stock market may seem to be suggesting.

Your journey to the comfort zone is about to begin.

Thomas Kee
PO Box 922
La Jolla, CA 92038

Acknowledgments

E conomics is all about people. Without knowing that, I would never be in the position I am today. Thank you, Mr. Wingate. Also, in fond memory, thank you, Jack Frager. You and Tom McMullen started me on my path. This book would have never been possible without each of you.

In addition, uniquely, I would like to thank everyone who believes that the current way is always the best way. My innovation would never be possible without you. You have driven me to think outside of the box, you have driven me to believe that the impossible is possible, and you have given me something we like to call Tommyland. Life is a little different here. Believe me, it is possible!

CHAPTER 1

The Investment Rate

The Investment Rate is the core of all of my analysis, and it is the catalyst for all of my trading strategies, too. It influences everything we do. Given the sweeping importance of this tool, I will start our discussion on how to make money in a volatile market by explaining the origins and properties of this tool and then build from that foundation as we move forward. Although proof of the Investment Rate is important, the discovery process itself is equally important as it reveals the simplicity of this model. Therefore, I think it is important to address this first. So, let's begin.

Economics Is All About People

My empirical journey to the land of economics did not begin with a Harvard MBA, or a doctorate from MIT. My drive to be the economist and independent market strategist I am today started another way. In fact, I confess that economics bored me in college. Although my grades were at the top of my class, I could barely stay awake during lectures. Initially, all of it seemed boring. The study of economics came easily to me, but the thought of applying those tools in the real world cast me from the science at that time. I was extremely social, and crunching numbers in a small office while surrounded by my intellectual peers seemed like the last thing I wanted to do. I was studying the works of Karl Marx, Thomas Malthus, and John Maynard Keynes, to name a few. The chairman of the Federal Reserve was Alan Greenspan, but he was not any different from the rest of them in my eyes. They were all bookworms; they were all number crunchers; and they all seemed to accept a lifestyle that did not interest me. Although I respected these intellects, I also feared the life that awaited me if I chose their path.

Without question, I was not a bookworm. Economics was just second nature to me. The number crunchers who were my peers in school had to work a little harder to achieve the same marks, but they did well and seemed satisfied with their results. Unfortunately, I was not satisfied with mine. Instead, to become satisfied I had to push myself in a different way. I did not need to study as much, but I needed to find motivation somehow. My peers already had it. Grades motivated them. However, because good grades came easily to me, that was not enough. There had to be something more, I thought, but I was not seeing it then. Every day my frustration grew, and I distanced myself from the science that I now find so compelling.

Imagine having a gift and not wanting to use it. What if you were a swimmer of the caliber of Michael Phelps but you decided that swimming was boring? What if you used to beat Kobe Bryant on the court when you were a child, but you stopped playing basketball because you did not like it anymore? What if your name was Tiger Woods, but because playing golf required so much patience, you decided to run track instead? I am not claiming to be in the same league as these athletes, but I did (and still do) have a skill, and I was not pursuing it appropriately. That was a major hurdle. Over time, I have found that everyone has hurdles like this. Helping us overcome them is one of my objectives. Everyone needs motivation— a drive, and a reason to move forward. I too was in desperate need of motivation as I pondered my future in relation to this wonderful science, which bored me before I completely understood it.

Luckily, my abilities and my diverging interests were clear to those who knew me. My economics professor at St. Mary's College of California, Stanley Wingate, sat down with me one afternoon after observing my disparaging attitude. Economics was already his life and his passion. Gracefully, he wanted to share some of his motivation with me. I cannot thank him enough for that simple half-hour conversation; it changed my life.

During our conversation, Professor Wingate explained that economics is all about people. If you understand people, you can understand economics. If you understand economics, you can understand people. Amazingly, in a blink of an eye, I found a parallel between my social activities and my education. I love interacting with people, and economics came easy, so synergies popped up everywhere. Eventually, I realized that economic theories—such as Random Walk theories—have a much broader range than just identifying opportunity. They apply in explaining many aspects of our social behavior. It is not about numbers; it is about people. Thanks to Professor Wingate, I was able to see this for the first time, and my eyes began to open. Almost immediately, I found correlations. Soon economics compelled me more than I ever thought it could.

Excited, I was motivated to move forward and to apply my new passion to my career. I did this by subtly changing the way I looked at the world. In turn, that opened a series of doors and provided endless opportunities for both inner growth and the expansion of my career. My transition was seamless and empowering at the same time. Eventually, I realized that this same simple revelation could change the perception of economics for many others as well. My drive, my passion, and my motivation have been unyielding ever since. However, I also realize that barriers to entry exist for many people, just as they did for me. Therefore, addressing these will be important to our end goal.

The Relationship Between Market Trends and Economic Cycles

After graduation, I entered the financial industry. Early in my career as a retail stockbroker, Colonial Mutual Funds approached me. Mutual fund companies often woo brokers to sell their funds. This gathers assets for the fund and generates recurring management fees for the firm. This Colonial wholesaler presented me with a sales kit for the funds he was pitching at the time. That kit included a comparative demographic study that pitted birth rates against the stock market. There were interesting correlations in that study. This was an eye opener. It was my first real-life exposure to this type of analysis. It showed me that the actions of people affect not only the economy, but the stock market, too. That broadened my interest even further. More important, it was also my first step toward developing the Investment Rate. Although the Colonial model was clearly flawed, it was on the right track. Over time, with that inspiration in hand, I continued to refine that imperfect model to produce a much more precise measure of current and future investment demand. That is the Investment Rate.

Although the Investment Rate includes variables, growth analysis, and quantum theories, its foundation is the simple study of human nature. It measures consumer demand for investments (demographic demand cycles). This is not a study of GDP. This is a study of investment demand, and it is extremely revealing. I will offer details in the next chapter.

Generally, most people experience similar personal financial cycles throughout their lives. In their early years, they are spenders; in the middle, they are savers; and from there until retirement, they are investors. Because I was looking for demand ratios, I was most interested in the third phase. Specifically, I wanted to know when people became investors. Interestingly, this is a consistent variable. Aside from unique circumstances, this happens at the same time for almost everyone. More specifically, skew is negligible over time, and demand cycles revert to the mean as well. As a result, investment behavior is predictable, and I have exploited that to identify longer-term economic cycles in advance. That is the Investment Rate. But, let me be more specific.

Everyone becomes an investor at some point in his or her life, and our aggregate demand for investments drives the economy. Because this is a demographic study, my references are to the entire population. When the overall demand for investments is increasing over time, the economy grows, and

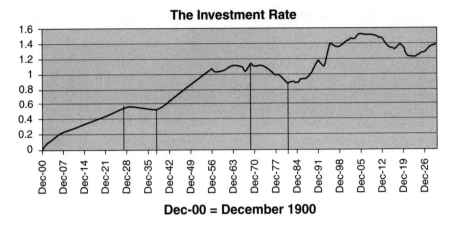

FIGURE 1.1 The Investment Rate.

the stock market rises. When net investment decreases over time, the economy comes under pressure and the stock market falls. This is the essence of the Investment Rate. The Investment Rate tells us when this happens.

Studiously, I compared my theory to the economic history of the United States from 1900 to 2009. The Investment Rate actually extends through 2030, but I was looking for correlations to past economic cycles in this review. My findings were significant. Importantly, my retroactive analysis proved that the Investment Rate has identified every major economic cycle throughout our history in advance. In turn, that past parallel suggests future parallels as a result. That is how my forward model began. This analysis accurately identifies periods of significant weakness, and it precisely identifies the boom periods, too.

Although I will go into more detail in the next chapter, Figure 1.1 offers insight into that relationship. The most revealing may be the first down period. After all, we all know what happened after 1929.

A Leading Indicator

I first offered the Investment Rate to the public in 2002. In early 2002, the market was reeling. Arguably, overall demand for stocks had dried up completely. Investors were scrambling to protect themselves from the Internet debacle, and meltdowns were occurring left and right. On the surface, this was very similar to our experience in 2008, but there are subtle differences. Panic drove the market lower in 2002, and although my proactive strategies were performing extremely well, the selling pressure was unnerving to my clients, too. Unfortunately, I later discovered that this uneasiness also prevented many investors from doing the right thing. Instead of protecting wealth and realizing opportunities within my well-established models, many investors sat idle and watched their wealth dissolve as the stock market declined around them.

Right in the thick of things, I launched the Stock Traders Daily website in January 2000. This was the peak of the Internet bubble and an extremely volatile time. Therefore, I began to offer proactive trading strategies without thinking twice. Longer-term investments were not even a consideration at the time. However, even though we focused on trading strategies, I also recognized the power of the Investment Rate, and I respected its influence on the economy and the stock market over time. Reasonably, this long-term theory of market cycles lingered in my mind, but it was not important to me when I first started. I was only interested in providing solid returns. The Investment Rate did not become important to my clients and me until the market began to fall apart.

Thoughtlessly, at the height of the Internet bubble, major brokerage firms (including Morgan Stanley, Smith Barney, Merrill Lynch, Prudential, A.G. Edwards, Goldman Sachs, J.P. Morgan, and others) had "strong buy" ratings on stocks like Amazon, Yahoo, CMGI, eBay, and others. If it had dotcom in the name, it was on their list. Therefore, if the retail clients of these firms were following the direction of those institutions, they were also holding significant positions in these overvalued Internet stocks when the Internet bubble peaked in 2000. From there, as we know, the resulting declines were detrimental not only to real wealth, but also to investor sentiment as well.

Expectedly, many retail clients were confused, and most investors did not know what to think. If these analysts were indeed superior prognosticators and if they believed those Internet stocks offered significant opportunity, then why not just ride out the storm?

Unfortunately, following the guidance of those analysts pushed some investors over the edge. Between 2000 and 2003, many investors learned the hard way. Major brokerage firms have arthritic reactions to policy changes and analysis for their retail clients. This is especially evident during periods of market weakness. In fact, and more specifically, according to many analysts who offered opinions on Internet stocks for these major brokerage firms between 2000 and 2003, those stocks were "strong buys" in the $100s. Then, sell ratings came when the stocks were in the low single digits. This was a classic case of buying high and selling low. Obviously, they got it wrong.

After the fact, we all know that major brokerage firms provided retail investors with some terrible advice during the Internet bubble. The subsequent freefall in many stock prices resulted in the collapse of many tech-heavy portfolios, too. My focus in 2002, when I developed and introduced the Investment Rate, was to address and quell the fears that resounded so heavily throughout the market as a result. Even though my proactive models were rewarding my clients with exceptional returns, surprisingly, fear still lingered. My clients, like most investors, seemed to be uncomfortable investing in a declining market. Underneath, they really wanted the market to increase, and frankly, so did I. Interestingly, as my knowledge grew, I discovered that this was a mistake.

Understanding and dealing with this emotion has become much more important to me now than it was prior to 2002. In fact, I failed to recognize the consequences of that emotional bias when I first developed my trading strategies. These strategies were essentially short term, and our trading discipline left little room for fear anyway, so I never paid much attention to emotional conditioning on a long-term basis. Reflexivity was part of our models already. At the same time, though, I had not yet applied the strategies stemming from my understanding of the Investment Rate to our longer-term investments. More important, we had not even considered longer-term investments until the going got tough. In 2002 that changed—the focus now is also on longer-term investments as well, and building and protecting wealth accordingly.

However, that does not suggest constant higher moves by any means. Instead, I have grown to recognize that market direction does not matter, even to longer-term investments. Opportunities exist on both sides of the curve, and we must recognize them.

Coincidentally, in 2002, an interesting phenomenon surfaced, and this influenced my study. During a period when the stock market was experiencing significant declines, positive flows of new money into our economy continued virtually unabated. The difference lay in the positioning of that investment money. Money began flowing out of the stock market and into real estate and private business. As a result, the stock market stayed under heavy pressure, and real estate prices began to increase.

Everyone can see that investment shift now, but very few were able to identify that simple transition in 2002. In fact, during periods of weakness in the stock market, almost everyone becomes blind to reason. Therefore, in 2002, investors were more concerned with the value of their mutual funds, managed accounts, and 401ks. If they were holding Internet stocks based on the "strong buy" recommendations offered by the major brokerage firms at that time, those concerns derailed structured and disciplined investment strategies even further.

My nervous clients and other concerned investors everywhere wanted to know if an improving economy would be enough to sustain a recovery in the stock market. I aimed to prove it one way or another. During my pursuit of insight into the future trend of the stock market, the main distinction I identified was that a simple shift in asset classes had taken place, and that was all. Otherwise, demand was still robust, and new money continued to flow into our economy. According to my theory, the Investment Rate, the market would recover swiftly from that decline. I said so in a work I published titled "Will an Improving Economy Be Enough?" That report included a concise understanding of the Investment Rate, a tool I had been developing for quite some time. Until then, I had never dignified this powerful theory with publication.

My report proclaimed that, according to the Investment Rate, there would be a prompt upward retracement in the stock market rooted in an overall increasing demand for investments. The report advised investors that investing in stocks would be intelligent again at some point soon. Therefore, with that evidence in hand, I knew that we should also be looking for precise opportunities to buy when the time was right. From there, I reviewed Fibonacci calculations and technical tools to help me identify the bottom within a few points. The result was not surprising to some of my clients who had already been following my proactive trading models religiously. The result of my preemptive analysis was that I defined the bottom of the market in 2002 almost exactly. More important though, that report also revealed important facts about the long-term health of the economy and the stock market that eventually reshaped the way we approach our long-term investments today.

As we know, in 2002, the market resumed a very strong upward trend that lasted until 2007. The Investment Rate had been a bullish leading economic and stock market indicator in the face of the Internet debacle, and it was virtually exact.

However, there is more. Attempting to defuse the fear of investing during the Internet debacle was initially restricted to proving that the market was still ascending. Inherently, most people held the misconception that they could comfortably buy the dips forever. However, as we have learned over time, it is also every bit as important that investors not fear participating in a declining market either, where opportunities also abound. To that end, the Investment Rate is equally valuable. It assists my clients to understand future economic conditions and market direction whether up or down. This goes a long way to unburdening their fears. With the Investment Rate, they have the tools to take advantage of whatever market opportunities exist. That is the first step toward the comfort zone!

Therefore, the Investment Rate, as I employ it for the benefit of my clients, is not limited to a demographic analysis. It must also include a second component, and that component produces actionable strategies in relation to the findings of the demographic study. The first component is a measurement of the increase or decrease over time of new investment into the economy. This is a predictor of economic trends. The second component is the technical tools I have developed to pinpoint support and resistance levels. These allow us to find turning points in advance. In my opinion, the combination of these components has produced the most accurate leading longer-term stock market and economic indicator ever developed. I will discuss both of these in the next chapter.

The Investment Rate is a long-term fundamental analysis of the economy and the stock market. It is the core of all of my research. It is rooted in all of my investment strategies. A review of the Investment Rate should be conducted before any investment decisions are finalized. This includes investments in stocks, bonds, real estate, businesses, and any other investment class that requires a positive inflow of capital to grow. I advise all of my clients to have a concrete understanding of longer-term trends before they engage any active (short-term) trading strategies, and I use the Investment Rate as a tool to satisfy this objective appropriately. If we can first understand longer-term cycles, we are more readily able to accept change—when change is required.

New Money Drives the Market

In summary, the Investment Rate measures the amount of new money available for investment into the economy over extended periods. In turn, that directly influences the demand for investments throughout that same cycle. Specific investments such as stocks, real estate, and other asset classes within the economy are impacted. The Investment Rate ultimately affects the value of all the investments we make, and that is obviously important to all investors. Nothing is sheltered from this demand-side analysis and that is why everyone should review the Investment Rate before making any investment decisions. Figure 1.2 explains how the Investment Rate affects the investments that are important to us.

The Investment Rate helps us to understand and to predict current and future economic cycles by measuring the demand for new investment, the prime driver of the economy. Simple in concept, it enables us to weed out the noise that clutters so many other economic models unnecessarily. This refined approach then allows us to focus on strategies designed to make us money regardless of market direction. More precisely, the Investment Rate gives us confidence in our strategies, and that is priceless!

The Investment Rate is powerful, it is far reaching, and it influences everyone. It should be used by governments to help them determine long-term economic policies. It should be used by corporations to help them manage business cycles. But most important, it should be used to help individual investors manage their wealth over time as well.

Appropriately, in the chapters that follow this will be a focal point. However, more important, our next step is to prove the theory I introduced here. In the next chapter, I will be specific, and the effectiveness of this demand-side analysis will come to light.

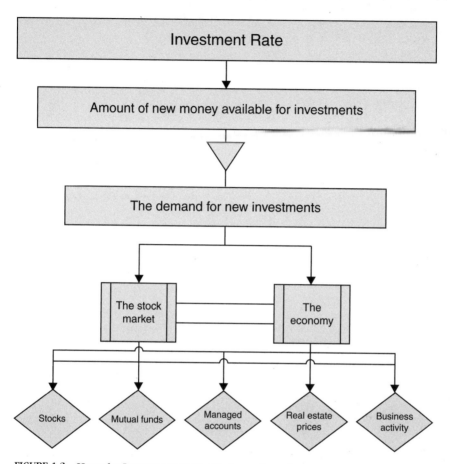

FIGURE 1.2   How the Investment Rate affects our investments.

Summary

Below is a summary of the most important topics in this chapter:

- Economics is all about people.
- The Investment Rate is a demographic study that measures the in-flows of new money into our economy annually and over extended periods of time.
- The Investment Rate reveals up and down cycles in advance, and accepting these as opportunities is the first step toward the comfort zone.

CHAPTER 2

Keep It Simple, Sweetheart

The Investment Rate is logical, comprehendible, actionable, and it can work for us to help us protect our wealth and take advantage of longer-term trends throughout fluctuating cycles over time. I have already outlined its origin; now I will illustrate past application and prove its effectiveness. Advancing this tool is integral to understanding our proactive models because it plays an important role in all of them.

Interestingly, though, the simplicity of the model is sometimes overwhelming to new subscribers. Surprising as this may sound, most people want to complicate the already effective contrivance stemming from the Investment Rate, and that usually curbs the effectiveness of this leading indicator with unnecessary variables. Sometimes these observations are sound, and I am always willing to entertain derivations, but not until a person first shows a complete understanding of my current model. In fact, more often than not, those persons who started by questioning the model begin to embrace it after they understand it, too.

Therefore, before I proceed with further explanation, I always challenge my audience. Until they finish the first phase of this lesson, I challenge them to stop listening to the noise. If they can do this, they can also accept the Investment Rate for what it is and see forward applications with ease. With proven effectiveness in hand, I will take that same stand here. Stop listening to the noise surrounding the stock market and the economy day in and day out. Instead, try to refocus on the foundation of economic science, which I described in the last chapter. Think about people, specifically about the people we might encounter every day, and think about the way they live their lives. Incorporate coincidental Random Walk theory into these observations, and draw parallels to the facts described here. As knotty as this may sound, all it really means is that we observe the people we know and take note of their occasional choices.

Specifically, in this case, we are interested in their financial behavior. Going so far as to interview people for discovery is not necessary. Because we all probably know the correct answers to the questions that influence this observation already, we probably do not have to dig any deeper than we already have. For example, think about when they bought their first home, how old they were when their kids started going to college, and when they chose to retire. These and other generalities will develop into specifics as we move forward, and from those specifics will come the action plans we are looking for.

At the same time, however, do not be immediately concerned with the direction of the stock market, or the current health of the global economy. Stop paying attention to interest rates, the housing market, libor, the dollar, oil prices, or anything else that might have investors on the edge of their seats. For the most part, none of these matter to long-term trends. Yes, they all matter to short-term trends, but none of them matter to long-term trends. Our goal is to define long-term cycles first, and then use them as a foundation for further analysis and immediate application afterwards. The only way to do that is to first weed out the noise so we can see the light at the end of the tunnel.

An Example: Interest Rates

Interest rates are a great example of noise. We have all heard the phrase "don't fight the Fed." This is often used to suggest higher market levels after Fed rate cuts. Interestingly, the opposite is usually true, and I will prove it. Listening to those prognosticators is usually foolhardy because they are usually wrong. Initial positive market reactions to Fed rate cuts are typically short lived, and the market usually continues to decline after a short honeymoon.

Interestingly, I do agree with that general phrase in a coincidental way. We should not fight the Fed. However, my approach is counterintuitive to traditional doctrine. Initially, it might seem ill founded, but my premise is well rooted and obvious if emotions are removed from the process of observation.

Rather than not fighting the Fed in the traditional sense, if the Federal Reserve is increasing rates, we should be buyers of stocks instead. In addition, on the other hand, if the Federal Reserve is cutting rates, we should seriously consider shorting stocks along with the decline in rates. Logically, save inflation concerns, the Federal Reserve increases interest rates because the economy is too strong. Conversely, the Federal Reserve cuts interest rates because the economy is weakening. However, as we know, during strong economies, the stock market trends higher, and during weak economies the stock market trends lower. Therefore, logically, we can rationalize the moves in the stock market based on the decisions of the FOMC (Federal Open Market Committee) if we can trust that they are acting prudently.

Assuming we do, we buy when the FOMC raises rates, and we strongly consider shorting when the FOMC is cutting rates. Instead, most investors listen to the noise, they follow the prognosticators, and it distracts them from obvious reality.

Look at this simple relationship in graphical format (see Figure 2.1).

Clearly, an initial short-lived easing cycle began in September 2008, and the market reacted negatively as expected. However, the relationship between the market and interest rates during that cycle is more difficult to identify because of its short-lived duration. Therefore, the following confirmation begins with the November 1998 tightening cycle. From there, longer-term correlations are clear, and our observations work to prove my

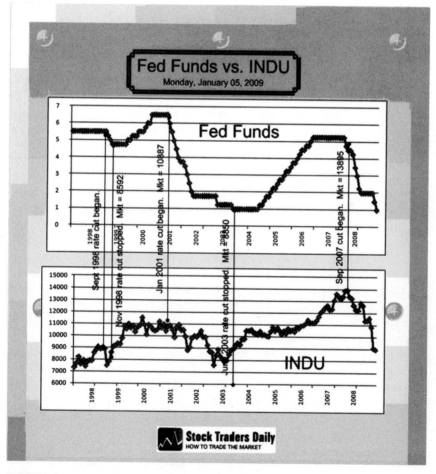

FIGURE 2.1   Interest rates versus the market.

TABLE 2.1   FOMC vs. INDU Confirmation Table

Duration	Cycle	Return
Nov 1998–Jan 2001	Raising	26.7%
Jan 1 2001–June 2003	Easing	−18.7%
June 2003–Sep 2007	Raising	57.00%
*Sep 2007–Oct 2008	Easing	−35.00%

theory. Compare the general trend of the market to the direction of the Fed Funds Rate during this ten-year span. The confirmation shown in Table 2.1 proves that the market performs well when the FOMC is in the process of increasing interest rates to curb economic growth, and it performs poorly when the FOMC cuts rates to flatten economic activity instead. This is counterintuitive to widely accepted intuition, and it elevates the value of thinking outside of the box at the same time.

I conducted this analysis in October 2008. The market was near 9000 at that time, and the Fed Funds Rate was 1 percent. However, the FOMC did not stop there. We all know that the FOMC cut interest rates again in December, and they were near 0 percent going into the new year. During that same time, the market continued to decline, and it established a low of 7438 in November 2008. This ongoing association continues to prove the counterintuitive relationship between the Fed Funds Rate and the market over time. Although the cycle arguably could have been considered complete in December, there had not yet been a turn higher in interest rates, and therefore our analysis will be left to October data. However, reasonably, the FOMC could not cut rates any lower after the December cut, and therefore the end of the easing cycle may have already been determined. If that is true, our analysis suggests that the market should increase for at least a short while after the final December cut.

Clearly, buying during rising interest rate cycles has worked over time, and shorting during easing cycles has, too. Since 1998, the market increased by an average of 41.85 percent when the FOMC was raising rates. It fell by an average of 26.85 percent when it was cutting rates. "Don't fight the Fed" is not all it is cracked up to be. In fact, investors should usually do the exact opposite of what that phrase traditionally implies. Unfortunately, they do not, and unwitting investors become emotionally bound to the influence of unfounded assumptions instead.

Don't Listen to the Noise

Interest rates are just one example of the noise that burdens investors regularly. Going forward, the next time the FOMC changes interest rates, determine why the FOMC made those decisions. If the purpose is to influence the growth of our economy, and not to combat inflation, we can be sure that history tells us to go with the flow of interest rates instead of against them. With this revelation, those pundits who would have us think otherwise will not be a distraction again, and we will retain the opportunity to realize gains from our advanced knowledge accordingly.

However, as actionable as it may be, this message carries a stronger meaning, and that new meaning will influence our purpose accordingly. More important, do not let other noise variables influence similar distractions as we move immediately forward either. Instead, KISS—Keep It Simple, Sweetheart! Forget about the news facing the market today, unburden those ties, and refocus on people until, at least, we are finished with this discussion. Refocusing on the basics is exactly what empowered my transition in college. It cleared my mind, and it allowed me to see the world in a slightly different way. Since then, I have been using a refined approach every day, and the results have been awesome. The power of simplicity is strong, if we allow it to work. Ultimately, it has put me in the position I am in today, and for many reasons I recommend a simplified approach to everyone. It all started with an evaluation of people.

Originally, I wanted to prove to my clients that demand for stocks would resurface again at some point. We all knew that a bubble was being dissolved in 2002, and we all recognized the turbulence in the market as well, but very few recognized that the demand ratios were still strong within our overall economy as assets shifted to real estate instead. Everyone focused on the crashing stock market and the resulting economic weakness of that era.

Nevertheless, I was able to identify solid existing demand ratios, and, because of the low interest rate environment at that time, others were unintentionally taking advantage of that asset class transition, too. Very few people knew why, but they were enthusiastically taking the plunge. They had the money, but they did not like the stock market, so they refocused on real estate. Across the board, overall demand was still robust, and new money was still coming into the economy. This was obvious to me thanks to my refined approach. I attributed that to the Investment Rate, so I leveraged this tool for my clients.

Informally, I had already been using the Investment Rate for years, but until 2002, I had very little reason to prove my theory. However, as the market began to crash, I was compelled to offer evidence. My clients were not interested in knowing why the market was falling, because that was already clear to all of us. Instead, my clients wanted to know if the market would stop falling instead, and if so, when. This laid the groundwork for a relatively exhausting study. Although it was a tough proof, after the fact the logic behind the Investment Rate is unparalleled and extremely easy to use. My clients, in turn, have embraced it ever since.

In 2002, I could see that demand ratios continued to be robust in our economy. My goal was to prove why. I started by reverting to the sales kit given to me by Colonial Mutual Funds. Ultimately, I found flaws in that report, but it was a great starting point. The direction it provided set me on the path to discovering the Investment Rate and proving my theories. The result is irrefutable.

Before I began, I made a few general observations. I already knew that the economy was all about people. That association, of course, was my found passion. I also knew, to a certain extent, that the stock market correlated to demographics as well. The sales kit from Colonial proved that to me. These two pieces of information were critical to my objective. With these in hand, I was able to move forward and dig a little deeper. My instinct was to revert to the starting point. Economics is a social science, and I appreciated coincidences, so I began to look for them amid these starting variables.

Mechanically, my next step was to look around me, specifically at the people I knew well. I wanted to identify coincidences and apply them to my combined analysis. Hopefully, I thought a revelation would appear.

Ultimately, my objective was to understand when people invest money into the economy, and why. I believed, if I could make these important determinations, I could measure the demand for investments within our economy over time, too, and then prove that an eventual transition back to stocks would take place. My initial goal was to measure the total amount of money earmarked for investments into our economy at any given time. I thought I could do this by determining when and why people invest money. In turn, I thought I could make relative observations about future transitions, and then predict future market cycles with these broad demand observations in hand. This seemed logical, so I pursued.

I started asking questions, I continued paying attention, but what I found was not surprising at all. People made investments when two important criteria were satisfied. First, they need to have money. Second, they need a reason to invest it. Initially, this was a tough hurdle. People had money to invest and different reasons to invest it at various times in their lives. In addition, people took money out of investments for differing reasons, too. There were no definitive correlations here. Bonus checks, inheritance, a great stock tip—there were all kinds of reasons and very few distinctive relationships. Pinpointing investment decisions on a broad scale seemed almost impossible at first.

Therefore, I skewed my ambition slightly. Instead of measuring all of the investments in our economy, I refocused on systematic and aggressive investments only. My new objective was to determine when people began to invest money systematically and aggressively into the economy. In addition, I was no longer focused on any one asset class, but all of them combined. By redefining the objective, I would be better equipped to measure correlations, I thought.

Ultimately, the same premise held. When people have money and reason to invest it, systematic and aggressive investments can take place. This time, though, the analysis was much more manageable. There were distinct relationships based on the systematic and aggressive investment patterns of people over time, and those did not exist in my initial observation. Those new relationships were critical, and they helped prove my theories.

Because of the uncanny accuracy of the model, what seems like rocket science to some began with simple cognitive integration. I just put two and two together to find my answer. Fortunately, I had already laid the groundwork when I negotiated my first hurdle, so I already had some tools to work with prior to my analysis of systematic and aggressive investment patterns. Therefore, with a new objective, I asked myself a few follow-up questions, and I looked for answers based on my prior analysis. The first question was when do people have money to invest aggressively? The second question was when do people have reason to invest it aggressively? This time, as I pursued my objective, the answers I was looking for began to fall into place. Eventually, I recognized that I had successfully laid the groundwork for my longer-term model, and I began to move ahead.

Sometimes economic models use a top-down approach to developing theory, but in other cases a bottom-up approach is more effective. In this case, I used a bottom-up approach to find the answers I was looking for. Instead of determining when people had money to invest, I found it easier to determine when people had fewer financial responsibilities. In addition, I wanted to know when those responsibilities declined without associated income contraction. This excluded retirement, of course. Although retirees often have fewer obligations, they also have lower incomes. I wanted to know when lower obligations were associated with the same or higher income levels uniquely.

With a little work, this was reasonable. My thought process suggested that if people were able to reduce their current obligations first, investment decisions could occur with excess free cash flow. This turned out to be a critical element to my equation. In other words, when people are finished paying for major lifetime expenses, they have excess money that can be allocated toward investments if they so choose. Therefore, my original objective had to be skewed slightly yet again. Instead of trying to identify when people have money to invest, I identified when major financial responsibilities stopped weighing on investment decisions instead. The logical follow-up question was what are the major financial responsibilities burdening people over the normal course of their lives?

After careful analysis, I determined that there were three major financial responsibilities affecting almost everyone. The first was a home. The second major financial responsibility was college education for their children. And the third was retirement. These, for most people, were as sure as death and taxes.

The next part of my two-part analysis was reason. I wanted to know when people had a compelling reason to invest money aggressively and systematically as well. Unfortunately, this could not be as simple as opportunity. Because opportunities present themselves for varying reasons and at sporadic times, those could not be a measure for this phase of my evaluation. Chance investments are not systematic, and they do not influence economic trends over time anyway.

However, other variables do affect these trends, so I remained focused on finding them instead. After careful evaluation, the measured criteria I studiously chose to evaluate in this second phase of my observation fell into one of two distinct camps. They were either expenses or investments. For example, buying a first home is less of an investment and more considered an expense for most people. Therefore, I did not consider buying a first home to be an investment. However, on the same note, planning for retirement was indeed an investment, so it fit perfectly. Retirement, by definition, is an investment in our future, so everyone is compelled to plan for retirement somehow. In fact, the government and major employers encourage retirement planning by law, and that was very important, too. Retirement planning gave everyone a reason to invest at some point in his or her lives, and it is the focus of the second part of my two-part analysis.

Initially, retirement planning fell into two categories. It was both an expense and a reason to make investments. However, the latter was much more important to my model, so the premise for my analysis changed accordingly.

Figure 2.2 shows a diagram that accurately represents this explanation.

Importantly, the image depicted in Figure 2.2 also includes subtle hints about the derivation of my analysis. First, it obviously separates our subtopics and that allows the logic to flow analytically as a result. I am an avid enforcer of structure and discipline, as I will reveal later, and this layout fosters both of these power points appropriately. Uniquely, it also weeds out the noise surrounding this observation as well. This will be important to our process going forward. Keep it simple, always, and seemingly complex theory starts to look a little clearer. In this case, a simple diagram distills otherwise confusing added variables, and it allows us to differentiate our constituents for application.

In addition, North America is shadowed in the background of Figure 2.2. Subtly, that is important, too. An evaluation of human nature as

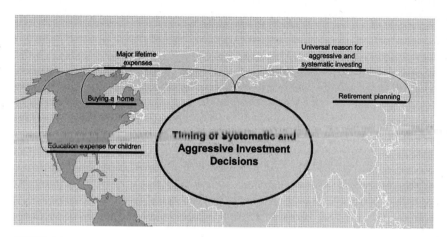

FIGURE 2.2   Most people invest money at the same time.

it applies to these critical lifetime decisions and obligations first requires an understanding of cultural normality. For example, although transitions to a formal contribution system were occurring as early as May 2007, Russia had a pension-driven retirement plan for its citizens. The comparative impact of retirement planning is significantly skewed in Russia as a result, and this model would likely break if it was applied to Russia without prior adjustment.

Therefore, the Investment Rate is culturally driven by societal norms within the United States, and largely, Canada. However, my focus was on the United States, and the cultural patterns I was already familiar with accordingly. My initial observations were within my social circles, and then I broadened that to include the national census. Reasonably, I can expand this theory to foreign nations, too, but I was immediately and specifically concerned with the economic conditions within the United States in 2002, so I stayed on track. My objectives were now explicit.

Refined and focused, I wanted to know when people within the United States finished paying for their first home and when they finished paying for their children's education. I also wanted to know when they started planning aggressively for retirement and when systematic and aggressive investments began. I tackled the expense variables first, using the same bottom-up approach as I used before. With structure and discipline, I proved my intuition, and the Investment Rate was born.

From here, I am going to summarize my findings. This book is not a proof of the Investment Rate, but rather an application of the model. The general derivation I used is important, and past application is eye opening because it confirms future correlations in advance, but this book focuses on application, not on the proof. Therefore, I will limit this to a summary, and possibly follow it with a formal proof at some point in the future.

With that, almost all of the information I was in search of was readily available through the government. Both census and housing agencies offer a vast array of data for researchers to use. These expansive resources provided most of the answers I was looking for. However, other statistical observations were necessary, too. These included collegiate data and associated expense ratios accordingly. As I worked, the data I found started to mount fast. If I allowed it to, this would have become overwhelming to my forward progress. Therefore, throughout my examination I continued to apply KISS theory to my process. I never overcomplicated my progression, and I maintained a simple focus with a concrete goal in mind.

For example, I did not modify the model to include second homes. In fact, I consider those investments, anyway. They were not expenses, so I did not allow that unnecessarily added variable to confuse the mean. I curtailed that risk at the onset of my research using the KISS method. Further, I did not account for student loans in my model either. Because they merely offset the cost of education, loans and grants only skew the longer-term cost analysis of education without changing it in any significant way. With the help of KISS, the answers I found were revealing, and not confusing. Because they were straightforward and logical, the coincidences that soon came clear were even more important, and they advanced the Investment Rate accordingly. I have since become a believer in KISS theory, and I recommend it to everyone for both analytical and investment techniques. I believe that a simplified process is usually easier to use and more precise than other complex models.

However, in this specific case I hit a major roadblock, which immediately curtailed my forward progress. Unfortunately, KISS cannot prevent these. KISS will not avert roadblocks, but it will help us pass roadblocks efficiently by simplifying the retracement process. Therefore, KISS adds value to adverse situations, too.

Encountering Roadblocks

Whenever we encounter roadblocks, we must go back over our methodology to identify and correct the problems that have surfaced. This is true always. However, if our process was complex to begin with, corrective steps are more complex as well. However, if the process is simplified at the onset instead, our resolution using the KISS method is much more fluid, as we would expect.

In this instance, my roadblock was troubling. I could not accurately identify the total amount of money that was readily available and earmarked for investment into the economy. That was my original goal, and I could not move forward without it. Even with the coincidences I observed, this data was not tangible. Although initial observations may suggest otherwise, the answer cannot be found in money supply or liquidity measures. These econometric variables added chaos boundaries to the figures I was in search of, but they did not provide specific answers. No matter what I did, I could not come up with an accurate measure. I could estimate cash and money supply, but I could not pinpoint the amount of money that individuals specifically earmarked for investments. Initially, this was troubling, and I had a hard time getting past it.

Eventually, though, I realized that I did not need an exact figure. Instead, I found that I could measure the rate of change of that figure instead and achieve the same result. As I proceeded, that became much more important anyway. Therefore, my focus shifted one last time to the rate of change in the amount of money earmarked for investments into our economy over time. The result was a defined growth rate model that measured the rate of change in the amount of money slated for investment in stocks, real estate, or other asset classes annually.

The resulting coincidences provided the exact answers I was looking for. Notwithstanding unique personal derivations, an average can be applied to all of these variables. Rationally, we can determine when people are typically finished paying for their first home. More important to my model, we can also identify when that mortgage payment becomes less of a burden as well. This figure is based on inflation-adjusted income streams, of course. Second, we can accurately surmise the average age of a graduating college student and apply that to census statistics to determine the average age of parents at that same time. Therefore, we can also determine when parents are finished paying for college education, with a reasonable degree of certainty. The retirement issue was a little different, though.

Retirement planning had unique characteristics. Typically, people start planning for retirement early. However, although early planning is indeed systematic, our studies determined that early planning was not aggressive by nature, in most cases. On a nationwide basis, most people are more concerned with buying a home or a car when they are young and less concerned about retirement. In fact, our studies proved that systematic and aggressive investments did not actually start to occur until people felt that retirement was near. In other words, people did not start to worry about retirement planning until they realized that they would have very little unless they started to take aggressive action immediately. This, unfortunately, is human nature. People do not take action until they have to. As fateful as human nature may sometimes be, this is a strong motivation factor, too, and it compels investments with the objective of building wealth for the relatively near future. This was the reason I was in search of from the beginning.

From there, I dug deeper and began the formal development of my model. The foundation was in place, and now the building blocks needed to complete the structure. The simple nature of the model made application easy. There were only three variables, mortgages, education, and retirement.

Importantly, as I continued, I found meaningful coincidences when comparing these three variables as well. When I compared the age of a parent after his or her children were finished attending college to the relative burden of mortgage costs at that same time, the end result fell directly in line with the aggressive and systematic investment strategies associated with retirement planning. That coincidence was our integrated coefficient. This was the age when people started to invest systematically and aggressively into the economy. They did it immediately after their children finished school, when mortgages were less of a burden, and when retirement planning became an immediate concern. The compelling force of retirement planning was the reason, and the coincidentally lower personal expense ratios that existed at the same time provided investors the ability to make those decisions. As I continued, my discovery proved that this happens at about the same time in everyone's life. Once again, the process has reverted to my definition of economic theory. Economics is all about people. This time, I just wanted to know when people began to invest money aggressively, and because I integrated the KISS theory from the beginning, the answer I was looking for became clear.

I called this the KEE AGE. Although it is variable over time, the current level of the KEE AGE is 48. At 48 years old, most people have just finished paying for school, they have a relative windfall, and they can start investing aggressively for retirement if they want to (see Figure 2.3).

Without a doubt, the driving force behind this model was my integral analysis of education costs. The coincidence was that when parents are finished paying for education, they refocus their funds on retirement planning. When they do, those investments are also systematic and aggressive in nature. That happens primarily because monies are suddenly available with which to make those decisions. Again, this is coincidental, but coincidences are very important. For the first time in their lives, most people realize a relative windfall when they are finished paying for education. That windfall is tied directly to the cost of education.

Education costs escalate much faster than inflation or normalized income levels over time, so this is significant. The cost of education, lodging, and living expenses per child can be overwhelming. My original 2002 report provided a reasonable example. It showed that the cost of education for two children attending Sacramento State University in California, and

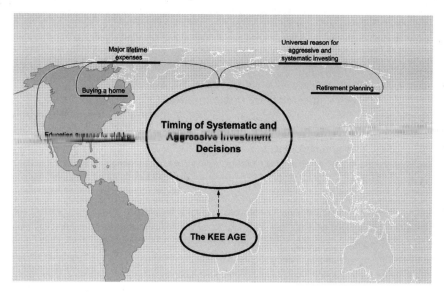

FIGURE 2.3   The Kee Age.

living on campus, was greater than $144,000. This represented a comparably inexpensive burden for two children, but the figures are still meaningful. Normal people have trouble with this expense. Nevertheless, that does not stop them. Instead, parents have a passion to pay for education and to further the growth of their children. Unyielding, they find a way to do it.

When introducing this concept to any audience for the first time, I always reference a unique motivation technique, which helped me advance my career. The analogy is a practice one of my past managers used to increase sales. His name was Joe Childrey. He was my manager at AG Edwards. Joe would encourage us to buy a nice car, or get the great apartment, even if he knew those added costs were a little beyond our means. In hindsight, his psychology was quite clear. He believed that if we had to work a little harder to afford a better lifestyle, we would. After the fact, I recognized his approach, and he was right. I worked harder because I knew I had to. That simple observation applies here, too.

The analogy is not perfect, but the same principle applies to parents and college education. Somehow, they find a way to pay for it. For some, that might mean tightening the family budget, or getting a better job. However, regardless of the means they use to reach that end, parents do whatever it takes because they know they have to. They assume added responsibility, and they find a way to handle it.

Notwithstanding loans and grants, when parents are finally finished paying for education, they realize a windfall of money. Finally, they can start thinking about themselves again. Many of them can afford a nice trip or a new car for the first time in a long while. Eventually, though, they also start to recognize the need for retirement planning again.

Coincidentally and universally, when parents finish paying for the cost of education, they have both a windfall of investable cash and reason to invest it. That is exactly what I was looking for when I started, and it is the answer that drives our demand-side analysis. Undoubtedly, my demographic studies prove that people encounter this windfall at about the same time. That is the KEE AGE, and that defines the Investment Rate.

Using a derivative demographic growth analysis based on normalized cultural trends adjusted for the KEE AGE, I was able to identify lifetime investment cycles within the United States. The result is a measure of the rate of change in demand cycles over extended periods. More important, this is also a measure of NEW inflows of money into investments in our economy over time specifically. New money drives the market, and that is the most important component of economic growth. The market cannot move higher by churning old money. Therefore, new money and new investments are required for growth in real estate, in the stock market, in business, and in virtually every asset class imaginable. As a result, I identified a measure of demand that forecasts growth in both the economy and the stock market over extended periods. From there, I backdated the model, and the result was the Investment Rate.

The Investment Rate is a measure of the rate of change in the amount of new money available for investment into the economy on an annualized basis. It identifies normalized demand ratios over extended periods. It does this based on a reversion to the grassroots concept and the foundation of economic theory, which is a simple study of people. New money drives the economy, not old money, and the Investment Rate tells us how much new money will be available to be added to the economy every year, over extended periods of time, and well into the future as well. The correlations between the Investment Rate and the market over time are staggering.

When you review the following graph, remember that the Investment Rate is one of the longest longer-term leading economic and stock market indicators available. Therefore, it does not measure small blips in the longer-term cycles, but rather, the complete longer-term economic cycle instead, save the noise.

This analysis dates back to 1900 and extends beyond 2030. In Figure 2.4, I have identified the major trends that define shifts in the slope of the Investment Rate over time with vertical crossbars. For example, the first

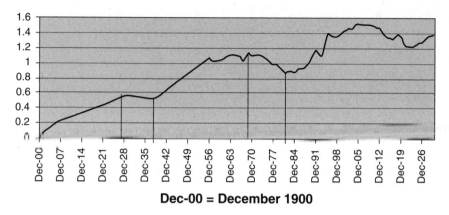

Dec-00 = December 1900

FIGURE 2.4   The Investment Rate.

down trend in the IR began in 1928, and the second began in 1969. The up-channels were longer in duration as well, as evidenced in Figure 2.4.

From there I compared the Investment Rate to both the economy and varying market trends during the relative periods of up and down cycles shown in Figure 2.4. The findings offered indisputable correlations. In effect, I had reached the top of my bottom-up analysis.

Confirming the correlations between the Investment Rate and the economy over time is important at this point, and it will validate the findings of my longer-term demand-side model accordingly. Eventually, everyone will come to realize that long-term demand drives the economy, and this is a measure of those demand trends. Because the Investment Rate measures the overall rate of demand for new investments, upward trends in the slope of the Investment Rate also suggest that an ever-increasing demand for new investments was taking place on an annualized basis through the extent of those up periods. Conversely, a declining slope in the Investment Rate suggests that less and less money was available to invest into the economy during the duration of the down trends, and therefore demand ratios decline when the Investment Rate slopes lower instead.

More specifically, an upward slope in the Investment Rate tells us that demand for new investments into our economy increases every year, and a downward-sloping curve suggests that demand declines instead. This helps postulate future economic conditions and influences current and future decisions accordingly. From there, not only does this help increase the proficiency of our personal investment decisions, but also it will positively influence proactive government policy and corporate decisions on a macro basis over time.

Back to Economics 101

If demand ratios decline and supply remains the same, prices decline. This is the proven relationship of supply and demand and the foundation of market-based economies. However, in my original analysis, supply was a dynamic measure and tough to quantify, so I put my demand-side analysis to the test all by itself. My perception suggested if demand increased and supply increased along with it, economic activity would increase anyway, and that eased the discount I imposed on the supply-side analysis of my model. As a result, I was confident moving forward with a standalone demand-side observation.

Eventually, I completely discounted supply-side theory as it relates to longer-term economic cycles, too. Irrefutably, this unique demand-side analysis was able to determine economic activity regardless of supply-side economic analysis altogether, which is taboo in modern economic circles. However, we cannot learn by following the leader, so occasional divergence can bring revelation.

Without a doubt, innovation is not furthered by stagnation. We need to think outside of the box from time to time if we want to remain strong and if we want to stay ahead of the curve. In turn, that allows us to discover a more efficient method of operation. By comparing my analysis to the economy and to the stock market over time, I was able to define long-term correlations, which superseded any relationships I had come across before. In fact, the market and my demand-side observations are directly correlated, and the Investment Rate is a leading indicator.

Here is a closer look at the correlations I have identified.

The bullet points below separate the relative periods of growth from the periods of contraction defined by the upward- and downward-sloping cycles in the Investment Rate respectively. In addition, I correlate the economic and market conditions of the periods in question. This is a summary analysis, and it makes the review easy to follow. However, a more thorough assessment is also encouraged. Specifically, related market information is available through historical journals like Dow Jones and Standard & Poors. That historical data will corroborate the bullet points below.

- The first major up period: 1900–1928
  - The Investment Rate was sloping higher.
  - This was an economic boom—the Industrial Revolution.
  - More money was available to invest into the economy every year.
  - Liquidity was plentiful.
  - The roaring 20s exemplified this boom cycle.
  - The up period lasted for 28 years.
  - Prosperity was seemingly everywhere as demand ratios increased.

- Some of this money went into real estate, stocks, and other asset classes.
- Everything performed well, and investors got used to it.
- Toward the end, investors grew comfortable with added risk.
- The end of this up cycle was an era of economic euphoria.
- The first major down period: 1928–1938
  - The Investment Rate was sloping lower.
  - This was the Great Depression.
  - Less money was available for investment into our economy every year.
  - Liquidity levels peaked in 1928 and declined for 10 straight years.
  - New money was not entering the market at the same rate.
  - Increasing growth rates were hard to produce.
  - Demand was declining.
  - Growth was stifled.
  - Multiple contractions occurred as a result.
  - The economy and the stock market came under severe pressure.
  - The market declined by 75 percent during this downturn.
  - Investments made at the beginning of the Great Depression were ill timed.
  - Full recovery took 26 years.
  - This was a natural phenomenon, and no one could stop it.
  - The Investment Rate proves that.
  - Reasonably, the impact was more severe because of poor economic policy.
  - Unfortunately, even sound policy could not have totally prevented this.
  - Sound economic policy could have provided a more resilient reaction.
  - The government did not recognize the pitfalls in advance, and it had to act reflexively and hastily instead of proactively and calmly.
- The second major up period: 1938–1969
  - The Investment Rate was sloping higher.
  - More money was available to invest into the economy every year.
  - Liquidity was plentiful.
  - This was an economic boom—the Technological Revolution.
  - Added investments spurred innovations.
  - This lasted for 31 years.
  - Market setbacks were short lived.
  - Buy and hold strategies worked well.
  - This growth phase was a natural occurrence and part of an irrefutable longer-term cycle.
- The second major down period: 1969–1981
  - The Investment Rate was sloping lower.

- Less money was available for investment into our economy every year.
- This was Stagflation.
- Decreasing demand ratios dampened economic activity.
- Real growth was virtually nonexistent.
- Demand peaked in 1969.
- The Investment Rate predefined this.
- Risks were high.
- The stock market experienced serious gyrations during this down period.
- Without sound policy, this could have been much worse.
- This natural oscillation resulted in Stagflation instead of depression.
- This could be the best-case scenario in a declining demand cycle.
- Investments took only 10 years to recover.
- Market declines were only 50 percent on a few occasions.
- *Only,* however, is a relative term.
- Although severe in their own right, these declines were less than the Great Depression, and recovery took less time accordingly. This was a direct result of more stable policy decisions.
- The third major up period: 1981, still moving higher in 2002
  - The Investment Rate was sloping higher.
  - 2002 is when I first published the Investment Rate.
  - More money was available to invest into the economy every year.
  - Liquidity was plentiful.
  - This was an economic boom—the Internet Revolution.
  - Added investments spurred innovations.
  - People first poured money into stocks.
  - Eventually, that transitioned to real estate, and the boom continued.
  - Demand was robust and unyielding.
  - Market declines were short lived.
  - These prosperous economic conditions were the natural byproduct of increasing demand ratios, and it was a natural occurrence.

In the next chapter, I will describe the end of this up cycle. For now, stopping here is the central point to my immediate observance. After all, I was in the process of formalizing the Investment Rate in early 2002. Not until afterwards did we apply it to our strategies. Therefore, I will address our application in the next chapter.

Before I get there, though, this illustration is extremely important to my purpose. It should be a lesson for modern economists and future policymakers as they make critical decisions. Of particular importance, the difference in the economic conditions during the Great Depression and the Stagflation period are significant. Even though each of these was also a period of decline in the Investment Rate, economic and market reactions were different in each case. There was a reason for that.

With certainty, government policy made the difference. Because each of these down periods, and the up periods too, were natural byproducts of concurrent demand ratios, they were also unavoidable. However, the down periods do not need to result in depressions every time, and the up periods can also be maximized. However, this will only be true if we recognize the risks in advance first. Specifically, policymakers should recognize when these up and down periods are close to coming to an end so they can make important adjustments to policy.

For example, when the major up periods in the Investment Rate end, they are usually met with economic euphoria, and growth usually peaks soon afterwards. The opposite happens at the end of the down cycles, when sentiment is capitulatory and the longer-term economic cycle bottoms instead. Obviously, pinpointing these transitions is the goal of policymakers. Striving to anticipate change is a catalyst to sound policy decisions, and the Investment Rate will help further that objective. With the Investment Rate, both governments and big business can recognize these directional shifts in advance. I will explain how this can happen. In addition, with this book, individual investors will also be able to do the same. In any case, during periods of euphoria, risks are assumed that should not be, and the result can be catastrophic if we are not ready for it.

My recommendation to policymakers specifically, but also to corporations and investors, is to be aggressive with policies designed to spur the economy during the late stages of the down cycles in the Investment Rate and to reverse that aggressive stance during the late stages of the up periods respectively. These are broad sweeping policy guidelines. If those guidelines are followed with policies that have the same objective, that simple observation would allow the economy to grow significantly during the natural up cycles defined by my forward analysis, and it would shelter the economy from disaster during the periods of declining demand. Because the Investment Rate is a leading indicator, it provides advance warning, so we can all be ready for these shifts. Therefore, individual investors and corporations can use it to make similar strategy decisions as well. I will be more specific in the next chapter.

Clearly, I was onto something. After my concise 2002 review, I found that the Investment Rate was more accurate than I could have imagined. Simple observations showed definitive relationships within these cycles.

Here is what I found.

During the up periods:

- Economic setbacks are short lived.
- Recovery from market declines is swift.

- Buy and hold strategies work for passive investors.
- Buying the dips works with proper selection.
- Positive sentiment overrides negative sentiment.
- More new money is available to be invested, and confidence builds.
- The average duration of the up cycles is 29.5 years.
- The market has increased by 394 percent through these cycles on average.

During the down periods:

- Setbacks have significant impact.
- Wealth deterioration is real.
- Buy and hold strategies fail.
- Buying the dips fails.
- Negative sentiment overrides positive sentiment.
- Less new money is available to be invested, and confidence levels deteriorate.
- The average duration is 10.5 years.
- Full recovery has been 16.5 years on average.
- Recovery can be longer than the duration of the down period.
- The market declined by 24.2 percent through these cycles on average.

From here, a few additional observations are important to reveal. First, the declines in the market during the down periods usually end a few years before the conclusion of that down period respectively. In other words, the market turns higher before the down period ends. Effectively, the market overreacts to the downside, and then starts to move higher in advance of recovery. Nonetheless, the period of weakness is still severe, but we can use this added information to our advantage. This will allow us to anticipate bottoms as well. Specifically, this will come into play when I introduce actionable strategies.

In addition, because the overall slope of the Investment Rate is positive over time, the notion that the market always goes up over time is supported as well. In this case, though, timing is everything. Regardless of pundit philosophy, timing is critically important to longer-term investment decisions. Investors cannot sit on their hands without adopting risk controls. The Investment Rate is first applied in 1900, and since then the slope is steadily higher with subtle undulations along the way. Appropriately, the market has followed in due course over that extended duration. Therefore, arguably, the market always goes up over time. The Investment Rate also suggests this. However, there are periods of severe weakness along the way, and those need to be recognized to protect wealth. Therefore, if investors ride out the storm, they are all but assured to make a solid return eventually, but they will also need to accept major losses as a natural byproduct of those idle strategies.

Specifically, if the timing of a long-term investment was associated with the beginning of the Great Depression, or the Stagflation period of the 1970s, those investments were also underwater by 75 percent and 50 percent respectively, and it took 16.5 years on average to recover from those declines. Even though the market indeed goes up over time, there are still periods of substantial risk along the way. If that associated risk matters, then timing matters, too.

Unyielding big brokerage firms will have everyone believe that the market always goes up over time, and they use that to try to prove that buy and hold strategies always work. However, their proof is both incomplete and based on underlying corporate directives as well. Of course, this was the adopted psychology of the market prior to 2008. Everyone knows the discourse that followed.

However, in 2002, when my original report came, investors were unsure. The market was under severe pressure, and it was getting worse. Buy and hold strategies were already failing. However, money flows were still there, and counterrelationships surfaced in real estate. Demand for investments still existed, and the Investment Rate proved why. My job was to relay this information to my clients, so I did. In fact, the Investment Rate proved that overall demand would actually increase for a number of years following that weakness, so buying stocks would indeed be smart again at some point. After all, the Investment Rate was still in an upward-sloping cycle in 2002 and still in the third major up period in U.S. history.

From there, I helped my clients understand that they should be buyers again at some point. Of course, that required a reconciliation of emotional burdens, but the Investment Rate helped with that. Then, with the help of timing tools, I told them exactly when to buy. Timing tools, as a result, are very important to correlate with the Investment Rate. Clearly, those tools will be an integral part of this book, and they will ultimately provide a means to our actionable strategies.

However, before we address this, we also need to lay some groundwork. In the next few chapters, I will provide the building blocks, the tools, and the strategies we incorporate into our investment decisions. This will allow us to move forward with proactive strategies. Proactive strategies, in turn, allow us to make money in any market environment, regardless of economic conditions. That is our goal.

In turn, the groundwork offered in the forthcoming chapters is critical to our continued progress. I will start with the basics and move ahead to specific strategies after those building blocks have been laid. I am an advocate of structure and discipline, and in many cases that requires a ground floor approach. Sometimes new clients want to start from the top, but that is far less efficient. We cannot expect to be experts without first learning the process. Even post-graduate MBAs need to take baby steps in the real world.

Traditional education provides us with the groundwork to move forward intelligently. However, true education comes outside of the books and within real-life application instead. In the real world, I was able to find my path, thanks to the groundwork that I laid. I learned how to learn, and I found that to be the most valuable construct I have ever retained. Learning to learn is a gateway to a much easier understanding of life's idiosyncrasies, and it can help revolutionize our approach to our investments forever.

In the next few chapters, I will pass on the qualities that allowed me to learn how to learn more about trading strategies and disciplines. I will examine real-world applications of the same principles and reveal the path to success, which we all are capable of achieving. These will act as the building blocks to our end goal and allow us to continue on the path to the comfort zone respectively.

Summary

Below is a summary of the most important topics in this chapter:

- We should stop listening to the noise.
- KISS: Keep it Simple, Sweetheart.
- The definition of the Investment Rate.
- Summary proof of the Investment Rate.

CHAPTER 3

Brackish Investors and Their Impending Doom

Although it sounds ideal, many investors thought the comfort zone was an unobtainable ideology in 2008. When this book was written, life was anything but routine for most people. Declining stock prices, declining real estate prices, and very weak domestic and global economies burdened investors worldwide. Nothing was working, and investors were unsettled. Safety was nowhere, except in government bonds, of course. However, those provided virtually no return, so alternatives seemed limited at the same time. Economists had a hard time rationalizing the widespread stress on all asset classes, and investors had a hard time trusting the prognosticators during the meltdown. Everyone seemed to have an opinion, but no one seemed to have trustworthy answers.

Understandably, investors were nervous because the playing field had changed, and they were realizing that for the first time. The natural byproduct of this uncertainty was fear. Initially, at least, the economic environment in 2008 appeared to be out of line with traditional doctrine. However, after this chapter, those conditions might seem a little more normal than they did at that time. In fact, by all accounts, the meltdown in 2008 was exactly in line with expected and predictable trends.

2008 was a rough year, and investors were learning the hard way that buy and hold strategies fail in down markets. Investors were confused at times, but the Investment Rate provides answers. The Investment Rate predefines major down cycles, and therefore it defines major economic weakness in advance. Similar pitfalls are also avoidable in the future, with the integration of the Investment Rate. The Investment Rate had already prepared my clients for the weakness in 2008, and I will explain how. This will also help with the policy decisions I referenced in the last chapter. Importantly, it also predefines major up cycles too, and that is where we left our recent discussion.

The Investment Rate has two integrated components. The first is a fundamental analysis of demand cycles, and the second is market timing and stock selection tools. We will discuss the market timing and stock selection tools in our later chapters. These will provide guides to actionable strategies in today's market environment, and I will offer past examples to reference for future application.

Predicting the Future

First, we must identify a much more important inflection point. The third major up period in U.S. history began in 1981, and we should indeed have been buying the dips along the way. But when does that up period end? This riposte is critical to our continued analysis. The derivation of the Investment Rate in 2002 paved the way for answers already, so this should come as no surprise to us now, nor should it have surprised anyone who knew about the Investment Rate when widespread economic regression began. In fact, astute readers of this book should have already been able to surmise the same.

According to our simple, yet effective leading longer-term economic and stock market indicator, the third major up period in U.S. history would end in 2007. We knew this in 2002. An advance warning came as the first report was published, and the Investment Rate told us to look ahead at the crest to anticipate a peak in liquidity and the top of the market accordingly.

Review Figure 3.1 of the Investment Rate again with the defined 2007 peak as illustrated.

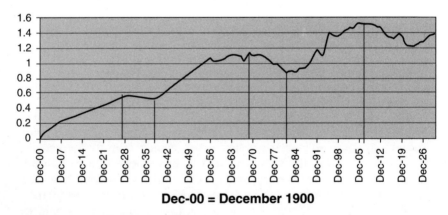

Dec-00 = December 1900

FIGURE 3.1   The Investment Rate.

During upward-sloping trends in the Investment Rate, buy and hold strategies work well for passive investors, assuming proper asset allocation and stock selection, of course. Mutual funds and managed accounts serve this purpose well, and they have become widely popular over the past few decades as a result. The most recent up cycle, the one that began in 1981, laid the groundwork for fee-based management, and investors have grown accustomed to sitting back and letting their money work for them along the way.

During upward-sloping cycles in the Investment Rate, a long bias with proper diversification should result in positive portfolio returns, without drawn-out setbacks, if investors are willing to buy the dips, especially the big ones, at all times. With that strategy, during an up cycle, positive performance will prevail in a relatively short period. The market recovers quickly from the declines, even the serious ones, during upward-sloping cycles in the Investment Rate. Even the crash of 1987, a historical occurrence by all measures, was short lived during the third up cycle. After a shocking crash, the market fully recovered in less than two years. Buy and hold investors just needed to add a little, as they were taught, and ride out the bear market environment for a while. Eventually, brokerage firms suggested the market would recover as it always had.

Unfortunately, they left something important out of their recommendation. This should come as no surprise—they always seem to leave something important out of the equation when their clients are concerned.

Although serious in nature, the so-called crash of 1987 was nothing compared to the declines during the down periods in the Investment Rate. Buying at the top of the 1987 collapse may have hurt for a while, but recovery was swift because demand ratios were still strong. However, what happens when demand ratios within the economy are declining instead? The recurring recommendations of big brokers omit this variable on a regular basis.

A Bad Idea

Buying at the beginning of the major down periods illustrated by the Investment Rate had a completely different result than buying the dips during the up cycles. The 1987 crash was amid an up cycle, and it was short lived. Had it been part of a down cycle, the result may have been dramatically different. Use history as an example. For investors who bought at the beginning of the first major down period, the Great Depression, any market-based investments would have declined by 75 percent, and they would have remained down for an extended period. Latent investments took 26 years to get whole again. Further, for investors who bought at the beginning of the second down period in history, during the Stagflation period of the 1970s, assets were down by 50 percent on occasion, and it took 10 years to get whole as well. Buy and hold strategies simply did not work within these environments. Yet, big brokers continue to recommend buy and hold strategies at all times, even though there are clear situations when these strategies do not work.

Admittedly, though, if an investor were willing to let his or her assets decline substantially, and if he or she were willing to wait an average of 18 years to recover, buy and hold strategies would have clearly paid off in the end. For investors who were able to sustain the duration of both the Great Depression and the Stagflation period of the 1970s, buy and hold strategies worked just as big brokers advised. The Investment Rate also suggests that an eventual recovery will occur over long periods of time. However, it continues to pinpoint the intermittent up and down cycles within that extended trend as well, and these are more important to measured wealth preservation.

Arguably, a buy and hold at all times approach lacks a considerate variable. It does not consider wealth preservation. In turn, that oversight could affect client affluence for decades. Therefore, the identified Investment Rate cycles offered above and included in our forward-looking statements could make the difference between personal wealth ratios over time. Those investors who recognized this when I issued my original report have had the opportunity to save themselves from substantial declines in advance. Protecting wealth and helping investors remain on the right side of the curve is my focus, and I use the Investment Rate as the foundation for my guide.

Because the Investment Rate offers conclusive leading economic and stock market indicators, investors should use it to make decisions about their financial future. Their choices to invest for the long term, become proactive, or remain in cash, should be grounded in the demand ratios offered by the Investment Rate accordingly. Specifically, that includes the intermittent up and down cycles referenced here. However, it does not end there. As we continue, additional correlations will also be included, and an associated parity analysis will help all of us determine the current state of the economy as it relates to the immediate position of the Investment Rate at any given time. That will be an example of the tools we use to predict future economic cycles. However, we are not ready for that quite yet.

Until then, we will continue to focus on the groundwork and first learn why we are able to anticipate these cycles every time. Overcoming that learning curve first will allow everyone to implement the associated strategies with ease. With anxious readers in mind, our incentive to cover the basics first should be clear. Our ability to identify economic cycles accurately could make the difference between a prosperous and meager existence, and that could affect our lifestyle forever. These initial steps are a means to an end, and therefore, our preliminary steps are very important to everyone as a result, too.

The First Line of Defense

Although the market indeed trends higher over extended periods, the undulating cycles defined by the Investment Rate are more important to my clients and me because they help us protect wealth and make proper decisions throughout the course of our lives. These cycles should also be extremely important to all investors, regardless of age. The Investment Rate tells us when to expect a healthy economic environment and when to anticipate weakness. Therefore, it also tells us when to make aggressive investment decisions, and when to stay in cash. Because of this simple observation, the Investment Rate is the first line of defense in the war on risk. In my opinion, an evaluation of the Investment Rate should be the first step to making any investment decision. This includes investments in the stock market, real estate, private business, and all other asset classes that depend on a steady flow of new money to prosper.

Before any other assessments are drawn, investors should first review the Investment Rate to determine if longer-term economic conditions are likely to improve, and if longer-term investments are wise as a result. This should be the first step in formulating economic policy on a government level as well. Before even Random Walk theories are applied, we should conduct a brief analysis of the Investment Rate. Doing this could make the difference between wealth creation and wealth destruction. For government officials and policymakers, the leading indicator that the Investment Rate offers could make the difference between a recession and a depression. These are important to me, so continuing discussions will consider government action and explain how the Investment Rate can help formulate proper government policy. In addition, I will further explain how that could have changed the scope of the economy in 2008 and beyond.

Understandably, even without the use of the Investment Rate, some astute investors remain ahead of the curve independently. In fact, many elite traders do this for a living. Because they are privy to successful investment strategies, they stay on the right side of the curve regardless of market direction by identifying these cycles in advance. They may not yet be able to assess their observations with pinpoint accuracy, as the Investment Rate often does, but they have learned to read traditional signals well. This ability allows privileged traders to protect themselves from major declines accordingly. They can do this because they have also learned to respect the warning signs, and that is a critical element to forward progress. In addition, other front-runners also have their finger on the pulse of the economy because they can interpret events with ease. They are able to separate the good news from the bad news, and that from the news that has no bearing on the economy or the markets at all. Those who are right every time avoid the big mistakes. This unique ability is not common, but it allows these select investors to stay ahead of the curve, and it is a full-time job. Luckily, for us, it does not have to be that hard. In fact, sometimes it can even be too easy.

In any case, if red flags are appearing, certain investors know there is a need for change, and they respect those warning signs accordingly. Unfortunately, though, normal people do not recognize these same pitfalls most of the time. However, as we have seen, after every major setback they wish they had. Hindsight is always 20–20; but foresight can be, too. Moreover, small investors are not the only ones prone to distress. Even those astute investors who are right most of the time are hurt badly by being wrong on occasion. This is true because of the large bets they make. Therefore, all classes of investor can benefit from leading economic and stock market indicators. That is where the Investment Rate comes into play. The Investment Rate puts everyone on a level playing field by accurately disclosing longer-term economic cycles clearly.

For example, it provided advance warning of the first two major down periods in U.S. history, and those warnings were immediately actionable. During the Great Depression and the Stagflation period of the 1970s, for example, who, if they saw the red flags in advance, would have been willing to let their assets decline by 50 to 75 percent? Furthermore, who would have been willing to wait 10 to 26 years to recover their wealth if they could avoid it? At first glance, the answer is no one, but that is not the right answer.

Instead, the answer might surprise you. Even intelligent and sophisti- cated investors are lumped into this category. Some have made mistakes over the past three decades; they have recovered every time, and now they believe that they can buy the dips every time and never look back. Money managers believe this, too, but like traditional doctrine, they do not recog- nize the longer-term cycles of the Investment Rate either. Passive investors have grown accustomed to delegating financial responsibility, and that has created a landscape prone to serious pitfalls.

George Soros provided us with an excellent example, but he averted the disaster, too. In his most recent work (*The New Paradigm for Finan- cial Markets*) George Soros talks about his delegation of responsibility. He allowed outside managers to invest his money for years, and he played a much more passive role during that time. This, in my opinion, was a brack- ish decision. Interestingly, that was fine because the Investment Rate was sloping higher at the same time. This lasted until 2007, when he astutely identified the end of his Superbubble. Because of his shrewd recognition, and because he was thinking outside of traditional guidelines, in 2007 he took measured steps to protect his wealth, and he reclaimed the onus of responsibility for his investments. Clearly, he identified risk on the horizon, and that prompted him to take action. Although he may not have read the Investment Rate yet, he also recognized the same behaviors as those pinpointed in my model. Interestingly, he is in search of reason to support his Superbubble and his Reflexivity theories, and the Investment Rate provides explanation for each of those.

For example, coincidentally, the third major up period in U.S. history started in 1981 and ended in 2007. Increasing consumer liquidity levels influenced this, and that is directly in line with Soros's Superbubble. In 2007, he balanced his portfolio with short positions as referenced in his book, and that timely move seemed to save him from the destruction experienced in the markets during 2008. Anyone who did not take similar action felt the pain levied by the market immediately afterwards. Unfortunately, this is exactly what happened to most passive investors in 2008, and this is why so many people were confused and under serious emotional strain during that time. Because most investors failed to take similar action, they were hurt by the market.

Unfortunately, most of us should have known better. We should not have been exposed to that degree. Nevertheless, most people also fail to act preemptively on a regular basis. This is human nature, and very troubling. We have already witnessed the result of laissez-faire regulation during both the Internet bubble and in the financial crisis of 2008; most of us lived through this, and these environments burdened investors in both instances. Unfortunately, investors have also adopted a follow-the-leader approach to investments as laissez-faire policies trickled down, and that has hurt them repeatedly. Because they do not learn, they deserve that added burden each time. If investors recognize the risks but do nothing to control them, they need to accept the harsh results as a logical consequence. The declines in 2002 should have been a call to action, but then every setback should serve the same purpose. Unfortunately, they often go unrecognized. My frustrations escalate when investors fail to learn from their mistakes.

Protection from the Mistakes of the Government

However, and equally as concerning as a citizen of the United States, investors are not the only ones who do this. The U.S. government has the same problem. But, this should come as no surprise. After all, the government is comprised of people, and human nature is prone to laziness and imperfection. Fortunately, well-established policies are supposed to prevent the government from making repeated errors over time. Our government has built in a system of checks and balances to prevent this. This was a brilliant observation during the formation of our Constitution, but unfortunately, that effort does not always work. These checks and balances are also subject to human failures. In 2007, for example, the government had already removed a number of restrictions from its spending policies, and investors found little need to tighten the reins on their own pocketbooks or their investments. Given the expected sanctuary of the market, and the contented assumptions associated with the economy, investors did not see the need to scrutinize either. The opposite should have been true, as we all know today. Eventually, those lax restrictions came back to haunt everyone.

Increasing debt ratios are an excellent example of follow-the-leader tendencies. The U.S. government, beginning in the Reagan Era, which was also the onset of the Superbubble, began assuming tremendous amounts of debt in the early 1980s. Growth fostered by debt issuance became widespread and mainstream for the government, where just a few years prior the opposite was true. Money inflows from foreign nations were finding shelter from relatively unstable foreign economies within a system originally designed with integrated boundaries and restrictions. Soon, those restrictions were lifted. In essence, the U.S. government began printing money to foster growth. Normally, we would expect the dollar to weaken in this situation, but the dollar remained strong due to the interrelationship of foreign trade that eventually defined the global economy we know today. In real terms, printing money became commonplace for decades. Even in 2008, after dollar risks had already become obvious, and even though bailouts and government spending were driving U.S. debt levels to historical highs, economists still did not seem to care. Then, in 2009, Americans began asking new questions for the first time in a long while. Finally, we wanted to know who would pay for it.

The debt without consequence leadership offered by the U.S. government eventually trickled down to financial institutions and the U.S. consumer. Soon carrying large amounts of debt was an acceptable way of life and a means for growth for both the government and its citizens. By mid-2007 household debt equaled GDP levels. The figure below does not include government debt or unfunded commitments such as Medicare or Social Security, but still it proves this point quite clearly. If added together, household debt, government debt, and unfunded obligations would be four to five times GDP or more. Estimates of unfunded liabilities vary, but they usually fit these boundaries.

Refocused, our point concentrates on the trickle-down effect of government policy to U.S. citizens. Figure 3.2 is limited to household debt, but it still sufficiently exemplifies the follow-the-leader laziness referenced above.

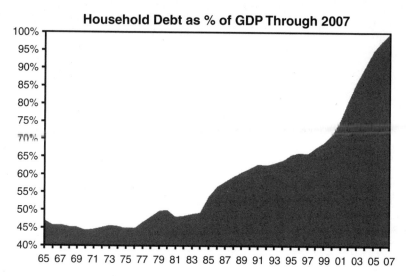

FIGURE 3.2   Debt versus GDP.

Source: Federal Reserve Z-1; Bureau of Economic Analysis.

Now that rational policy is finally surfacing again, the world is quickly realizing that growth based on debt assumption cannot last forever. The foregone disciplines of the U.S. government allowed debt ratios to skyrocket first on a government level, then on a corporate level, and finally on a consumer level. Now, because they followed the leader, U.S. consumers, who have been the driving force behind the global economy thus far, are in trouble. Laissez-faire regulations and a skewed order of precedence by U.S. policymakers caused this. If they had recognized the shift in the Investment Rate, though, they could have taken steps to lessen the impact.

Protection from Big Brokers and Money Managers

Evidenced during the Internet bubble, brokerage firms have a skewed priority scale. During the bubble, lax oversight by investors existed at the same time as easing policy referendums were put into place. This is a recipe for disaster. The first priority of any publicly traded brokerage firm is to grow revenues and earnings to satisfy the street. Although their clients are the bread and butter of these firms, client wealth preservation comes somewhere further down the list of established priorities. During the Internet bubble, for example, these brokerage firms maintained strong buy ratings on overvalued Internet stocks to win their investment banking business.

They made decisions at the expense of client portfolios by encouraging investments into these stocks with visions of windfall investment banking revenues offsetting the obvious risks to client accounts. We already know the consequences of these actions and the long-term adverse impact they had on client wealth. We should have also learned our lesson. Obviously, client-based wealth preservation is not as important as corporate earnings to these firms. This lesson has already been learned, repetitively, but many investors do not seem to get the point, so I am repeating it again with the hope that everyone will eventually understand.

My experience as a financial advisor provided additional insight to this practice. Office managers encouraged the financial advisors who worked under them to build businesses based on professional management fees. In fact, my practice of stock selection and position trading was frowned upon, because commissions were sporadic. Management fees, after all, provide a stable and predictable income stream for the broker. In addition, the firm was able to offer reasonable earnings guidance to Wall Street analysts by using this practice as well. From a business standpoint, recurring revenue models made sense.

In addition to identifiable revenue streams, this practice also reduces the responsibility of the broker and the brokerage firm as well. For example, if one manager is underperforming, there are plenty of other managers to choose from, and the decision to choose a new manager is relatively seamless. Therefore, the risk of losing a client and the revenue generated from his or her account based on an underperforming managed account is far less than if poor stock selection within the broker-client relationship caused the loss instead. As a result, big brokerage firms prefer to leave all investment decisions to the hired money manager, and they advise their brokers and their clients to do the same. Eventually, the title of stock broker became outdated. Brokers began to focus on gathering assets, selling managers, and growing their identifiable revenue streams by the guidance of their firm instead. This worked well for everyone during the most recent up cycle, and assets under management seemed to grow measurably for everyone I knew in the business. On paper, this was an excellent model.

However, most money managers did not even keep up with the market anyway, so I seriously questioned the practice when I was a broker. In the late 1990s, an estimated 95 percent of all mutual funds and money managers underperformed the market over a 10-year timeframe. That number is similar in today's market. For example, I remember being approached by Russell Asset Management, who wanted me to sell its risk-conscious products to my clients in 1998. However, the portfolios this company referenced did not even come close to the returns of the S&P 500. The lag was about 30 percent. However, there was a slight reduction in volatility, and they touted that as a key selling point. Even so, I considered the reduction in risk marginal. Why, I asked myself, would I ever place client's money in the hands of a manager who did not even keep pace with the market? Show me a manager who beats the market over time, and I will consider it, I thought. My focus was on equity portfolios, and therefore I measured the performance of managers against the market itself. Very few impressed me over extended durations, and the ones who did had very large minimum investments, which made them difficult to approach.

Eventually, associations that are more negative became apparent to me as well. Over time, after exiting the brokerage industry, I came to other startling conclusions, and the losses that resulted from that investment style during the down markets I experienced in my lifetime verified that. The most revealing were the inherent restrictions of those accounts. Most managed accounts actually dampen an investor's ability to react to market fluctuations, while also struggling to keep up with the performance of the market itself at the same time. That prevents investors from controlling their risk. Specifically, a portfolio of 50 to 75 stocks, which is normal for most managed accounts, is difficult to liquidate quickly. Therefore, managed accounts actually restrict proactive investment strategies and expose those housed assets to market corrections. Modifications to these portfolios take time, and more often than not, the market has the ability to move before portfolios adjust. In addition, although the client usually remains in control of these assets, he or she is also encouraged by his or her broker and the brokerage firm to let the paid professional money manager make all of the investment decisions, and that often keeps clients at bay until it is too late. After all, clients are paying fees for that service already, and a reputable firm in most cases has recommended these managers to them. Therefore, psychology supports the notion of letting the manager make these decisions accordingly. Unfortunately, that is not always the best practice. Sometimes, as George Soros did, reclaiming responsibility is required.

Unfortunately, large financial institutions have brainwashed investors into thinking that buy and hold strategies using professionally managed accounts are the best approach to long-term investments strategies forever. In actuality, they are not. Instead, this practice secures substantial income streams for these brokerage firms, and it limits the flexibility of the client at the same time. Interestingly, it does this within the guidelines of traditional doctrine. More interesting, though, traditional guidelines frown on strategies designed to profit from both up and down market conditions as well. I attribute this to the laziness integral to human nature. Money managers, who are human beings, would much rather invest money in companies deemed to be sound, and let the market do the rest, instead of actively managing risk at the same time. Unfortunately, that presents major problems and puts assets at unnecessary risk as a result.

Even a simple index fund or a market-based ETF with minimal fees is almost always a better alternative to managed accounts or mutual funds because of the added flexibility, the lower associated fees, and the higher overall returns. This practice, however, removes the warm and fuzzy feeling associated with the broker-client relationship, and it breaks the recurring revenue model encouraged by major financial institutions as well. Therefore, big brokers prefer and press managed accounts instead.

Large financial institutions encourage investors to stay the course, pay the fees, communicate with their broker, and believe that the market trends higher over time, no matter what. Depending on an investor's timeframe and his or her need to access capital, this could be the most obvious fallacy in the financial industry today.

During upward-sloping trends in the Investment Rate, the market trends higher over time, declines are short lived, and investors are less concerned with relative performance than they are with overall positive returns. Earlier, I offered an example of the 1987 market crash. The Internet bubble was a more recent example of the same phenomenon. Demand ratios were still strong, and buying the dips was still a good idea. Brokerage firms were doing well and assets under management were growing. At the same time, so were the recurring fees associated with managed accounts, so there was no need for the brokers to change anything materially.

Brokerage firms offered that same point of view going into 2008 as well. They recommended staying the course. In fact, they have been making this same unyielding recommendation since the upward-sloping trend in the Investment Rate began in 1981. This time, though, the landscape was a little different, and we know why. In addition to the findings of the Investment Rate, 2008 was a time when the financial system was on the brink of collapse. Yet money managers and mutual funds maintained their defined buy and hold strategies. Even though the economy was failing and other financial firms were dissolving in front of their eyes, a reversion to cash was virtually nonexistent in most managed accounts and mutual funds. Either they did not recognize the shift in demand as we have, or they did not want to sacrifice their revenue streams instead. In either case, this was a clear red flag, and it defined the self-interested corporate policies of these firms.

Brokers Are in It to Make Money!

Nevertheless, faulting brokerage firms or mutual fund companies for an aversion to cash is sophomoric. They are paid when they invest money, not when they hold it in cash. They are not paid to protect wealth; they are paid to place assets. In some cases, they are also paid because they have convinced someone they have built a relationship with to stay the course as well. In fact, this is an integral part of the relationship and a key to retaining business during the tough times. Brokers are the conduit. Never expect a broker to contact a client and tell him or her to move to cash, sell a mutual fund, or fire a manager, unless there are other investment alternatives to consider. Brokerage firms want their clients to remain invested at all times, and they preach buy and hold strategies to incentivize brackish investment decisions to retain fees. They preach this to their brokers first, and then teach them how to relay that information to their clients. Rationally, corporate policy drives the firm, and the broker is a pawn in the process.

Possibly, in 2008 many firms may have shut their eyes to the economic landscape that sat directly in front of them. Almost surely, they had not yet realized the findings of the Investment Rate either. Unfortunately, though, that probably would not have mattered anyway. After all, brokerage firms rely on these revenue streams to survive, so how could they reasonably recommend cash and allow their revenues streams to dissolve? The adverse impact this would have on their stock would be detrimental, and the board of directors would never consent to that associated risk. Instead, from a corporate perspective, the better action in their opinion is often no action at all.

Eventually, I believe that will be one of the biggest mistakes in the history of our financial markets. From a client perspective, brokerage firms chose revenue streams over wealth preservation at the beginning of the third major down period in U.S. history. Our record books will tell the story from there.

According to the Investment Rate, the third major down period in U.S. history began in December 2007. This down period will last 16 years. In addition, the duration of this decline is substantially longer than the Great Depression or the Stagflation Period of the 1970s. Specifically, the third major down period in U.S. history ends in 2023. The projected economic weakness during this downturn should continue to be severe. In turn, this weakness will continue to affect all of the investments that are important to us as well. Nothing will be sheltered from these declining demand ratios. This will affect all asset classes. Review the familiar image in Figure 3.3 once again, but recognize that this derivation represents a declining Investment Rate specifically.

Don't Be a Brackish Investor

Brackish investing is a term I use to describe the inactions of that portion of our population content to take whatever the economy or the stock market dishes out.

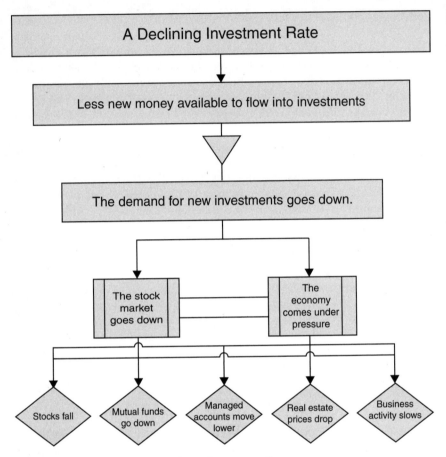

FIGURE 3.3   The impact of a declining Investment Rate.

Brackish investors are content to let their assets sit in a mutual fund, or in the hands of a money manager, without oversight or restriction. They continue to believe that their assets will be managed with wealth protection in mind, and they believe their assets will grow over time regardless of economic conditions. Brackish investors live well in longer-term economic up cycles, but brackish investors are often devastated during longer-term down cycles as defined by the Investment Rate.

The impending doom of brackish investors lies within their laissez-faire approach to their own investments. During major down cycles in the Investment Rate, investors cannot sit back and let their investments work independently as they can during the up cycles. Demand ratios are deteriorating during these declining environments, and we cannot expect a prompt recovery as we can in upward-sloping cycles. Unfortunately, many investors have only lived through the 26-year up cycle that began in 1981, so they are not yet familiar with prolonged periods of weakness, and they do not remember the devastation associated with buy and hold strategies during these down cycles. Sadly, major brokerage firms failed to recognize these risks as well, even though most of them have been in existence for quite some time. The government is no exception either. So far, the U.S. government has failed to shelter the country from impending economic disaster. As bleak as this may sound, this book will open their eyes as well.

Without question, buy and hold strategies fail at the beginning of the major down periods evidenced by the Investment Rate. Based on historical trends, recovery has taken 18 years on average, and assets are significantly underwater along the way. Accordingly, fee-based management fails during down periods, too, and that happens because of the brackish nature of their structure. Therefore, the guide of major brokerage firms is flawed as a result.

Direct comparisons have already been drawn between the previous two down cycles, but this down cycle could be much worse. Not only is the duration of this third down cycle greater than the previous two, but the current and projected household and government debt ratios in the United States loom over the economy and impede resiliency. This will eventually influence higher taxes and create a circular impediment on economic recovery. Investors need to be proactive, and they must re-establish oversight, reclaim responsibility, and implement conditional measures for wealth preservation accordingly. The risk of a Greater Depression is real.

Although this circumstance appears dire based on traditional doctrine, this unique situation still provides opportunity. The cup is half full, but that positive approach must begin with a realization of the drawbacks associated with traditional guidelines; they are ineffective during periods of weakness. However, with slight skew investors can still realize positive returns in down markets. Therefore, my focus from this point forward will revert to the positives associated with this leading indicator entirely. With advanced knowledge, we all should be able to protect our wealth and realize opportunities after we complete this lesson. In other words, if we know what lies ahead, we should be able to use it to our advantage, and my strategies point us in that direction appropriately.

Acting as an alternative to traditional buy and hold strategies, the third major down period in U.S. history promotes a resolve of proactive trading disciplines instead. Proactive trading strategies apply to all durations and asset classes as well. They apply to long-term investments, retirement plans, real estate, and businesses. Proactive and risk-averse investment strategies need to be applied to any and all investments in any and all asset classes that rely on a positive inflow of new investment capital to grow. This broad range suggests that everyone needs to take a close look at his or her current holdings and ongoing investment decisions, then relate them to the findings of the Investment Rate and develop a conscious understanding of the future economic landscape before moving forward. These are, after all, where most people have their wealth, and wealth protection is our first goal. Recognition is therefore the number one step toward a proactive lifestyle.

Investors cannot sit back and watch their wealth dissolve during these down cycles, and then expect to recoup those losses immediately in the face of deteriorating demand ratios. Recovery takes far too long during declining demand trends, and most investors do not want to wait that long, or they cannot afford to. Therefore, flexibility and a reversion to cash are required from time to time. I hope that a professional investment advisor can help foster a proactive approach with wealth preservation in mind, but managed accounts restrict flexibility and may not be the right choice given the proactive requirements of the current and future economic landscape.

Brackish investors have an impending doom, but they also have alternatives. As we progress, I will reveal a handful of immediate options. The groundwork will continue to build until everyone is capable of protecting wealth and realizing opportunities regardless of economic or market conditions.

However, additional resolutions still exist within the scope of the financial industry today, so our next chapter will address those ongoing concerns specifically. Objectively, I will dispel additional widespread notions imposed by big brokerage firms, so we can revert to the mean. The mean is our starting point.

Summary

Below is a summary of the most important topics in this chapter:

- The third major down period in U.S. history has already begun.
- Even so, brokers recommend buy and hold strategies at all times.
- Brokers are in the business of generating fees, not protecting wealth.
- They will never tell anyone to move to cash.
- Major losses are a normal part of buy and hold strategies.
- We must take control of our own risk to avoid those losses.
- Proactive strategies help everyone protect wealth and realize opportunity regardless of market direction.

CHAPTER 4

Golden Handcuffs

Faulting brokerage firms for producing a functional recurring revenue model is slightly misplaced, as I have already shown. A recurring revenue model is arguably the best-equipped method of sustaining revenue and cash flow in a capitalistic economy. Growth companies may not see it this way, because revenue is consistent, often negotiated, and simply trickles in slowly. However, recurring revenue models have far less assumed risk in times of economic weakness and therefore they add significant value over time. International Business Machines is a great example. In 2008, while most companies were struggling to increase sales, or merely sustain sales in extreme cases, IBM's services division, a division whose principle is recurring revenues, fared comparably well. Then, in 2009, the same thing happened. These same results seemed lackluster during the boom periods, but they proved to be firmly grounded as the economy turned.

Faulting big brokers for pressing a recurring revenue model is unfounded from a corporate perspective. Yet clients must recognize these practices because they affect the trickle-down policy that passes through to their financial advisors and ultimately to their portfolios as well. That is where the negative influence exists. Unfortunately for the clients of these big brokers, they must wear two separate hats when evaluating their housed investments and the recommendations associated with them. The first hat should be an objective one, which observes the business practices that ultimately drive the company to whom they have entrusted their wealth. Those observations should be noted and compared to their personal interests. Only after an analysis of corporate objectives is compared to the best interest of the client can a rational conclusion be drawn.

For some, the proposed brackish investment policies of large brokerage firms will be the best choice. Brackish clients are content with losses for one reason or another. Potentially, this could mean that the impact of portfolio-related decline does not affect their real wealth. However, others in this category don't see the associated risks at all, they don't monitor their portfolios, and they erroneously entrust their broker and brokerage firm almost blindly. This can spell trouble, as I have pointed out already.

Fortunately, on the opposite side of the spectrum, an obvious dissociation will appear more clearly to other astute investors at the same time, and a transition to a defined proactive approach will immediately follow. That was the case with Tom, the client I reference in the Real-Life Example at the end of the book. He saw the pitfalls, and with the help of the Investment Rate, he was able to sidestep them. Without using the Investment Rate directly, this is what George Soros did. However, as I have already shown, the Investment Rate proves his Superbubble, so he indirectly used it, too.

However, a larger percentage of the investing public will probably be stuck on the fence as they contemplate a potentially life-changing decision. That's where I come in. Not only will I help everyone make this decision, just as I helped Tom, but I'll prove that we can empower the markets to work for us over time as well. We can make money in any market irrespective of economic woes or direction. From there, I'll also demonstrate the guidance I provide to my clients that keeps them on the right side of the curve as well. With a little luck, a transition to a proactive lifestyle will be relatively seamless for everyone as we move forward.

Although I have disproved the main investment vehicle offered by big brokerage firms, most brokers could actually help investors understand proactive strategies from time to time, so I encourage a consultation with personal financial advisors on a regular basis. Before policy shifts are made, most investors can use the added advice of professionals. In fact, advisors can help in a meaningful way if they are pointed in the right direction. Often this involves a divergence from already ominous pre-existing corporate policies, but it is not impossible. Therefore, when addressing proposed investment policy transitions for our advisors, make sure to adequately reveal all underlying objectives. Only then will we be able to determine if our broker or advisor is on the same page. Developing actionable investment policy is our objective and it should be the objective of our advisors as well.

The Path to the Comfort Zone Starts Here

The path to the comfort zone will become clear from this point forward.

Past experience has proven that investors often develop a reliance on passive tools. This is human nature. We tend toward those things that are easy, or familiar to us. We also tend toward those things that seem less arduous, or more satisfying immediately. Most of us also surround ourselves with people who appreciate our company because it makes us feel good. More important to this conversation, though, we often engage in strategies that have been engrained in our trading psyche over time. This was particularly dangerous in 2008, and it will continue to be dangerous for the next handful of years, given the transition defined by the Investment Rate.

Indirectly, the past success of any investment technique satisfies human nature and implies that those tools will work again and again regardless of current or future market conditions. For some, these habitual tools are mutual funds. For others, their money managers have acted as a security blanket between them and market risk. And for others, like the buyers of Internet stocks in 2000, simple techniques are repeated until such time as those techniques dissolve wealth altogether. This was the situation during the Internet bubble, and it has been defined as the cause of the credit crisis in 2008. In every case, past-proven professional money management techniques include carefully developed stock selection engineered to balance risk and provide return in equity-based portfolios. This often offers immediate solace to some investors. But these techniques have a vested interested to produce revenues for the firm as well, and they do not work in all market environments.

Specifically, as we have already proven, equity exposure is not always the best path to wealth preservation, and money managers get paid to have our money invested at all times. Therefore, from time to time money managers may not be the best path to wealth preservation. Sometimes cash is king, and because we have already proven that an aversion to cash is inherent in the brokerage industry, a conflict of interest presents itself.

Ultimately the responsibility of wealth preservation must be passed on to the client if part of the definition of preservation includes cash on occasion. Brokers and brokerage firms cannot be expected to advise cash positions because they don't receive consideration for those recommendations. Therefore, clients are left responsible for making the decision to move to cash from time to time, and that leaves them wanting answers that may seem difficult to produce at first. But rest assured, those answers are far less difficult than we might think. I'll gladly prove that as we move forward. Nonetheless, with very few resources to draw from at the beginning, many investors become confused, unsure, and eventually they remain willing brackish investors for at least a short while longer. Eventually, though, as they are backed into a corner, their decisions turn into all-or-none decisions in down markets.

However, in this reference even a decision not to make a decision is still a decision. Either people are all in and let their money manager control their wealth, or they are all out and they convert 100 percent of their assets to cash instead. Indeed, that sounds aggressive, but it might not stop there. Sometimes the envelope is pushed even further. In 2008, for example, investors preferred Treasury bonds to cash because they were considered a safer haven than money market accounts or CDs. Treasuries were considered the only asset class guaranteed to return principal.

Ultimately, the choice to remain invested or move to cash depends on the relative performance of the portfolio and the risk assessment of the client. There is another lingering component here, though. Thus far the prospects of capital appreciation have been left out of our discussion, and we have focused on wealth protection instead. However, capital appreciation is very important, too, and we will address this issue accordingly. For now, our first focus is on risk control, and specifically wealth preservation as it relates to the client-broker relationship. Capital appreciation will be discussed as we proceed.

With our immediate focus in mind, after a series of like encounters clients eventually realize that a reliance on their broker or brokerage firm for wealth preservation is likely to result in investment transition rather than cash allocation. If this has not been realized already, be warned. Brokers rarely recommend a transition to cash because they don't get paid to do that. Therefore, if cash is required given certain market conditions, and if brokers rarely advise cash, then independent investors are left to determine when the time is right. That's what I do. I make these transitions easy to anticipate and even easier to take advantage of, and that helps clients make confident decisions.

Reasonably, the question is when should our money be exposed to the market, and when should we short or move to cash? I will teach everyone how to find those answers. However, there is an important revelation to make first.

Timing is important to achieving this objective, and this is a skill I will pass on in later chapters, but we can't afford to rush in and begin using these important tools without full disclosure. First, a more important step must be taken. We're going to tackle the process one step at a time, and we will cover all bases, but we cannot start at the end and work our way back. We must start at the beginning and work forward. Otherwise, we will be prone to serious mistakes. I use a similar approach for all new members who join Stock Traders Daily. Given the success of my trading models, many new clients want to jump in with both feet without first understanding the premise that defines those models. In turn, many of them make avoidable mistakes. Only after they take the time to understand the foundation that has tenaciously built the models I offer do they begin to make timely decisions efficiently.

Therefore, before I introduce timing techniques, I must first attempt to ensure that all investors have the ability to make the necessary transitions to cash when the time is right. This is a requirement before we move forward and a significant leap ahead at the same time. Interestingly, though, ability, as it is used here, does not reference cash on hand or sophisticated trading platforms. Instead, ability refers to a mindset and a comprehension of our strategy definitions instead. Afterwards, timing tools can be introduced and used effectively to move positions out of investments and into cash to protect wealth at the right time. For most, these decisions will not require sophisticated tools or in-depth research. All it takes is discipline.

Start with the Basics

Herein lies the structure of this book. We all need to have the ability to make these decisions, and that ability is found within an obligatory framework. Initially, a few preliminary measures must be taken to avert potentially slothish reactions to essential compulsory investment decisions. Then we can move forward with the building blocks I mentioned before. In the end, with proactive strategies we will all be capable of pursuing our objectives independently and with confidence.

Always, we must start with the basics. However, in this model, the basics are rooted not within education or experience, but within ourselves and our personal attachments.

First, investors must not have an emotional tie to their investments. Emotions have no place in this business. For those who allow their emotions to get the best of them, failure is almost surely imminent. Emotions can be harmful in a number of ways, and therefore they must also be controlled. An example might be an emotional apprehension to taking a small loss early, which then turns into a big loss over time. Or it might be rooted in a callous disregard for proactive decisions that eventually replaces well-defined risk controls. Unfortunately, this happens all the time. In fact, I witnessed this firsthand as well. One of my best friends watched his portfolio decline from $430,000 to $30,000 in 2008 because he was heavily weighted in Citigroup stock. On November 24, 2008, when the government offered a bailout strategy to Citigroup, he was on the brink of a complete loss. The reasons for this might have been the emotional ties he had to the company he worked for, his aversion to risk control, or both. After 2008, we probably all know someone like this.

Regardless of the representation, emotional bonds are tied to failed strategy over time and they have no place in any of the decisions we make about our investments. This is true regardless of situation or condition. When emotions start playing a role in our investment decisions, a red flag should tell us that we are doing something wrong, and a reversion to the mean needs to take place.

Although it is statistically derived, my reference to mean refers to the starting point from which all decisions are made. This is a predisposition with rules and disciplines proven to work over time. A reversion to the mean wipes our slate clean, if it needs to be, so that we can start fresh. This starting point, because it is intended to be a healthy reversion, also restarts our mind so we can approach our strategies with a level head again. I relate this process to taking a nap; sometimes we just need to shut down for a while and let the dust settle. Afterwards we are more capable of getting back on track.

In turn, this gives us the opportunity to make productive trading decisions once more. Sometimes we lose focus on otherwise obvious rules; almost everyone does this at one time or another, and this process helps restore those conditions accordingly. A reversion to the mean is necessary when emotional distractions take us off course. Expect to have a reversion to the mean a few times a year. I consider this normal for most people. Unfortunately, some take longer to recognize their divergence and the emotional ties associated with it than others. Regardless of individual propensity, however, throughout time our responsibility is to recognize this condition in ourselves, and heal the diversion before it becomes destructive. A refusal to revert to the mean can lead to significant losses, so careful attention must be paid to our emotional hazards at all times. Luckily, once we recognize that a problem exists, a reversion is both a logical and seamless transition. Clearly, the first step is admitting we have a problem. Once we recognize a divergence, we just have to shut down for a short while. That usually satisfies the return to the mean we are looking for. Specifically, that means no computer, no news, and no economy.

Recognize Potential Pitfalls

With the mean in our back pocket, the next expected step in our process is presenting examples of potential problems. Hopefully, that will offer a starting point for cognitive recognition. We want to identify problems before they begin to affect our decision-making process, but there could be a number of those, so initially that sounds difficult. Fortunately, though, potential hazards can be identified relatively easily. Instead, if we allow ourselves to be hurt, it is the healing process that may take time. In addition, our inaction may also avert accomplishment if we allow it to. Once again, this reflects back on human nature, and it transcends investment strategy to affect our personal lives as well. Diets are an excellent example. Many people know that their diets are poor because they have already identified personal health concerns, but very few know what to do to change their bad habits. Instead, they turn to a nutritionist, hire a personal trainer, or start reading self-help books related to health and well-being to fix their problems. The same process exists here. Most investors know that problems exist; they just need to fix them. That starts with recognition, and then translates into action.

Luckily, identifying emotional discourse as it relates to our investment strategy is not nearly as difficult to identify as internal health concerns.

Frequently used words and phrases, and associated thought patterns, often provide ample red flags. Many of these identifiers are used regularly by both novice and professional investors, and in almost all market conditions as well. Akin to diet concerns, this is far too widespread, and it needs to be stemmed. For those capable of doing so, the prospects of proactive investment strategies will surface. But if emotional conditions dominate mental capacity, and if investors begin to use jargon like hope, feel, believe, think, pray, need, must have, it later increase, I might be wiped out, or anything similar to those obvious predispositions, pitfalls will almost surely lie ahead instead. If an investor finds himself facing this realization, he should immediately understand his divergence and revert to the mean quickly. From there, if this idiolect becomes commonplace, take it even further, and consult a professional. Doing so will help clear the mind, refresh the psyche, and allow the process to restart seamlessly again without those lingering concerns. As our building blocks come together, this will play an integral role in our constant development. Emotional conditioning is critical.

With that understood, continuing with our disclosure of the preliminary measures designed to ensure proactive investment decisions in any market environment, investors must also always have a broad understanding of the current economic landscape. We cannot shut our eyes completely. This secures a more prompt reaction to shifts in the market, and it prevents retracements that subsequently cause delays. Investors should never have to re-evaluate learned information prior to making an investment decision. If retracement, or re-evaluation, is averted, the result is improved efficiency. Efficient behavior is important in proactive models that incorporate risk controls. Although it might sound like work, this is a routine and a lifestyle, not a chore. Most of these steps are regular for us already anyway, and therefore very little additional work needs to be done in order to keep pace with current affairs. We don't need to develop economic policy or dig through corporate earnings releases to keep up. All we need is a broad understanding of current conditions. The steps are straightforward. Read the paper, watch the business channel, and stay informed of recent happenings on a regular basis. Most important, consider an unbiased market evaluation the best path to predefining market direction. This simple approach will usually suffice.

With constructive tools in hand, investors are more able to react appropriately in a relatively timely manner. Investors must be able to react to shifts in the market if they intend on using proactive strategies. This requires investors to understand what is happening, what will happen, and why. Although I offer my proactive disciplines through automated venues, I also require everyone to understand them before using them. Depending on the chosen strategy, time constraints will vary. I offer five different strategies in this book, and one or more of them are appropriate for most people. My strategies range from longer-term proactive models to active trading models, with specialized systems in between. The common denominator in all of them is risk control. This is integral to every strategy we incorporate.

However, as efficient as these strategies may be, they still require a time commitment to be used effectively. In turn, this requires emotional conditioning and an understanding of current conditions. No one will do this for you, unless of course you pay them to, so some time is required to use each one of my strategies. Eventually, that time commitment becomes infinitesimal. Reasonably, certain strategies are more intensive than others, and therefore time may eventually be an integral component in deciding which strategy or strategies are immediately actionable, but others are not demanding.

For some, proactive strategies that integrate risk controls can be adopted without sacrificing time or lifestyle at all. Some of the tools I offer allow investors to work, play golf, or trade other stocks while knowing that a proactive risk-control strategy is working for them while they go about their normal day. Other strategies, however, require a hands-on approach. These are more intended for investors who prefer to make their own decisions, rather than let a machine handle the work for them. There are positives and negatives to each strategy, and we will address all of these in the final chapters, after our predefinitions are offered.

The Emotional Ties Levied by Big Brokers

Next, we are going to tackle the most important action item in this chapter, emotional control. Emotional control is the most important throttle we can impose on ourselves. We have already discussed the impediment of emotional decision making; now we are going to take it a step further and discuss the capture of those emotions. We must respect the power of our emotions and our mind in order to unbind our aptitude for investment strategy. Everything reverts to human nature, and this section is specific to that. If we continue to revert to the basics, as we are doing here, we will find this process quite simple. I will do this throughout the rest of the book. Using KISS theory, we have already quelled the noise that otherwise confuses economic policy, and we uncovered the Investment Rate as a result. The same principle applies here. We need to quell the noise.

Emotional ties restrict everyone's decision-making process, and they are not limited to investments. From relatively simple decisions to more complex ones, emotions can play an integral role in our lives if we let them. This happens in all walks of life, and in varying business and interpersonal situations. Unfortunately, sometimes we can't avoid it. For example, struggling to decide where to spend Christmas is difficult for many married couples, and that simple resolution doesn't usually impact personal wealth ratios like our investment decisions can. Therefore, the pressure should be more constrained, but it is obviously not. Because it is personally important, it also weighs on our emotions. If only there were a way to alleviate the burden of concern. If only we could be sure that Mom wouldn't mind if we spend Christmas with the in-laws. Unfortunately, she probably always will, so there's nothing we can do about it.

Luckily, though, that does not apply to our investment decisions. We do not need to remain emotionally tied to any of our investments, and we shouldn't be. Instead, we should position ourselves to react to shifts in the market whenever those signals present themselves. This is the only way we can be successful in all market environments. This is the only way we can effectively use the strategies I just mentioned. We need to be free from investment-based distraction and pre-existing carryovers. For many this refers specifically to current positions, especially long-term holdings.

Let's begin this part of our discussion with a conscious understanding of the implied emotional constraint imposed by big brokers. We have already begun to discuss this. They pass these down through their financial advisors and on to their clients accordingly. While they often advise buy and hold strategies that impact longer-term strategies, they also impose indirect emotional ties to those positions and the relationship itself.

Using longer-term investment objectives, big brokers want to capture our investments for life. With that goal in mind, they use specific procedures designed to keep us bound to the firm, or mutual fund, or money manager at all times. But these can be impediments to our progress. Therefore, investors must recognize these restraints in order to move forward on the path to the comfort zone. Sometimes, unwinding emotions means breaking these ties. However, reverting to the mean as it relates to this established relationship is fine in theory, but that cannot be applied correctly unless we are also free from the pre-existing psychological ties we might already have to our investments. That unwinding starts with an understanding of the corporate policies big brokers are bound by and then it builds from there. These are the same conflicts we discussed at the beginning of this chapter, but now I will reveal that the web of capture imposed by these brokers extends much deeper than simple capitalistic growth models.

Obviously, the broker-client relationship plays an integral role. In fact, brokers were our sole resource for information just a handful of years ago. Prior to the advent of the Internet, market-related information was hard to come by. Instead, brokers controlled information flow and distributed it as they saw fit. More important, information flow was the underlying reason that many of these early relationships existed in the first place. Smart money, for example, wanted to know all the facts, and brokers seemed to have the information they were looking for. In many instances, investors relied on their brokers for information about companies, valuation, and economic implications. This was true especially as policy shifts impacted client portfolios. Without knowing any better, clients assumed that big brokers had their finger on the pulse of the market.

However, over the past 10 years, the balance of power has shifted, and market-related information is now readily available to all of us. In the current era, more often than not, brokers are actually a little behind the curve with respect to information flow. Most of the time, brokers are not allowed to find information the same way we do. They are restricted from surfing the Internet, they are restricted from signing up for third-party research or investment newsletters, and they are advised against passing along any other information for fear of liability. Most firms don't allow and definitely don't condone these practices. Instead, brokerage firms supply their brokers with the information they feel is important about individual stocks, the economy, and the stock market itself. This is the same way they have always approached the market, but now that has become outdated. In turn, the broker supplies that information to her clients with the objective of advising them on strategy, but the flow of information remains controlled by the firm.

Therefore, the hierarchy of big brokerage firms often limits the supply of information afforded to their clients. Information flow is restricted to what the firm deems appropriate. This brings up a more obvious conflict. First, this assumes that the firm is always right. Then, this assumes that the firm has the best intentions of each client in mind. Each of these is heavily debatable. Immediate concerns start to surface as we directly relate this conflict to the control of information during the Internet debacle, and the conscious and obviously misplaced strong buy recommendations that were given for Internet stocks at that time. In addition, the lack of corporate transparency in 2008, specifically the lack of risk disclosure during the credit crisis, was another excellent example of the potential hazards that exist within broker-imposed hierarchies. Although there are meaningful debates to be had on both sides of these topics, those are better left to another discussion. Instead of trying to fix the internal problems of big brokers, I only intend to point them out so investors can make conscious decisions for themselves.

The important point is, in-house policy and research restrictions curb a broker's ability to make objective and timely recommendations. These bureaucratic procedures not only limit the reaction time in managing retail accounts during adverse market conditions, but they also limit the research available to financial advisors, which in turn limits their ability to guide their clients properly.

Nonetheless, the warm and fuzzy broker-client relationship remains, and it is an integral part of "keeping the business" for the firm. A broker acts as a link between the firm and the client. That link then acts as an information conduit for brokerage opinions and approved research. In most cases, this is a perfectly healthy association, so please don't misconstrue my enlightening of policy for discouraging the relationship. Many people need the added support of a broker or an investment advisor to help them make formidable decisions. So long as that broker is being proactive, he is at least giving wealth protection the consideration it deserves. That consideration is critical and it can add significant value. But the underlying problem still exists; they are controlled by the firm.

Before I move ahead, I'd like to point out a subtle difference between independent advisors and those who work for large institutions. Independent advisors and brokers have fewer bureaucratic limitations and they are, in general, more free to advise their clients objectively. However, although independents have a wider array of resources available to them, they also must have a reverence for the financial markets at the same time. Independents must have a prowess that allows them to excel beyond their peers; otherwise, their information flow can be flawed as well. Although they have access to more information, they must also disseminate it independently and formulate accurate opinions themselves. If those observations are wrong, their clients pay the price. Therefore, drawbacks could exist on this side of the spectrum as well. As a result, when evaluating an advisor, these criteria, in addition to investment-related experience and expertise, should be considered carefully.

In any case, levied emotional ties start with the broker-client relationship, but large brokerage firms also seduce clients with proprietary products. The next observable ties are in-house investment vehicles that cannot be transferred outside of the firm. These include in-house mutual funds, private money managers, unit investment trusts, hedge funds, and in many cases initial public offerings (IPOs) and other investment banking opportunities. Some brokers shun these proprietary products. Interestingly, in-house products can also tie the broker to the firm, not just the client to the firm. If, for example, a broker decides to move from one firm to another, but her clients are invested in proprietary mutual funds, her clients are not able to move with her unless they liquidate their holdings beforehand. This could be troublesome, and it often causes brokers to advise clients against in-house products accordingly. In addition, this also offers insight to other restrictions imposed on individual clients as well.

Similarly, IPOs are a different animal, but they are used to solidify a bond, too. Most large institutions have access to IPOs. However, only investment banks can satisfy the appetite of the wealthy for these sought-after equities. Investors of the highest caliber, who were clients of these investment banks, relished their position on the totem pole while it lasted. Regrettably, the glamour of pure investment banks may have been fading in front of my eyes as I wrote this book. The forced conversion of Goldman

Sachs and Morgan Stanley in 2008 may have marked the end of investment banks as we have grown to know them. We will only be sure after the fact, but the ax head was swinging over these investment banks as I wrote this piece. Regardless, these entities and other big brokers that were part of the syndicate created emotional ties between themselves and their clients with the lure of private offerings. The thought of being able to get something that others could not has strong appeal in the financial world, and it creates a value perception that is hard to match. Be it an IPO or a proprietary fund, investors often feel bound to their firm for giving them the opportunity to access these products. In the case of Goldman Sachs and Morgan Stanley, investors not only felt bound to these firms, but uniquely indebted to them for providing otherwise unobtainable institutional quality products, too. That emotional tie was strong.

Both the broker-client relationship and in-house products are binding the emotional ties levied by big brokers. All of these have the same objective. The intention is to retain the client for life by making it difficult for him or her to separate from the firm. Powerful as these two obvious ties may be, they don't even compare to the binding diversification models that eventually seize control of the relationship. Diversification models are broken down into two subsectors, asset allocation and balanced portfolios.

Reflexively, the thought of proper asset allocation and strategic balance attracts many clients to big brokers, and it keeps them there through thick and thin. After all, who would be better equipped to offer asset allocation and diversification models than large financial institutions? This is a value-added proposition that is hard to match. This time, though, the instrument is less elitist and more a necessary component to sound investment strategy. Because this impacts everyone, this could be the strongest emotional tie of them all. Brokers use it to capture assets, retain assets, and increase fees in line with corporate doctrine. In turn, investors use these tools because they don't feel as if they are able to diversify properly without the support of their financial institution.

Ultimately, some investors consciously choose to hand over their assets to big brokers and entrust their wealth to a system riddled with conflict. Unknowingly, the decision to hire a broker or a money manager is often coupled with the silent acceptance of a golden handcuff. This is a powerful tie. It couples real wealth with potential pitfalls, and therefore could be problematic for investors who are not prepared properly. Therefore, the decision to hire a money manager or a mutual fund company requires careful consideration prior to the agreement. Investors must acknowledge the probability of restrictive golden handcuffs prior to entering into any relationship that concerns personal wealth, or more important, wealth preservation over time. If this recognition is not made in advance, a constrictive tie will almost surely restrain proactive decisions when our timing tools call for adjustments or reversions to cash. If we don't understand that these handcuffs exist, we can never take them off. Therefore, not only are we acknowledging the existence of these handcuffs in this section, but we are also learning how to pick the lock. Recognition is the key.

Immediately, our goal is to act reflexively when defined trading signals present themselves, and this explicit revelation is a preemptive step that betters our ability to do that. Relationships with money managers or mutual funds are not necessarily bad relationships if they can be managed properly on a broad scale. That starts with an understanding of these implied emotional ties, and it carries over to proactive portfolio adjustments from time to time. If we understand that emotional ties exist, and if we dispel the handcuffs from our reaction process, we will be able to react to risk controls when necessary. But failure to manage the broad strategy can be problematic. The earlier reference to George Soros, when he regained control of his assets in 2008, applies here as well. Although he allowed managers to make stock selections within his portfolio, he decided when his assets should be exposed or protected, and that saved him from potential disaster. This should be implemented on an individual level as well. We need to be able to tell our managers, freely, when our assets should be in cash, and when they should be allocated to equities. This empowerment begins with the recognition of hidden golden handcuffs prior to entering into the relationship. From there, we should be able to make the same type of proactive decisions seamlessly when protectionist measures are necessary.

We cannot move to cash if we are tied to our investments, so this chapter helps dispel that tendency. But there is more to it. In the next chapter I will review performance, and a more obvious resolution will present itself accordingly. After that step, I will have broken down many preconceived notions, and our transition to a proactive lifestyle will continue from here. I will be free to disclose the proactive strategies that act as alternatives to buy and hold strategies afterwards.

Summary

Below is a summary of the most important topics in this chapter:

- Barriers exist for most people, and they need to be broken down.
- We are responsible for managing our own wealth.
- Emotional control is necessary to move ahead.

(continued)

(Continued)

- We must identify potential hazards.
- Wealth preservation always comes first.
- Capital growth comes second.
- Brokers are behind the curve due to restrictions.
- Brokers impose ties with golden handcuffs.
- Brokers make us believe we cannot do it ourselves.
- However, with proactive strategies we can.

CHAPTER 5

Since When Has Losing Less Become a Winning Strategy?

Slowly, the seemingly well-intended objectives of big brokers are becoming transparent. That's my intention. I want everyone to understand the benefits and consequences of these policies at all times. After a while, we will all begin to realize that the emotional ties levied by these firms can be avoided and used to our advantage instead. If nothing more, they surely can be anticipated and understood so as not to impact our proactive decisions or our intention to preserve wealth in the future. In fact, aside from diversification models, most of those ties are rather flimsy anyway, so we should use a more constructive approach as we move ahead.

However, diversification is a unique subject. It is extremely important, so we will need to address this in more detail. Portfolio diversification carries with it subjective consequences that prevent inconsequential escape. Diversification is required in all successful longer-term investment strategies, and it cannot be brushed aside. We must always be diversified regardless of our preexisting relationships, and diversification is supported by large financial institutions. Therefore, this subject should be addressed independently and in greater detail.

Specifically, the differentiation within normal diversification models should be observed. In fact, these differences often go overlooked. Asset allocation and balance are not the same, but brokers lump them together. Although they are both defined components of diversification, there are distinct differences between these two subcategories. Unfortunately, investors often group them into the same category without consideration, and that is usually the direct result of established or developing trust relationships. Eventually, asset allocation and balance are treated the same way because investors are not able to immediately identify the difference. Big brokers usually offer these tools in a combined diversification package, so investors rarely know which is which anyway.

Consequently, over time misconceptions can result in portfolio stress when risk-aversion techniques are implemented improperly. With this in mind, the forthcoming section aims at alleviating that possibility using the same cognitive tools we have been using already to remove other emotional ties. In order to do that, linear perception needs to be broken, and we must unbind the emotional ties that restrict timely decisions in association with this false impression. The process will be similar to the one we used to remove the golden handcuffs, but the result may be more substantial. Record the following two definitions for future use.

Asset allocation involves the diversification of assets between different asset classes over time. Typically, a rebalance occurs every quarter in institutionally managed accounts. Asset classes are investment vehicles used to take advantage of growth trends. Certain asset classes perform better than others given current economic conditions or policy, and therefore diversification among various asset classes allows investors to have some exposure to the better-performing asset class in the spectrum at all times. Superior models successfully overweight select asset classes given current or future economic or policy considerations resulting in relative outperformance. Interestingly, though, during declining periods in the Investment Rate, all asset classes suffer, and therefore the normal benefit of asset allocation is discounted. Unless, of course, one of the asset classes is cash, asset allocation is moot during the major down periods in U.S. history. However, when asset allocation becomes applicable again, the better-performing class is often determined by current policy. The noise that surrounds the economy on a daily basis, the same noise that we quelled when discovering the Investment Rate, might determine which asset class performs better than others at any point in time. Specifically, this could mean bonds, stocks, private equity, hedge funds, businesses, cash, foreign investments, and other asset classes that make up the spectrum of potential investments evidenced in the demand ratios offered by the Investment Rate. Asset allocation is a key component to wealth preservation and long-term growth.

Portfolio balance refers to the diversification between sectors of the stock market. As noted above, the stock market is an asset class all by itself. Therefore, balance is a refined focus on one asset class. However, in our economy stocks are typically the investment vehicle of choice for most investors, so the importance of balance should not go overlooked. The stock market is made up of a variety of different subsectors, and balance allows investors to take advantage of the subsectors that are performing well given current market conditions. But that doesn't set it apart. The same principle applies to balance as it does to asset allocation in relation to the Investment Rate.

During the major economic down trends in the Investment Rate, all subsectors of the market decline in relative unison. Therefore, the supposed benefits of a balanced portfolio are muted as well. In 2008, we witnessed this as even conservative equity portfolios, which are expected to hold up, often had equal if not greater percentage declines than the broad market. In any case, balance needs to be linearly divided from the concept of asset allocation because it focuses on a subsector of one asset class. Those subsectors include growth stocks, value stocks, small caps, large caps, technology, biotech, utilities, consumer staples, and the like. The market itself is pre-diversified among all potential subsectors already, and that acts as a starting point for most professional money managers. In fact, managers and mutual funds often base their adjusted models on the dynamic structure of the market itself. The unique objective of enhanced performance or reduced risk is usually defined in the prospectus of the fund, and it is usually achieved by skewing the preexisting balance of the market accordingly. That differentiates the performance of the asset manager from the market at any given time. However, balance does not reduce the exposure of those assets to the market.

Like asset allocation models, balanced portfolios strive to overweight or underweight subsectors of the market to enhance performance or reduce risk. In addition, certain funds strive to do both. Expectedly, some are more successful than others, and it is this relative outperformance that separates top managers from those lower on the totem pole. From there, investors strive to differentiate between them to make sound decisions, but they need a little help most of the time. Therefore, they seek out established resources. One good example is Lipper.

Specifically, Lipper Analytics is a common resource for mutual fund investors. Its slogan is "Leading Fund Intelligence," and it ranks fund managers based on peer results. Furthermore, Lipper produces a benchmark for specific fund classes, called the "Lipper Average." That Average sets a standard against which managers and investors are able to gauge the relative success of the manager and the fund he or she oversees. In turn, that allows investors to better understand the efficacy of those investment products during the investment decision process. This is extremely important, and balance often distinguishes equity managers accordingly. Therefore, balance, like asset allocation, is an integral component of proper investment strategy and it should be considered before any investment discipline has begun.

Diversification Does Not Protect Against Broad Market Declines

Without refute, the common denominator here is diversification. It is a key element in successful investment strategies over time. Diversification tools, including both asset allocation models and balance, are key elements of the binding policy enforced by big brokers. Emotionally, investors realize they should be diversified, but the models offered by big brokers are ingrained in complex strategy that dissuades investors from going it alone. However, this perception is masked as well. In fact, diversification is much easier than anyone thinks. It can be achieved without complexity, and I will prove it. KEEP IT SIMPLE. For now, consider pre-diversified market-based ETFs, and I'll detail the simplicity of diversification later in the book. These ETFs satisfy the requirement of diversification automatically. Still, brokerage firms, with carefully constructed diversification models, integrate themselves into client portfolios and create an emotional bond using the broker-client relationship. On the surface, and in upward-sloping trends in the Investment Rate, this relationship seems perfectly healthy.

However, the emotional ties levied by big brokers often perpetuate brackish investment decisions and therefore wealth preservation becomes a secondhand concern. These emotional ties need to be broken before we can move forward and approach our investments objectively.

Unfortunately, for some, reality hits hard. The perception that a manager knows best, or the firm looks out for our best interests, dissuades investors from taking the necessary steps to preserve their wealth over time by creating a false sense of security. Instead, the firm encourages the client to stick with the plan, pay the fees, and ride out the wave no matter what the economic conditions might be. The firms are not geared toward wealth preservation, but rather toward satisfying the revenue objectives of the firm instead.

Resoundingly, two additional emotional caveats present themselves. First, the portfolios developed by professional money managers often include top-tier companies like Johnson & Johnson, General Electric, IBM, American International Group, and Cisco Systems, just to name a few. The inclusion of top-rated companies in client portfolios suggests an added level of comfort that, at the end of the day, is also unfounded. Astute market observers already recognize that the simple list offered above includes AIG, once the largest insurer in the world and a victim of the financial turmoil in 2008. We could easily have lumped Citigroup into this category, too. Smart money, educated investors, and institutions around the world were subject to significant losses as a result of their holdings in these unfortunate firms and their brackish investment discipline. This happened even though the companies were considered to be some of the best companies in the world, and even though these investors were supposed to be some of the smartest on the street. Therefore, the names of the companies we hold in our portfolios should not be considered shelter or protectionist in any way. At best, they only have a fractional bearing on wealth preservation, and in worst situations they can dissolve portfolios completely, as we all witnessed with Bear Stearns and Lehman Brothers as 2008 wore on. Top-tier companies are not sheltered from the storm, as we have seen. Yet, a lingering emotional tie keeps some investors exposed when they should otherwise be in cash.

From personal experience, I have heard new clients claim that their portfolios include great companies time and time again, so many of them come to me believing there is no reason to worry. My response usually offers a reverse analogy of the old adage: A rising tide lifts all boats. In other words, when the market is trending higher, this simple philosophy seems to hold water, and good companies perform well. However, when the market begins to retreat, flaws begin to appear. After a while, investors realize that the adage works both ways. Not only does an ebbing tide bring all boats down with it, but some boats are left stranded onshore as well. This was the case with AIG, Fannie Mae, Lehman Brothers, Washington Mutual, Bear Stearns, Citigroup, and the others. All of these firms were unable to keep their heads above water as the economy contracted in 2008, and they helped prove the misconception that good companies are safe investments.

Admittedly, the companies listed in the preceding paragraph had internal problems, management made poor decisions, and stockowners were left holding the bag. But many of them were still considered good companies at some point in past history. Regardless, in every case, excessive risk was assumed at the expense of shareholders. In most cases, that added risk was also assumed to further corporate revenue objectives. Therefore, poor corporate policies impact owners and creditors of the company, and that makes investors look for shelter.

With bad apples in mind, an argument could be made for a broad sector allocation and a reversion to conservative stocks in weak market environments. In fact, for most prognosticators, that was the first guess in 2008. There is one main reason for this: Conservative stocks are supposed to hold up. The purpose would be to protect assets with a more conservative diversification when the going gets tough. But there are subtle problems with that theory. First, converting a moderately aggressive portfolio to a conservative portfolio is not as easy as it sounds, and it takes time. Unfortunately, the imposed workload is exhausting on an individual basis and time consuming for professional managers, too. Therefore, it is often put off in favor of alternatives.

Obviously, the objective of a conversion to a more conservative portfolio would be to protect wealth. Even though it might take time, the effort seems to be properly rooted with good intentions. Reining in risk variables makes sense during economic weakness, so at first glance a conservative reversion sounds like a great idea when market risk escalates.

Understandably, this practice appealed to many accredited investors during the credit crisis, especially when those first inclinations were met with like recommendations from their advisors. Investors had learned with past experience that this process makes sense, but it's not flawless. In fact, most investors were not aware of the underlying risks at all. However, in 2008 that changed, and they found out just how dangerous conservative stocks can be. Reasonably, individual investors may not have remembered adverse conditions based on experience, but their advisors surely did.

Unfortunately, Wall Street forgets fast, so supposed intelligence did not matter anyway. The news from today often trumps the news from yesterday as it is, so the risks associated with market conditions in 2008 were discounted as typical of past experience instead of being evaluated for what they really were. Those risks were treated the same as the risks experienced during the most recent up cycle in the Investment Rate, and the same old recommendations were made. Even accredited investors missed the red flags. The substantial declines associated with the major down periods in the Investment Rate were already forgotten. Again, that's human nature. People take the easy road until they are forced to learn again.

Accordingly, this is probably the root of policy deterioration on a government level, too. Officials forget why risk controls are in place during boom periods, just as investors forget the risk of equity exposure during major down trends. Not until major catastrophe hits again do governments reinstill protectionist policy. It takes a while, but eventually investors begin to remember the flaws of a more conservative reversion during the major down periods. The broad assumption that conservative stocks are the best place to be in down markets, a technique that had been true during the entire 1981–2007 up cycle, no longer holds during major down cycles. Conservative sectors are not sheltered from down markets. In fact, conservative stocks are hit hard too.

In the Market Trends section of the November 10, 2008, issue of *USA Today,* an illustration explained this point clearly. Preconceived and propagated notions exist throughout Wall Street, which suggest that monies should be replaced in utilities or consumer staples when the going gets tough. This point of view is entrenched in the belief that the revenue streams of these firms are reliable, and the stocks therefore hold up better than others when the market comes under pressure. At first glance this makes sense; however, it is not completely true. These are equity instruments, and although the underlying businesses may be sound, share prices can still fluctuate wildly. When broad-based selling hits the market, when mutual fund redemptions begin to escalate, and when forced selling takes place, even conservative stocks are sold. Utilities or consumer staples are no exception. The *USA Today* article represented these broad sectors by comparing their relative year-to-date performance ratios to the market. The graphic showed that consumer staples were down approximately 15 percent and utilities were down approximately 22 percent through the first three quarters of 2008 respectively. Although the market was down by about 32 percent at the same time, the sector-specific declines were still severe in nature. They should be construed as serious. A portfolio decline of this magnitude is intolerable as far as I am concerned and cannot be justified regardless of relative performance.

During that same time, analogous to the Internet debacle in 2002, comparative performance ratios began to surface that contained unique observations. Touting outperformance in the face of negative returns became commonplace for mutual funds and money managers as 2008 was coming to an end and as 2009 began. They did the same thing in 2002 when the market was in a trough, and they will almost surely do it again whenever they have to. Although actual portfolios had lost 20 to 30 percent year to date, managers and fund families found reason to celebrate. Their Lipper Averages provided the rationale. Luckily, for some fund companies, those comparisons were based on peer performance, not on actual results.

Expectedly, most portfolios are beaten down when market declines occur, and therefore negative returns are a reality in most cases. But that doesn't prevent the praise of either the fund or the manager. Managers still have the ability to evaluate their performance against their peers, and that changes the playing field completely. If, for example, a manager is down 20 percent, but his peer group, according to Lipper, is down 25 percent, he has reasonably outperformed his peer group. From there, he is considered a superior manager because of it. As odd as that sounds, this is tradition on Wall Street. Negative returns are considered positive returns sometimes.

Beating their Lipper Average was reason for some mutual funds and money managers to celebrate in 2002, and it has already begun to happen again in 2008 and 2009. Mutual funds relish relative outperformance statistics when those results work in their favor, and they use them to encourage clients to stay the course and continue to pay fees. Ultimately, this tool is used to exemplify the value attributed to professional management techniques. However, during these same times most firms were also repressing the actual net return of their funds, so the results are deceiving. In most cases the net returns in 2008 were seriously negative, even if relative outperformance was solid. From the point of view of the money manager, his or her added value was seemingly revealed to current and prospective clients with those comparative loss quotients. However, so was the brackish nature of mutual funds and managed accounts, in my opinion.

Conservative Stocks Fall, Too

Prudently, an advisor might recommend a more conservative equity allocation if he or she anticipates a tough market environment, but that doesn't protect client wealth from decline. It may alleviate some of the risk, but cash would be a much better option. Unfortunately, brokerage firms have an inherent aversion to cash, so the next logical alternative recommendation they come up with is a more conservative allocation.

But why should an investor have constant exposure to equities during down market cycles at all? A cash option would be a much better approach to risk control and wealth preservation than redefined asset allocation.

Even if a conversion takes place, the inclusion of top-tier stocks in a managed portfolio predisposes a developing emotional tie, which prevents investors from making efficient investment decisions. Notwithstanding the adverse notion of liquidating companies perceived to be leaders in their respective industries, the difficulty associated with liquidating 50 or 75 stocks at the same time influences the perpetuating brackishness supported by big brokers and managed accounts. For good reason, brokerage firms encourage delegation practices.

Accordingly, this gives me the opportunity to illustrate a few additional restrictions. A money manager for a large brokerage firm typically manages all of the accounts under her umbrella in the same relative fashion. Clients all hold the same stocks, they are all balanced in a similar way, and decisions are made for all accounts at the same time. Typically, these money managers manage billions of dollars in assets as well. To the layman, this suggests that the manager is worth her weight in gold. However, behind the scenes, those managers are handcuffed instead and prevented from taking action. With education and knowledge of the financial markets put aside, these managers could be the best managers on the street, and they still wouldn't have the same proactive abilities that individual investors do. They simply manage too much money, and they are governed by restrictive corporate policies designed to maintain income streams for the firm at the same time.

Applicable to mutual funds as well, money managers could not move fast enough in volatile market conditions even if they wanted to. In fact, we can take this a step further. In order to efficiently manage their account mutual funds, money managers also encourage investors to stay invested even though volatile conditions exist. With the underlying assumption that the managers are monitoring the investments closely and that they will make any necessary adjustments on behalf of the client, investors are advised to stay invested. This affects the cash position of the fund, and the performance over time. If a mutual fund, for example, can offer reasonable assurance that redemptions will be small, cash positions can be minimal too, and the fund can remain fully invested. This reassures the fund families of revenue streams and satisfies corporate policies at the same time. After all, they are paid based on the size of the underlying assets in the fund.

However, as we witnessed late in 2008, redemptions can change the allocation of funds considerably. Forced liquidations of fund assets drove the market lower in 2008 because mutual funds had to sell into a declining market to cover rescinded investments. Arguably, consumers empower institutions, and therefore they control the market. This is one of the founding principles of the Investment Rate. Consequently, when the masses run for the exits, both the markets themselves and the specific holdings of those funds decline. Because of the large dollar amount involved, this usually causes the fund's share price to decline as well. Still, individuals can be relatively comfortable that a money manager is doing what he is commissioned to do. Usually, unless the mutual fund manager or money manager has completely dropped the ball, managers indeed provide a worthwhile service. Some are expectedly better than others, but most managers will continuously review their portfolios against the market itself and make educated decisions based on current market conditions. Asset allocation within a diversified equity portfolio is their goal, usually, and regardless of any manager's individual success, managers are forced by law to adhere to the objectives defined in the prospectus. Therefore, don't completely discount the value of a money manager; just recognize his or her objectives and make sure those objectives are in line with current market conditions.

Clearly, the objective of most equity-based managed accounts and mutual funds is to earn fees based on invested assets. They encourage clients to remain invested so they can generate fees at all times. Ultimately, this is the root of the problem. In turn, the allocation of investable dollars to a professional money manager should also be considered an allocation to an investment, not an allocation to cash. Furthermore, investors should never assume that any of their invested assets are protected from the market when it is in the hands of a money manager because the prospectus usually defines investment strategies instead of cash management. Unless money has been taken out of the control of a manager and reverted to cash by the client, equity exposure should be expected at all times in long accounts. Clients are responsible for making cash allocations most of the time, as a result.

Furthermore, if the market declines broadly, a reversion to conservative stocks is not the answer either. Specifically, if a declining market hurts good companies as well as brackish investments, managed accounts and mutual funds during a period of decline are also doomed to fail. This is true even if they adopted a more conservative approach.

Risk Control Is Our Responsibility, Not Theirs

Ultimately, the onus rests on the client. Brokerage firms will not recommend cash but instead a more conservative approach in the face of perceived market risk. This, of course, assumes that the bureaucratic brokerage firm moves swiftly, before adverse economic conditions impact the market and client portfolios first. Unfortunately, they are usually behind the curve in this respect.

After careful evaluation, a conflict of interest arguably exists between big brokers and their retail clients. The main objective of the corporation is to realize an increasing revenue stream that is directly tied to recurring management fees. This influences policy designed to perpetuate investment exposure at all times. Therefore, individual clients cannot rely on the guidance of their money manager, broker, or brokerage firm to protect their wealth. Instead, investors must make the decision to move to cash from time to time on their own. This is where my services come into play. My objective is to eradicate brackish investment patterns, and that begins with dissolving the adhesion that encourages us to stay invested in the face of negative economic and market conditions.

The emotional ties that might bind investors to their money managers or their mutual funds must be broken in order to empower the freedom of occasional cash allocation. These ties vary from person to person, but I have offered a few examples here for consideration. Investors must realize that wealth preservation is a secondary concern to everyone in the hierarchy, except them. Therefore, investors must also assume individual responsibility for wealth protection. The tools that I provide allow investors to accomplish this goal independently.

Using proven techniques for evaluating current and future market conditions, I have been able to provide an advance warning of both adverse market conditions and windfall opportunities over time. I will explain those techniques in this book. For example, during the Internet bubble and the subsequent meltdown of 2002, we were able to identify the bottom within a handful of points. In 2007 we were able to identify an overshoot of our predefined demand ratios and anticipate a return to parity, which resulted in a market decline and the beginning of the third major down period in U.S. history, too. These are more obvious because they are defined, longer-term inflection points, but my interim models work equally well. Accordingly, identifying undulation cycles in between these major inflection points has redefined the dynamic skill that I will pass along as we proceed. Thus far, it continues to work, and I expect this same process to carry on well into the future. The Investment Rate is and will continue to be the foundation for all of my analysis. In fact, the first tool I will offer is a parity analysis of current demand ratios as they relate to the normalized demand trends offered by the Investment Rate. This will tell us if demand will improve over time and if economic conditions will improve accordingly.

Before we get there, though, I have a little more to do. Clearly, the first step to realizing these opportunities includes breaking the emotional ties we might have with our brokers, our money managers, and our investments. We have started to do that here. But there's more to it. The references in this chapter were intended to help us understand the ties that are levied by the financial industry itself. Our eyes should now be open. My initial effort is to enable us to sidestep pitfalls like George Soros so nimbly did in 2007.

However, additional factors need to be considered as we transition to a proactive lifestyle. Comprehension of intention is fine, and over time this could prevent serious missteps, but it does little to help us manage our current or future emotions. The groundwork for breaking those ties has been laid, but now our real emotions need to be addressed. The end goal is to lift all current and future emotional burdens so we can approach the market with an open mind and with the confidence to react when the time is right. In turn, emotional conditioning acts as a catalyst to the tools that keep my clients on the right side of the curve when everyone else seems to be asking questions.

As we move ahead, level heads will prevail, and that carries with it a strong meaning. Our job is to define what that means to us individually. Luckily, there are defined guidelines for us to follow, and that makes it easier. In the next chapter, we will begin to address those specifically. We have already broken down misplaced truths, and that has probably left many people questioning their next steps. Responsibly, we will start to build again from here. Now, we can move ahead without restraint.

Summary

Below is a summary of the most important topics in this chapter:

- Diversification does not shelter us from losses.
- Conservative stocks are not protected from decline.
- Traditional remedies do not work when the Investment Rate declines.
- In negative markets, negative returns are regularly touted as positive results.
- Since when has losing less become a winning strategy?
- We have successfully dispelled misplaced doctrine.
- Now we can begin to build again.

CHAPTER 6

Redefining Balance

Reasonably, this chapter could be construed as prophetic in nature, but it is required because a balanced mind promotes emotional freedom. This is our first building block. Emotional freedom opens the doors to a proactive approach toward investments, and that furthers our journey toward the comfort zone. In direct relation, a healthy mind and a healthy body are also integral to a proactive investment competence.

Early in this book, I referenced Deepak Chopra and his teaching of Perfect Health. At first glance the subject of personal health and investment strategy may seem divergent, but a second glance reveals much more. Over time, I have grown to appreciate the coincidences that shape the world in which I live. Although the Chopra Center would argue that coincidences are a fallacy, I still respect the recognition of synchronicities. Indeed, things happen for a reason, and those can reshape our lives if we recognize them. More definitively, I will explain how I have reshaped select and revered coincidences into sentiment indicators that help me determine market direction over time as well. Eventually, these have become very important to me, and they influence my ability to see the economy in a clear light. In any case, I have also identified similarities between the teachings of the Chopra Center and my promotion of proactive trading strategies. Those twists of fate have redefined the use of the word *balance* in my financial capacity, and that notion drives the visionary compound within this chapter.

It Is a Lifestyle

Balance no longer refers to the diversification of assets, but rather to a mindset that allows investors to approach the market objectively and free from concern. The traditional definition of balance is far less important than asset allocation in diversification models anyway, because there are pre-diversified tools at our disposal already, like the ETFs, and this new definition is much more meaningful. Therefore, from this point forward, balance should be referred to as a mindset that allows us to achieve an efficient investment strategy. The efficacy of a balanced mindset allows investors to achieve emotional freedom, the key element of our primary concern.

Everyone finds balance in slightly different ways, but the Chaos theory of life that points us to that common goal typically evokes similar conduits. My significant other brought this to my attention. She is a teacher of Perfect Health at the Chopra Center at La Costa Resort and Spa, and I thank her for this revelation. The emotional cleansing taught by the Chopra Center is analogous to my effort here.

Indeed, the science of life and the promotion of efficient strategy are contiguous. They are bound by the conception of a healthy mind. This coincidence cannot go overlooked. Coincidences are far too important to pass up most of the time anyway, and this one trumped all the others I had come across.

In turn, a healthy mind is a byproduct of a healthy body, so the concept of Perfect Health envelops both. A healthy body and a healthy mind are the conduit to a lifestyle free from emotional burdens. Therefore, the objective of achieving Perfect Health should be part of our combined effort here.

I am not a health expert nor a nutritional consultant, spiritual healer, or psychologist. I am a lowly economist who understands that a healthy lifestyle promotes a conscious awareness integral to sound financial disciplines. Because the root of economics is people, the concept of personal health plays an integral role in the complexities of reflexive theory. Achieving a sound mind, healthy body, and balance within ourselves opens the door to engaging disciplines that attract strategic and unemotional reactions to pronounced shifts in the market before they occur. In essence, a healthy mind has a greater likelihood of accurately anticipating variable shifts, market corrections, and economic cycles before they happen. Accurate and acute reflexivity is made possible because of aspirant health predispositions on an individual basis.

Unfortunately, most people do not understand this interrelationship. Most people in fact neglect their personal health for their career, or other selfish interests that are furthered by financial successes. Interestingly though, most super-successful businessmen have a discipline beyond their corporate lifestyle that defines their character. That discipline often contains a natural byproduct in a health-conscious lifestyle. Coincidentally, those persons are typically ahead of the curve and leading the way for others to follow. That should be telling on its own.

Positive personality traits, sharp reflexes, and a universal awareness of immediate and global surroundings often embody health-conscious professionals. Although not set in stone, odds also favor a more positive and rewarding career and personal life, provided homage is paid continuously to our mind and bodies. It is not a one-time trip to the gym or a singled-out choice to eat right. Instead, it's a lifestyle. The same qualities further our goal toward constructive, disciplined, and successful proactive trading strategies. Uniquely, our minds are typically more free to accept the dynamics of proactive models when we are physically healthy. Conversely, a predisposition to insensible health concerns could also explain why so many people fail to make proper investment decisions on a regular basis.

Admittedly, though, the definition of physical health differs from individual to individual. However, Chaos theory applies here, too. Everyone understands the same general definitions, and everyone accepts them. But reasonably, for some, achieving that end goal is harder than others. Recognition of physical ailments provides an obvious divergent from our universal definition of the norm. Admittedly, impaired individuals are not capable of achieving the same physical strengths as professional athletes, and in some cases, incurable disease has reshaped the boundaries of health in their lives altogether.

Constructively, achieving the end goal of Perfect Health is less important to our efforts than the path to achieving that goal instead. Therefore, I am not suggesting that we need to be perfectly healthy in order to reach the comfort zone. However, I am suggesting that we should make a meaningful effort to remain healthy and stay on that path.

Successfully reaching an ultimate goal of perfection might be an eventual target for some ultra–health-conscious individuals or die-hard athletes who have the drive to be the best they can be. But our references and my recommendation are not suggesting that we strive to achieve these extremes. In fact, extremes may even detract from certain aspects of the conscious understanding of strategy that I am suggesting instead.

With that, the path to a healthy lifestyle should be an integral part of life. That should be enough to free ourselves from some of the emotional burdens, which may bring about irreflexive decisions. Immediate emotional cleansing may be required for certain people to find this path. Reasonably, we all have our idiosyncrasies, and therefore we all need to address these similar issues in different ways. However, with a healthy objective in mind, everyone is capable of moving forward in this regard. Even if the trek is a little different for all of us, we all can weed through the noise and aspire toward our end goal in a relatively similar fashion.

Luckily, these paths are not too different, and the following common denominators apply to almost everyone interested in realizing a healthy lifestyle:

- Regular exercise
- Proper nutrition
- Mental stimulation

Before we discuss these individually, we should also recognize a universal underpinning. The KISS theory mentioned earlier in the book has relevance here as well. Mental stimulation is a great example. An overstimulated mind is no more free from emotion than an unhealthy body. Each of these promotes brackish or unresponsive reflexive actions and could result in poor decision making as well. Therefore, in every instance, try to keep it simple. In the case of mental stimulation, try to limit the noise.

Excuses Result in Losses

The bullet points mentioned earlier are probably already well rooted in our definitions of conduit as that applies to health-conscious lifestyles. Unfortunately, although we often recognize these as important contributors to a healthy being, we also find ourselves neglecting one or all of these important sub-catalysts from time to time. Simple excuses arise, exceptions are made, and the path to the comfort zone breaks down for a while as a result. Until we are able to get back on this path, our lives are a little out of touch with the global environment. Our minds are not as healthy as they should be, our skills are not as sharp as they could be, and eventually our proactive reflexivity dampens. This is a circular process and it manifests in itself.

Occasionally, for example, isolated excuses not to exercise become commonplace. Then, eventually those are also accepted as the norm. Sooner or later, for some, the road less traveled is the road to financial prosperity, which has been neglected or truncated by routine excuses. In extreme incidents, the only option in reverting back to the path toward the comfort zone is to reverse to ground zero and start again from scratch.

Before we make any extreme observations, though, a discussion of these simple disciplines is warranted. These are broad categories, and the options are seemingly endless. Exercise could encompass trips to the gym, running outside in the morning, fast-paced walks, swimming, playing basketball, or lifting weights. Mental stimulation for a Princeton Eco-Physics Magna Cum Laude may encompass a universal understanding of cold water tides as they disperse through arctic channels in direct reaction to global warming trends, where most of us are content reading the paper and formulating opinion based on revealed policy or corporate action. And in extreme cases, vegan practices define proper nutrition, where most people are well served with an unprejudiced vitamin-rich diet. Restrictions are not imposed anywhere, yet a common goal is defined for each sub-category. A divergence from the common goal in either case could eventually circumvent the road less traveled.

Therefore, I not only encourage and promote the active catalysts mentioned above, but I will also offer an additional encouraging incentive, which is designed to maintain the path from which we draw our internal skills. Any decision not to exercise, any decision to allow unhealthy radicals into our bodies, and any decision to forgo simple mental stimulation for an easier way can eventually lead to unfound financial decisions and significant losses. Poor decisions can come full circle, and in most cases, they do.

My advice on this subject is clear. Stay healthy, exercise regularly, eat right, and stimulate the mind every day. Otherwise, the path to financial prosperity may be averted for a while, poor decisions could lead to major mistakes, and personal finances could become an extreme emotional burden for many years to come. The next time we decide not to go to the gym, the next time we eat at McDonald's and supersize it, or the next time we neglect simple mental stimulation, remember that we could also be adversely impacting our financial future at the same time.

Is it worth it?

Clearly, I am making suggestions here because I know they are effective. For many people, their personal routines need to change. Maybe the simple outline I have offered in this chapter will be a good beginning. However, additional encouragement may be needed, too. Therefore, in the next chapter I will show how we can leverage the simple challenges of this chapter into being the best investors on the street.

Summary

Below is a summary of the most important topics in this chapter:

- Regular exercise influences positive performance.
- Proper nutrition influences positive performance.
- Mental stimulation influences positive performance.
- A healthy lifestyle influences financial success.

CHAPTER 7

Contemporary Darwinism

Our prior discussion encourages a healthy lifestyle. But that notion runs deeper than conditioning to include a parallel to Darwinism. A healthy lifestyle must also be one capable of surviving environmental changes. In our modern economy, assuming that capitalism prevails over socialism, contemporary Darwinism takes precedence. In order to survive, contemporary species, which include investors, corporations, and governments, must adapt to changing economic conditions over time. Survival of the fittest applies here. However, that does not mean that investors need to be healthier, faster, or stronger to flourish. Instead, other resounding qualities do exist, and I will define those in this chapter. In the end, we will realize that our modern economy is itself an environment subject to the same definitions offered hundreds of years ago by Charles Darwin. Furthermore, we will find that we are merely part of that evolutionary process. Uniquely though, unlikely the species that Darwin defined, we can also control our fate.

Charles Darwin changed the world's perception of evolution in the mid-1800s when he introduced his theory of natural selection. Most of us have already studied Darwin's theory, at least to a certain degree. His science suggests that species evolve from a series of mutations and extinctions over time. In the end, only the strongest survive, but the definition of strongest varies from species to species. Mutations for some may provide necessary defenses that allow continued survival. For others, brute strength is the dominant force necessary to be left standing at the end.

From almost every angle, these same theories apply to the modern world of finance. Therefore, I believe our modern financial world is subject to contemporary Darwinism. Arguably, contemporary Darwinism again became obvious to the world in 2008. The failure of major financial institutions and the extinction of investment banks as we know them caused some of the most tumultuous financial conditions the world has ever seen. Although immediate government intervention delayed some catastrophes from occurring, past laissez-faire government policy and lax corporate risk controls proved that even the strongest, most well-equipped companies can face extinction given changes to their respective economic environments. Although the strongest indeed survive in a laboratory environment, global environmental changes allow less strong, but properly mutated species to survive worldwide catastrophes over time as well.

Now, if world leaders would refrain from supporting deteriorating companies, the same premise would hold true in our financial world. My argument suggests that any company that is ill-equipped to handle current economic and market conditions must either adapt to those conditions or face extinction. In addition, those companies who are equipped to prosper in current conditions should have the opportunity to do so. Survival, in turn, depends on adaptability, especially in adverse economic conditions. Growth, on the other hand, depends on many additional variables and is only indirectly included in the first stage of our contemporary analysis. However, in the second section, growth will become a more prominent consideration of ours. Until then, this stage of contemporary Darwinism focuses on survival, not on growth. Natural growth variables can be left to Fibonacci for now. Given our current economy, a subdued growth environment is something Wall Street has not seen in decades. Therefore, Wall Street has largely ignored contemporary Darwinism until the credit crisis began.

Natural Selection in Modern Economies

Far from the Ice Age, the credit crisis of 2008 marked the beginning of a cataclysmic change in the global economy. This change has already claimed the lives of many contemporary species. New corporate policies, renewed oversight, restrictions, and a shrunken financial system have thus far been natural byproducts of current contemporary Darwinism. Similar corrections and continued natural selection are likely to persist until such time as a more harmonic financial system inclusive of proper oversight and regulation prevails. More important, there is very little anyone can do about it. This is a natural occurrence, and subject to natural selection. During this washout, some companies will survive, some companies will fail, but an intelligent few will flourish. Contemporary Darwinism will ultimately be the determining factor. Even though government intervention has supported many weak companies to date, those weak companies still cannot survive unless they too adapt accordingly. The government cannot support floundering companies forever. Instead, unless those companies adapt as needed, government intervention will only prolong the inevitable.

General Motors is an excellent case in point. General Motors, along with Chrysler, requested government assistance in December 2008. The company questioned its ability to survive as a standalone entity and went to Congress for help. However, its poor business model coupled with deteriorating market conditions made the intervention questionable at best. Had the government satisfied its initial request, General Motors almost surely would have been asking for more money a few months later, and the entire investment would have evaporated. Interestingly, in an effort to help our government I also independently developed a formal proposal for the auto companies at the same time. This was based on contemporary Darwinism. I submitted this to our government and the media for consideration, and I encourage everyone to review the article. My proposal included a real life application of contemporary. Darwinism, and it was designed to protect the U.S. economy while also allowing the auto industry to survive. Unfortunately for taxpayers, the government ignored my proposal and opted to fund a weak entity instead. Between the United States and Canada, General Motors was given $18 billion to help it survive. Arguably, that's better than the original proposal, but probably a waste of money nonetheless. The market cap of General Motors at the time was less than $2 billion. The problem with that bailout is clear. The bailout package was nine times the value of the company itself. Now, I expect General Motors to come back to the well sometime in 2009. (When this book was in the last stages of editing, GM had filed for bankruptcy.) In addition, I also expect all other weak companies to do the same if they receive a lifeline they do not qualify for.

Any company that is unwilling or incapable of adapting to current economic conditions will either dissolve or feed off the government forever. AIG, Citigroup, Bank of America, Morgan Stanley, and others are capable of doing exactly that in years to come unless they make fundamental changes to their business models immediately.

Although the government has good intentions, the practice of supporting the weak adds prolonged pressures on immediate economic conditions. It also delays a rebound to a healthier economy, and it makes recovery more cumbersome over time as a result.

However, an adherence to contemporary Darwinism would prevent this from happening. Using this model, the washout would be swift, and the companies left standing should be stable and prosperous. Some of these companies may be stronger than others. Some may possess natural defenses against potential economic depressions. And others may simply have been in the right place at the right time. Interestingly, those left standing in the end may not be those you expect. But this assumes an unabated capitalistic model. Instead, the modified version of contemporary Darwinism that existed in 2008 allowed select major institutions to drain the economy at the expense of debt consideration and fiscal policy.

While the U.S. government transitioned to new leadership, a debate loomed about ongoing government direction. Investors want to know how anticipated regulatory changes will affect the corporate world and the global economy. First and foremost, expected changes in policy will have the ultimate goal of ensuring that the mistakes made between 2000 and 2007 will never be made again. In addition, of course, the initial changes in policy are also likely to be designed to alleviate the immediate strain on the economy. Unfortunately, government is as shortsighted as Wall Street, and I expect the government to make similar mistakes again at some point in the future. Therefore, we should not count on an error-free transition. Obviously, we should not expect the same mistakes to be made again immediately either, but over time we can be assured that similar conditions will surface even if prudent policy is adopted now. The current credit crisis, for example, was avoidable based on lessons learned many years ago. We learned this lesson during the Great Depression, and over time, we forgot what we learned.

Specifically, the demise of the stock market during the Great Depression was caused in part by bucket shops, which operated like betting parlors. They allowed bets for and against the movement of stock prices over time. Legislation was passed shortly after the 1929 stock market crash prohibiting such activity, and that legislation stood fast until the Commodities Futures Modernization Act of 2000. In Section 408-C of that Act, Congress, which was admittedly in a lame duck session and eager to recess at the time, repealed the current policy, which was premised on the demise of the stock market during the Great Depression. That, in turn, opened the door for "bucket shops" to resurface once again. Either the new Act was passed because the government failed to recognize the purpose of the existing law, or the Act was passed to foster growth at the expense of assumed risk. In any case, the failed recognition of our Legislature ultimately led to the credit crisis experienced in 2008 and the demise of our financial system as we knew it.

Here is a direct excerpt from Section 408 of that Act:

> c) PREEMPTION—This title shall supersede and preempt the application of any State or local law that prohibits or regulates gaming or the operation of bucket shops (other than antifraud provisions of general applicability) in the case of—
> (1) a hybrid instrument that is predominantly a banking product; or
> (2) a covered swap agreement.

Arguably, the seemingly simple subsection quoted here was the root cause of the financial crisis in 2008 because it allowed the formation of unregulated swaps. In essence, these were bets on the direction of the housing market, and they were allowed by the preemption excerpt from the Commodities Futures Modernization Act of 2000. However, more important to our modern economy, those bets were being made with trillions of dollars at the same time. This was a far greater amount than anyone imagined, and much larger than the initial reference to bucket shops above. Therefore, the impact will likely trump that of the bucket shops during the Great Depression accordingly.

For some reason, the same mistakes that happened in 1929 happened again. This is human nature. People repeat their mistakes, almost always. Unless emotional conditioning is implemented, people repeat bad decisions all the time. Interestingly, a reversion to our grassroots concept has happened again. The economy is all about people, and now we have learned that government is, too. Therefore, we should expect the mistakes of the recent past to happen again as the economy oscillates within its longer-term cycle over time. Admittedly, this may take 40 years, but eventually our government will forget about the risks again, and the economy will ebb. In the meantime, other mistakes are sure to happen; we just need to keep our eyes open and be aware of our environment.

Repetitive errors have fostered a circular evolutionary process in historical economic dynamics. History is repeating itself. This is a natural occurrence in contemporary Darwinism, and it should be recognized. Proven mistakes were made in the 1920s, and those were corrected with well-founded regulation. Eventually, those laws were repealed in 2000, and now the process has begun again. Therefore, new regulations should be expected going forward that are designed to protect the economy accordingly. This example is clear and the inherent circulatory theory is proven easily, given the macro impact of recent history.

However, this is not the only case of circulatory economic policy. Be assured, similar instances of short-sighted policy occur regularly on a micro basis as well. Check local government records to find specific details.

Corporations and Governments Are Different

Recurring circulatory policy is not limited to government. Corporations often repeat errors, too. However, these errors are subtly different. Instead, corporate errors are more often grounded in greed as that relates to potential windfalls, rather than on neglected observation, which is more normal for the government. A great example is the greed associated with big brokers in relation to their anticipation of windfall investment banking fees during the Internet bubble. Following the demise of dotcom, risk assumptions were throttled in 2002 only to be reasserted during the cheap money period that almost immediately followed. Short-sighted, in this case, is an understatement. Financial institutions were hurt by their actions during the Internet bubble already, and then they made risk adjustments to avoid those pitfalls in the future. Soon though, they jumped right back into the fire without a second thought when new opportunities surfaced again.

Obviously, a different catalyst than government motivates corporations. For the most part corporate repetition is also coupled with a willingness to assume excessive risk. This, in turn, is associated with hopes of related profits. Circulatory policy and repetitive risk assumption on a corporate level are typically conscious and willfully assumed as a result. However, governmental circulatory policies may not be. We hope, at least, that government is not driven by greed. Unfortunately, that's not entirely true. In fact, given the possibility that the removal of policy in the Commodities Futures Modernization Act of 2000 could have been the direct result of a conscious willingness to assume risk in order to achieve renewed growth during a period of recession, President Clinton and Congress may have been subject to a derivation of greed in 2000 as well. This would have obviously incorporated a benevolent desire to produce a healthier economy, and it could be acquiescent. Nonetheless, a byproduct of either fear or greed could have influenced this action, and in turn it may have allowed the mortgage crisis to manifest throughout our economy. Unfortunately, we are not likely to know for sure. All we will know for sure is that the same mistake was made twice. In turn, we know that repetitive circulatory missteps need to be recognized in advance to avoid similar pitfalls in the future.

Unfortunately, contemporary Darwinism warns us that mistakes will inevitably occur again. Even though recognition may be made now, governments are likely to succumb to these mistakes again over time, and corporations can be assured of doing the same when faced with new opportunities. Therefore, investors must remain aware of current economic conditions, policy shifts, and corporate initiatives if they intend on sheltering themselves from poor policy and corporate greed. This requires a conscious understanding of the impact government policy and corporate action could have on their personal finances over time and an appropriate reaction to the same.

Sometimes professional advisors should be requisitioned to help navigate these changes as they occur. With their added observations, appropriate portfolio shifts can take place that shelter investors accordingly. This is a dynamic process, however, and also prone to miscalculations. 2008 was a great example: During 2008 investors made mistakes based on an assessment of corporate growth forecasts, economic data, and government policies. Even with the help of financial advisors, these mistakes were consistent, but avoidable at the same time.

Adapting to Contemporary Darwinism

Alternatively, investors can position themselves so these matters do not influence their decisions at all. This option is the path of least resistance over time, although it might contain immediate caveats. Instead, if investors recognize the issues at hand, they can negotiate around major setbacks at all times. This nimble position is not taken on a case-by-case basis, but rather broad in scope. A sweeping effort to sidestep these eventual pitfalls requires a lifestyle change for many investors though. Call it a mutation in the face of contemporary Darwinism if you will, but it is a healthy adaptation to changing conditions at the same time. Interestingly, this adaptation almost only occurs during times of trouble and is often forgotten during the good times. Resoundingly, the same principle applies to government, corporations, and individuals over time.

In turn, investors themselves are subject to contemporary Darwinism. In this instance, survival of the fittest refers to the investors who are aware of their exposure to excessive risk and who choose to control it at the same time. The strongest investors in times of trouble could be those who decide to shelter their assets from perceived economic weakness. In this instance too, the strongest may not be the biggest, or the most powerful. In fact, risk aversion was commonplace in 2008 as investors moved into Treasury bonds and drove yields to zero. In effect, some investors were paying to have their money in Treasuries because that seemed to be the safest place during the credit crisis. However, although assets seemed to be protected, they also were unable to produce meaningful returns. Interestingly, return on investment was less important to many investors than the eventual return of their capital. In fact, very little consideration was paid to growth at all in 2008. Arguably, no return was far better than a negative return in the eyes of big money, and these risk-controlled investments were considered stronger, relatively speaking, than all others. If nothing more, an appropriate adaptation to the economic conditions in 2008 was made irrespective of growth.

However, in 2008 some investors were still interested in receiving a positive return on their assets. Arguably, many people wanted to recover losses, because 2008 was a tough year. Regardless, neither aspirant was willing to sit in Treasuries for the next few years while watching opportunities pass. Instead, they chose to position themselves to take advantage of opportunity on occasion. In any case, those who fit this demographic have found shelter in my proactive strategies. Because those strategies provide opportunity without sacrificing risk controls, they were attractive during the deteriorating market conditions of 2008. Already experienced losses had proven the necessity for risk controls beforehand, so this process was not nearly as difficult to promote as it was in 2007. In 2008, investors wanted to control their risk and realize positive returns at the same time, and that is part of what proactive strategies provide. These are alternatives to buy and hold strategies accordingly.

Interestingly, brackish patterns are part of contemporary Darwinism as well. Only when necessary conditions exist do investors take action and adapt to the economy. Otherwise, investors sit on their hands and let the system flow accordingly. Instead of proactive, the process is reflexive by nature. Almost always, investors react to changing economic conditions, instead of reacting before conditions deteriorate. Reflexivity, as defined by George Soros, is therefore an integral part of contemporary Darwinism.

Expectedly, and evidenced by the demise stemming from the credit crisis of 2008, most investors failed to act proactively before that collapse started. This caused severe portfolio instability, and substantial loss was a natural byproduct. Sometimes people need to have a slap in the face before they wake up and smell the coffee. In this case, before they realized the landscape had changed, many investors were already underwater. However, anyone who had engaged a proactive model prior to those declines had little concern about their portfolios as the economy came under pressure. The warnings stemming from the Investment Rate laid the groundwork conceptually. Instead of brackish tendencies, a proactive model transitions investments automatically as the market turns. In other words, those investors who took steps to control their risk in advance just needed to transition with the model, instead of evaluating the overall economy every step of the way.

Understandably, general concerns about the economy surfaced for everyone in 2008. Admittedly, the same thing will happen again at a later time, during the next down cycle, I expect. Regardless of personal financial stability, though, we will always be concerned during periods of weakness because we all have ties to the economy outside of our investment activities. If nothing more, we care about those people who are losing their homes, jobs, or savings, because this is part of our human nature. We will always have concern, but we don't always need to be subject to the same risks. A proactive lifestyle helps alleviate the strain that a declining market might otherwise bear on our decisions, and it allows us to rationalize economic cycles objectively instead. In many cases proactive models eliminate that stress altogether. Instead of dissemination, investors ride the wave up, down, and in between established channels over time. Eventually, the process becomes as easy to follow as that.

Although it sounds similar, this is not the same method used by hedge funds. Hedge funds place large sector bets and balance their risk with complex instruments instead. In the end they usually squeak out a gain by assuming a high degree of risk. However, in 2008 that was not the case. Hedge funds lost 18.9 percent on average instead. Accordingly, some of their bets work, some fail, but educated and disciplined hedge fund managers are typically able to offer a competitive return. Again, however, like most money managers, hedge funds rarely keep pace with the market either. Competitive return, in this instance, is based on peer references again. In addition, hedge funds should work in both up and down markets by definition, but hedge funds are usually considered more worthy only in down markets. This characteristic is not the same as the proactive models we incorporate regularly. High degrees of leverage are not required in our models, and large sector bets are not the best way to make money using proactive strategies.

Instead, a simplified and refined process equipped to react in advance to shifts in the market and the economy works best. My systems operate without leverage, options, or derivatives, and they don't require users to incorporate any other synthetic instruments into their activities either. Proactive models don't require accurate economic analysis or market perception; they just require an adherence to discipline. Initially, in 2008 many people failed to take these important steps. However, after the realization hit home, they are finally adapting to the environment, too. Some are making the transition gracefully, and some are kicking and screaming, but most investors have come to the same striking conclusion. Given the turmoil in the economy, and the significant losses that occurred in 2008, most investors understand that they are responsible for managing their own risk. They also realize that their money managers, advisors, and stockbrokers are usually behind the curve, and usually governed by conflicting interests at the same time.

Contemporary Darwinism tells us that periods of weakness will undeniably surface again, and risk management is therefore required at all times to avoid exposure, protect wealth, and take advantage of necessary transitions when they occur. This will happen regardless of the findings of the Investment Rate, but more probably in line with the trend we have already outlined. Contemporary Darwinism is a separate interpretation, but it points to the same conclusion. Proactive strategies are the best way to prosper in virtually any market environment. In the next section, we will delve into this association and exploit opportunities going forward.

Summary

Below is a summary of the most important topics in this chapter:

- Contemporary Darwinism affects investors, governments, and corporations.
- It is a natural occurrence and circulatory by nature.
- We all must adapt to changing environments.
- Without change, we will not survive.
- Proactive strategies help us dynamically change with the environment, and that provides opportunity every step of the way.

CHAPTER 8

A Proactive Aversion

Before I continue, I need to make a distinction. Reflexivity theory, defined by George Soros, has a negative slant. However, I look at it in a slightly different light. I embrace the reflexive nature of human being instead, and I have incorporated that into my proactive models. We use it to our benefit. Therefore, from time to time, I will reference reflexivity as a positive attribute, and rightfully so. Our reflexive nature allows us to react to changes in advance. I will prove that this is not a contradiction in terms as well. Until then, back to our steady forward progress.

With contemporary Darwinism revealed, my job transitions and my focus shifts to protecting my clients from circular pitfalls. We can do that in one of two ways. Either we can try to pinpoint periods of weakness in advance and hope we are right, or we can adopt a proactive strategy and never look back. The former is a strategy often used by professional money managers. They try to pinpoint ebbs and flows in the economy, and they skew the diversification models that they use accordingly. Exposure still exists, of course, but they make every effort to stay ahead of the curve by trying to identify these cycles in advance. This creates two difficult scenarios. First, if they are wrong, the shift in balance that has taken place will need to be parsed. Their portfolios usually control billions of dollars, and therefore the losses are usually meaningful. Missed opportunity is the best-case scenario though. If, instead, a period of weakness occurs, like the one experienced in 2008, the identification process and the repositioning that may have been prudently endured doesn't matter at all. In this case, declines exist anyway. Therefore, attempting to identify periods of weakness in advance can be futile.

Obviously, some professionals are very good at predicting periods of weakness as well as periods of growth. In fact, I would argue that I am very good at doing the same. Unfortunately, though, we are all wrong on occasion. This is normal, and everyone recognizes and accepts imperfections as a way of life. However, if our mode of operation transitions to a proactive model, those same imperfections dissolve, and we are much more capable of going with the flow of the market at all times. Therefore, not only will analytical pressures be removed, but also risk will be controlled and prowess will improve accordingly. The benefit is not only realized during periods of weakness. Unlike hedge funds, proactive strategies work well in any market environment. Up, down, or sideways, proactive models have the ability to produce returns at all times, while controlling risk, of course. Going forward, so long as those persons who adopt a proactive strategy continue to use that strategy at all times, future adverse conditions will not have the same material impact as they did in 2008. Further, investors in proactive strategies will likely be positioned well to realize opportunity during periods of growth, or periods of decline, whenever they might surface in the future. Routine discipline soon becomes integrated into the strategy. Over time, eventually, this becomes a lifestyle instead of a strategy shift. This lifestyle then leads directly to the comfort zone, which is our ultimate objective.

The First Step Is the Hardest

Unfortunately, some investors remain slightly behind the curve. They know they should take control of their risk; they just haven't done so yet. Luckily, investors who are interested in adopting a proactive approach are not required to start from the same place as everyone else. Instead, opportunities present themselves on a regular basis, new investors can participate at any time, and selection can be natural. In addition, investors who use a proactive model can make the conscious decision not to make a decision from time to time. Because cash is an integral part of the model, this is not only possible, but a common practice as well. There are requirements, though, and adaptation is mandatory before proactive models can be used effectively. Investors need to accept the weakness in our economy first, then avoid fighting it. Next, they must treat that observation as an opportunity to adapt and become proactive. Over the course of years, a proactive approach will seem less important than it does today, but because the economy, policy shifts, and corporate greed are circular, this process also allows everyone to avoid those pitfalls again in the future. Gladly, this cautious approach does not sacrifice return on investments. In fact, the process usually improves returns significantly, even in the face of economic distress.

Many investors become afraid during periods of economic weakness, and that prompts action. Unfortunately, investors only act when they have to. At least this is true most of the time. Fear and greed drive investment decisions on a broad scale, and in 2008 fear was the dominant emotion. The option to transition to a proactive lifestyle becomes obvious to many investors during these times. When their backs are against the wall, and when alternative strategies fail, investors look for something that will work regardless of market direction. Therefore, for some, the findings of the Investment Rate and the theory of contemporary Darwinism have been blessings in disguise. They have rationalized the weakness during the credit crisis, and that has made their transition to a proactive lifestyle seamless.

Although pinpointing periods of weakness is important, a transition in investment doctrine carries much more weight. That comes from the Investment Rate. A change in the way an investor approaches the market can have long-lasting effects, where the policies of most money managers are prone to periods of extraordinary risk along the way. Longer-term cycles are still important, but they only provide a rationale for current conditions. Longer-term observations do not influence immediate strategy most of the time. Instead, they usually provide the general guidelines for our continued approach. Occasionally, though, longer-term cycles may experience an ultimate peak or valley, and that would be construed as immediately important. In turn, that cusp would immediately influence investment decisions in stocks, real estate, businesses, and other asset classes. 2007 was a case in point. The economy was at a high point. Liquidity had peaked according to the Investment Rate, and a major down cycle would begin immediately afterwards. We knew this in advance, so in 2007 the longer-term strategies were also actionable. However, the next immediately actionable period in that long-term cycle will not occur until 2023. Clearly, longer-term strategies are important because they rationalize the longer-term direction of the market and the health of our economy over time, but they rarely offer actionable strategies unless additional analysis is conducted.

Developing strategies will be important as we progress, but these observations act as the foundation for those strategies, so they need to be addressed first. The market has clear longer-term cycles defined by the Investment Rate, and changes in our economic environment will occur over time, and along those lines. More important, problems will surface again as economic cycles also oscillate according to contemporary Darwinism. Good companies will fail, and smaller companies who have structured their business models to take advantage of adverse conditions will flourish from time to time. This is survival of the fittest.

These are warning signs, though, and not strategies. Nonetheless, they do offer important insight. Sometimes the warning signals identify adverse conditions. But sometimes the advance indicators show us that a positive economic environment is likely to present itself instead. Either way, these identifiers do not influence strategy. Instead, they promote awareness. Investors feel more comfortable with their decisions because these tools help them understand the conditions that broadly exist and that immediately follow. This step is critically important to investor psyche.

However, even though these theories are proven, and even though some investors already feel comfortable with their conclusions, investors cannot stop there. This realization and rationalization is the first step. People who stop here will still be in search of a strategy. They will be looking for something to help them control their risk and provide opportunity regardless of economic conditions or market. Therefore, most investors are left with one more important question before they can constructively move forward. They must identify a strategy suitable to their objective. If the objective is risk control, if the interest is to protect wealth and take advantage of opportunities from time to time, and if their long-term goal is to avoid serious pitfalls again in the future, a transition to a disciplined strategy is the answer every time. This is a natural byproduct, and flows seamlessly after the Investment Rate and contemporary Darwinism have been accepted. Afterwards, all investors need to do is modify the process they use to make investment decisions to incorporate proactive strategies and disciplines. From there, burdens are lifted, and investors are free to make money irrespective of the environment.

The Right Lifestyle and Mindset

Understandably, a change of this magnitude is easier for some to accept than others. Although the adaptation is subtle, it is a lifestyle change, not a onetime decision to control risk. I made reference to wealthy families earlier in the book, and the lifelong investments that burden their decisions specifically. That's a great example, but somewhat isolated. An apprehension to adapt to changing economic and market conditions stems from much deeper and is found throughout all aspects of the investment community we know today. This is true for almost everyone because it is well rooted in human nature. The commonly used phrase "you can't teach an old dog new tricks" goes a long way. However, in this instance it could also cause material setbacks to real wealth. In turn, this brackish posture and a universal refusal to adapt to current conditions could impact retirement and change the course of lives forever.

Unfortunately, most people have grown accustomed to holding investments through periods of extraordinary weakness without controlling their risk. They have conditioned themselves to accept serious declines as a natural part of investing. In most instances, they have done so because their financial advisors have influenced them to accept declines as part of market cycles. These advisors are not wrong. Declines are part of normal oscillation cycles. However, submitting to wealth deterioration does not need to be. In fact, I don't consider that acceptable.

Losing less is not a winning strategy. Dissolving wealth is a serious issue and investors should not be conditioned to it. Clearly, losses need to be taken from time to time, but a brackish posture prone to wealth deterioration during varying economic cycles is not part of that equation in any way, shape, or form.

Still, most investors will remain apprehensive, regardless of the longer-term cycles that are now clearly identifiable. So long as they are, they will continue to expose themselves to these major setbacks as well. If this brackish posture continues to be acceptable, setbacks will occur repeatedly for those who fail to adapt. Over time, this will cause comparable wealth deterioration. But because proactive investment strategies have the ability to perform regardless of market conditions, proactive strategies also have the ability to significantly outperform brackish buy and hold strategies over time as well.

For example, if a buy and hold portfolio declines by 50 percent, a 100 percent gain would be required to get whole. A recovery of this magnitude can take a significant amount of time. Unfortunately, many people had losses of 50 percent in 2008. However, a proactive strategy that performs during all market cycles can sidestep those setbacks and accelerate ahead of the curve as a result. In addition to avoiding the losses, a proactive strategy will also allow investors to realize new opportunities, while brackish portfolios are still in recovery mode.

Afterwards, assuming losses are curtailed, full recovery could take quite a while to achieve for those persons who allow the losses to occur in the first place. In recent times investors have been accustomed to recovery within a few short years. Therefore, with recent history supporting their decisions, investors tend to sit on their hands and wait for the market to recover before they take action. First, they ride the wave down and do nothing. Then they become afraid to take losses and convert to a more effective strategy when the going gets tough, so they nervously sit exposed to market cycles and hope for a recovery. Finally, if a recovery comes, investors lazily avoid conversion to proactive strategies most of the time as well, because they are no longer driven to act. When the cycle completes itself, the circular pattern of human nature shows its face. This is a pattern most of us recognize, and it is part of the problem.

Because the conditions within the economy or the stock market may have improved when portfolios return to par, investors forget about the pitfalls associated with the brackish strategies that got them in trouble in the first place. Instead, they remain in the same position, with the same approach and the same risks, and they never learn. Most brackish investors will fall into this category. After a while, as a result, the circular process repeats itself and major setbacks happen again, and again, and again. Most often, investors remain brackish throughout the entire cycle, but they don't have to. If buy and hold strategies have already been identified as hazards over time, and if alternatives have already been proven to work as well, investors can make the choice to adapt to current and future market conditions at any time. This requires a conscious decision, though, and a subtle change. However, the results are immediately rewarding most of the time.

Although making this transition is logical, some investors never change. Therefore, for brackish investors, not only is there a period of negative return during market declines, but those negative returns are followed by prolonged periods of no growth and missed opportunities most of the time, too. Obviously, when investors are recovering losses, they are missing opportunities for real growth at the same time. Until those losses are fully recovered and positive headway is made, real returns are negative.

Clearly, had losses not occurred within those brackish portfolios in the first place, growth could be realized immediately instead. Growth, in fact, is realized immediately in proactive strategies that are able to produce results in negative market environments.

Proactive Strategies: The Only Ones That Work

After careful evaluation, proactive strategies may be the only strategies that work when everything else fails. In 2008, even hedge funds were caught on the wrong side of the curve on a regular basis. These are some of the smartest people on Wall Street: They are supposed to be able to identify opportunities well before everyone else does, and they are supposed to be able to incorporate risk controls in case they are wrong. However, they are also paid on performance, so this creates a familiar conflict of interest. Hedge fund managers often accept high levels of risk and routinely incorporate exponential leverage ratios only to produce marginal returns. Interestingly, most hedge funds underperform over time as well.

Excessive risk assumption is the underlying reason so many hedge funds were down significantly in 2008. They were overexposed to the wrong side of the market on a regular basis. Even though they are able to balance their risk, most of them did not do so successfully, and that was a conscious decision most of the time. The conflict of interest referenced above may be an underlying reason why. After taking losses early in the year, many hedge fund managers become more aggressive as the year progressed. They were willing to make big bets by way of less risk control with the hope of recovering those early losses. Most bonus checks are based on positive performance, so they needed to get their heads above water at any cost. Instead of prudence, many bets were made incorrectly, and their investors paid the price. In 2009, most of them are expected to fold as a result.

Alternatively, proactive strategies are not complex, they do not incorporate high degrees of leverage, and risk controls are integrated every step of the way. This happens regardless of market direction or economic conditions, of course, and that allows them to be used at all times. Although most hedge fund managers would argue they do not bet on market direction, in effect, that is what happened in 2008. Those managers who failed to control their risk properly made bets on market direction, and most of those bets didn't pay off. Over time, I have found this to be true almost always. In fact, we all know this to be true. When we are in Las Vegas, almost everyone loses money. The same principle applies here. When bets are made, risk controls are sacrificed, and investors pay the price. Therefore, every time an investor makes a trading decision without incorporating risk control, he or she is also making a bet. In my opinion, and as we witnessed in 2008, the house wins over time. Although declines are less likely to happen as quickly, investments without risk controls are akin to rolling the dice. Not only is the potential for loss similar, but emotions increase exponentially when the dice are rolling as well. Therefore, if one of our goals is emotional conditioning, investments without risk controls need to be avoided at all times.

Because our proactive strategies do not place bets, they are more effective. Market direction is important, but proactive strategies allow investors to remain nimble and control their risk at all times. Hedge funds are not only less nimble, but they are also arguably burdened by the excessive leverage they use. Our proactive strategies don't have these problems. In turn, that increases the proficiency of these strategies in all market environments. Nonetheless, investors expect hedge funds to perform better than the market during periods of decline, but that did not happen in 2008 either. In fact, that rarely happens in increasing market environments, as most equity managers would willingly point out. Instead, the complex nature of the funds, and the high degrees of associated risk caused many hedge funds to fail in 2008, while our easy-to-follow and easy-to-understand strategies prospered.

Accordingly, this gave way to proactive strategies because investors began to look for alternatives. Nothing else was working, so investors finally accepted the only strategies that work regardless of market direction, volatility levels, corporate scandals, or economic collapse. The stock market was declining, Treasury yields were zero, real estate prices were in free fall, and money market accounts paid nothing. Money managers lost credibility, Bernie Madoff caused shock waves throughout institutional investment communities worldwide, and hedge funds stopped letting investors have access to their money. In every respect, turmoil rippled throughout the global economy, and investors were not only losing money, they were also mad.

Unique circumstances existed in virtually every financial institution that comes to mind, but the worst case that I was aware of came from Citigroup. In January 2008, investors in Citigroup's select Corporate Special Opportunities Fund, C.S.O, requested access to their money, but they were denied. The sector in which the fund invested was under pressure as the credit crisis began, and apparently Citigroup wanted to mitigate the potential impact of a disorderly liquidation. In effect, it shut the door on these clients in January, hoping to stave off redemptions until the market stabilized. The managers of the fund may have argued that the market was near the bottom of a cycle, and liquidation at that time was unwise. If they did, they were wrong. Regardless, Citigroup made a conscious decision to deny investors access to their monies, and that enraged those accredited investors accordingly. They no longer were able protect themselves from the credit crisis that had just begun. Finally, in November 2008 Citigroup announced that the fund was being dissolved, and the investors would be left with virtually nothing. The fund, whose value was $4.2 billion at its peak, was worth $58 million and carried $880 million of debt at the end of 2008. If investors were allowed to liquidate in January, they would have received much more, but they were denied.

Events similar to these were occurring on a regular basis in 2008, and wealth was being dissolved without recourse. Investors were frustrated, but there was little anyone could do in these specific circumstances because hedge funds were not required to provide access to monies. In most instances, mismanaged companies were passing along their mistakes to investors, and then making more mistakes on top of those.

Corporate and Government Missteps

At the same time, amazingly, the government was supporting the cause. By doing so, the government was also preventing contemporary Darwinism from separating the weak from the strong. With specific reference to Citigroup, the government allowed a weak institution to survive and burdened the health of our economy in the process. Although the infusion of $300 billion helped Citigroup avoid the imminent dissolve that awaited the company in the middle of 2008, it also slowed our transition to a healthier economic environment by slowing down the government's ability to address internal issues related to fiscal policy and the escalating debt burden of the country. While Hank Paulsen favored an allocation of TARP (Troubled Asset Relief Program) funds to financial institutions like Citigroup, the Treasury secretary did not respect the negative impact those bailouts would have on the health of the economy or the value of the dollar over time. He also did not foresee the muted impact those infusions would ultimately have.

Although he was an intelligent executive, Hank Paulsen was not a proactive Treasury secretary, and he did very little to protect the economy during his tenure. Prior to the realization of the credit crisis, Hank Paulsen knew about the potential negative impact of the massive collateralized debt market because he had firsthand knowledge. Prior to being Treasury secretary, he was president of Goldman Sachs. In that role he absolutely understood the process of the derivative market and the lack of regulation that defined both the creation of and the trading of those instruments. Thus, as Treasury secretary he understood the potential impact the unregulated swap market could have on the economy. Arguably, as Treasury secretary, he was also obligated to protect the economy, but he did not act in advance.

Instead, possibly, he trusted that financial institutions would do the right thing and that capitalistic cycles would prevail. Interestingly, in the end capitalism may indeed have prevailed, just not the way he expected it to. In turn, he took no action to mitigate the risk associated with the mortgage-backed derivatives that ultimately caused the credit crisis. Some might argue that he wasn't aware of the potential impact. Others might argue that capitalism should have protected the economy. However, capitalism isn't designed to do that. If the definition of capitalism is taken into account, if periods of excess are accepted byproducts, if corporate objectives are also taken into consideration, and finally if his objective was still parallel to those he had as president of Goldman Sachs, Treasury Secretary Paulsen may have believed his distance would allow those major financial institutions to flourish. That, in turn, would provide immediate economic prosperity and a healthy economy in his opinion. Unfortunately, he did not look ahead.

Logically, he was aware of the risk, he understood the greed cycles of capitalistic economies, and he consciously chose not to regulate the industry. He therefore allowed financial institutions to push the envelope as far as they could, and he did nothing to control the risk associated with the derivatives he was already familiar with. Eventually, the economy and the wealth of our nation paid the price. Instead, brackishly, he reacted after the fact. Only after problems began to surface did he take action. Unfortunately, by then, it was too late. With his back against the wall, he floundered to find a solution, but nothing offered resolution. Instead, he did the opposite of logical discourse and the opposite of contemporary Darwinism. He tried to save the economy by propping up distressed financial institutions like Citigroup. Interestingly, these were the same companies that caused the crisis in the first place, and the same ones he allowed to flourish without regulation. He was wrong to turn a blind eye to risk then, and I believe his efforts will prove ineffective here as well. Reasonably, the prior few paragraphs include opinions as well as observations. However, if anyone believes these are speculative or conjecture, I strongly encourage them to review his exit interview. On January 12, 2009, Hank Paulsen openly admitted that he anticipated a financial crisis when he first came into office. According to his account, he met with the president at Camp David when he first became Treasury secretary, and he warned the president that the economy was poised to pull back during their term. In addition, he also stated in the interview with Maria Bartiromo that he did not know what the impact of the new credit swap would have on the pullback he anticipated. Instead of taking action, he told the president they would just have to wait and see what would happen. Therefore, other than admitting he did not protect the economy by acting proactively, he has already confirmed my points. I have simply added in the obvious. Anyone interested in reviewing the interview should contact CNBC and reference his exit interview. It supports the entirety of my argument.

Take a look at the timeline once more:

1. Paulsen managed Goldman Sachs.
2. He was aware of the potential adverse impact of credit derivatives.
3. He warned President Bush that a decline was coming many years before it started.
4. He did nothing to protect the economy from what he knew.
5. He let the credit bubble escalate in the face of risk.

With pause, I do not want to conclude this point with the wrong idea. I am not suggesting that Hank Paulsen is a bad man. Instead, he is a superior executive and a savvy investor. He was extremely good at managing Goldman Sachs. He is a corporate leader. That is what he knew best. However, he was not familiar with the role President Bush assigned to him. He was not a government man, and errors were made because of it.

Thus, my purpose in telling his story is to point out that errors were made during his term, recognize that we have seen errors in the past, and admit that we will see errors again in the future as well. We can never be sure where they will come from, but we can be sure they will come, and we need to protect ourselves from them.

Admittedly, protecting ourselves from mishaps like this is hard to do, especially when we let our emotions play a role. However, proactive strategies make that a non-issue. In fact, proactive strategies protect us all from the mistakes made by governments, corporate greed, and ourselves. If nothing more, they need to be recognized for that.

In any case, after the capital infusion by the TARP program in 2008, Citigroup still had the same problems. The infusion simply afforded the company more time to adapt to the environment. Unfortunately, the operations at Citigroup had not changed meaningfully by the end of 2008, which is when I wrote this. The company announced layoffs, and that cut costs of course, but internal operations had not changed, and Citigroup did not seem to be adjusting to the economic landscape. Unless it does, I expect contemporary Darwinism to catch up with the company again. Like many other companies who accepted handouts from the U.S. government in 2008, including General Motors, I expect a regression in Citigroup and an eventual collapse unless they immediately adapt to the change in demand cycles evidenced by the Investment Rate. Unless they do, our government will be left with the expense, and contemporary Darwinism will still have prevailed. In fact, even if these companies do successfully adapt and prosper, contemporary Darwinism will have prevailed anyway because they had to adapt to survive. Companies like Citigroup need to change if they intend to survive during times of economic distress.

During this time, with floundering policy and corporate concerns mounting, investor frustration grew. Nothing else was working. Even government intervention had little impact on current economic conditions. For example, global interest rate cuts did not spur economic activity at all, and investors were looking for shelter. They needed something they could trust. That meant a few things in 2008. First, investors needed to understand the risk associated with their investments. Prior to 2008 those risks were not properly disclosed. From mortgage-backed securities to hedge funds and back, the investment community was experiencing a revelation. Risk perceptions were changing. That started at the top and worked its way down quickly.

Notwithstanding the escalating debt levels that occurred during the Bush administration, regulatory agencies also failed to do their jobs. The SEC dropped the ball numerous times, Moody's and Standard & Poors improperly evaluated debt obligations of major financial institutions, and the risk levels on Wall Street were far greater than anyone had perceived as a result. Those failures were the fallout of the economic euphoria of years past, and proof that the third up period in the Investment Rate had ended.

Proactive Strategies Control Risk

Investors normally are not averse to risk, but they need to understand the risks associated with their investments so they can evaluate them properly. Because risk assessment was increasing as a result of the doubts that clouded the financial community, many investors opted to assume no risk at all. Unfortunately, this too may have been a misconception. Throughout 2009, Treasury bonds are likely to create their own circular trap and also limit economic recovery.

Unfortunately, this compounded the problem that already existed at big brokerage firms. Investors had already found out the hard way that money managers and mutual funds don't protect their assets, so the big brokers were already bruised. However, because those professionals are responsible for identifying opportunity and disclosing risk to their clients, and because many advisors failed to do so, investors became even more distraught. They relied on their brokers for these things. Without these added values, investors didn't have much need for them anymore. In fact, many believed that brokerage firms were behind the curve and expensive anyway. That encouraged a transition. Initially, everything seemed complicated as investors began to realize that risk levels were much higher than they otherwise thought. They could not trust the government, they could not trust their advisors, and many were in search of an alternative.

Astute investors, who realized that zero yields in Treasury bonds might not be the best place to invest, looked for a viable alternative. Hedge funds were out, money managers seemed like a losing proposition, and buying stocks in general seemed risky because the economy was still extremely weak and Wall Street expected it to get weaker. The 20 percent bear market rallies that occurred from time to time even made short selling risky. At first glance, nothing seemed to work. However, those investors who dug a little deeper were handsomely rewarded.

In 2008 intelligent investors were looking for investment alternatives that were clean, easy to use, and effective in up or down markets. Risk needed to be obvious, and it needed to be controlled at the same time. The only logical alternative was proactive trading strategies. To integrate proactive strategies, the general idea is easy to understand, so some investors engaged these disciplines independently. Many of them decided to jump in without learning the trade first. After a while, they discovered the nuances of these strategies on their own as well.

Unfortunately, many of those who jumped in without understanding the logic also failed to adhere to the emotional conditioning and trading disciplines, which are required to succeed in this sector of the financial industry. Independent traders and investors are the backbone of our niche, but they cannot sacrifice the set of guidelines integral to these strategies or they are bound to fail. Positive results are achievable by every level of trader and investor, but all of them must control their emotions and adhere to disciplines in order to succeed. These are the foundations of proactive trading strategies. Emotions have no place in this business, and discipline is required at all times. All of my clients understand that. I ingrain these two fundamental concepts into my analysis every day, and remind my clients of their importance so they never go astray. Although most investors who learn proactive disciplines are able to start using them appropriately, most end up diverging from strategy over time unless they are constantly reminded. This is human nature. Eventually, everyone who works with me accepts these truths as part of their normal activities. This is what sheltered my clients from the devastation in 2008, and this is why they use my tools in their investing activities regularly.

Although they were first designed to protect wealth and provide opportunities, my strategies have done much more than I ever imagined. When I first started Stock Traders Daily, I thought I was only providing a better way to make money in the stock market, but the proactive strategies that I eventually developed do much more than that. They also remove doubt, clarify risk, protect wealth, and allow individuals to feel much more comfortable with their decisions. Prior to 2008, most investors didn't seem to care about these things, but now everyone does. The result that this added degree of financial stability has had on the personal lives of my clients is amazing. At the end of this book, I provide a Real-Life Example that should help everyone understand the potential impact proactive trading strategies can have on a case-by-case basis. I am blessed to have had this opportunity.

I have been offering proactive trading models since January 2, 2000. Therefore, I also consider this a millennium discovery. Over time we have experienced pitfalls, adjusted strategy, and refined our process to work in any market environment. The current models have been working wonderfully, and that makes everyone happy. But we never become complacent, especially in the face of success. In addition, we never expect anything from the market. Expectations are just another form of emotion, and they have no place in this business either. Instead, we embrace reflexivity and react to changes instead.

Slowly but surely, the subtle change required to engage proactive strategies is being revealed. We need to change the way we approach the market altogether. Old school techniques are outdated, and success is no longer directly related to those aged concepts. Instead, success stems from discipline, nothing more.

Although proactive strategies are consistent, and the methodology I will explain in later chapters is unyielding, we also need to adapt to changes in the market when conditions call for it. Fortunately, this happens automatically, most of the time. Thus far we have been successful, in part, because the models I have developed are also designed to adapt to changes in market direction without any additional input. I will also detail how this works in later chapters. However, even with a powerful strategy that adjusts automatically to changing market conditions, some investors still fail. This happens, in almost all circumstances, because they have stopped adhering to discipline. Instead, my successful clients adhere to structure and discipline at all times.

Appropriately, proactive strategies help us protect our wealth, and that is our primary objective. However, because wealth preservation also requires an independent evaluation of circumstances from time to time, our next discussion will address that obvious concern. Independent traders who assume the burden of wealth preservation themselves will embrace the following chapter accordingly because it is all about independence.

Summary

Below is a summary of the most important topics in this chapter:

- The Investment Rate and contemporary Darwinism tell us to become proactive immediately. It is a lifestyle choice, not an investment decision.
- Proactive strategies work in up or down markets because they control risk and provide opportunities.
- We should embrace the opportunities the market provides.
- Our proactive approach can be adopted at any time.
- Risk controls, emotional conditioning, and discipline are integral to proactive rule-based models.
- It is time to start looking ahead and preparing for action.
- Rule-based proactive strategies are the way of the future.

CHAPTER 9

Embracing Independence

For good reason, big brokerage firms do not want us to think that we can do it ourselves, but we can. In fact, not only can we embrace the process, but we can do a better job, too. All it takes is structure. That will be our focus from here.

Understandably, many people are not accustomed to structure, and they have never been taught the discipline of risk control. This usually differentiates my new clients from my grandfathered clients. After all, the brackish investment vehicles that big brokers offer don't incorporate these integral components by rule, so prior to 2008 only a select few felt the need to learn. However, that disinterest dissolves fast when they see the results. Structure, discipline, and risk controls are clearly defined in direct correlation to performance. This relationship usually starts the ball rolling. Understandably, most investors have questions and concerns as they learn the process. Therefore, because I recognize that most investors are not accustomed to controlling risk, I have also taken steps to accelerate their learning curve by incorporating educational tools into my models. Doing so allows them to begin using these strategies proficiently, and much sooner than they would otherwise be able to. Not only does this help them immediately stabilize their portfolios, but it also adds value in the realm of contemporary Darwinism because it provides them with tools necessary to adapt to the ever-changing environment. This could separate them from the weak as the conditions detailed by the Investment Rate are realized.

Therefore, many frustrated investors who searched for alternatives in 2008 welcomed my services when they found them, and I expect that to continue indefinitely. In the midst of a global economic collapse and despite widespread panic in the financial industry, the subscriber base of Stock Traders Daily grew by over 150 percent. We were one of the few companies positioned to experience exponential growth during the credit crisis, and we are one of the few positioned to do well during the struggling environment that lies immediately ahead as well. Arguably, this is a direct result of our competitive advantages. However, that is just another way of saying that contemporary Darwinism is playing an integral role. In no uncertain terms, the strongest do survive.

Proactive Strategies

Noticeably, in 2008 some investors began to realize that proactive strategies are the best way of approaching the market during periods of decline. My clients also realize that proactive strategies are the best way of approaching the market when it trends higher, too. Nonetheless, proactive strategies are the best resource for investors in any market environment, and I don't consider them an alternative. Instead, I consider them a fundamental element for all investors to incorporate into their routine. Even the professional traders and money managers that comprise the panel of "Fast Money" traders on CNBC supported this notion going into 2009. Still, most investors do not yet incorporate proactive strategies into their investment discipline. They continue to create barriers to entry and convince themselves that the old ways are best. Instead, they remain positioned in brackish investments and hope for a reversal. For many of those persons, recovery of wealth is psychologically necessary before any transitions happen. However, given the findings of the Investment Rate, that could take a while.

Consequently, and even during normal pullbacks, prolonged periods of no growth are part of the natural process after portfolios decline. Clearly, the most logical way to avoid this pitfall is to prevent losses at the onset, but very few strategies offer this as an option. Alternatively, investors could choose strategies that afford them the opportunity to make money during otherwise weak market conditions. This, at least, would present a viable alternative to buy and hold strategies. After all, buy and hold investments are the most vulnerable to decline during weak market environments anyway. Therefore, as long as investors refuse to adapt to evolving market conditions, they must also wait for a full recovery before they experience real growth as well. However, that assumption is risky. That assumes the market will recover quickly.

In fact, most investors expected a rather prompt recovery after the pullback that occurred at the beginning of 2008, but they were wrong. It kept on declining instead. Understandably, no one wants to sell at the bottom, so when the market was down in early 2008, most investors chose to sit tight and let their money managers handle all of their investment decisions. The aftermath is clear. The market continued to slide, and brackish investors stared at their computers, or watched CNBC or Bloomberg like a deer in the headlights as their wealth deteriorated in front of their eyes. But other investors chose a different path. Even though their portfolios were likely underwater as well, some investors opted for proactive trading strategies. Either they realized the potential impact of the credit crisis early, or they luckily stumbled into proactive strategies on their own. Either way, they adapted to the conditions and mutated into a stronger species of investor. Those investors who found the most viable option for making money in 2008 appreciated the results.

During that same time, when most buy and hold investors were significantly underwater, proactive strategies were working well. For example, one of the more basic strategies that I offer provided results of 60.82 percent. As the year came to an end, this strategy had outperformed the market by almost 100 percent. Accordingly, many buy and hold strategies were down as much as the market. However, because managed accounts often underperform the market over time, a surprising number were down significantly more than that. Nonetheless, they all had a long way to go before they recovered those losses. With respect to the average, before any portfolio that declined the same amount as the market in 2008 begins to produce positive returns again, it first must increase by approximately 58 percent. Although the market only declined by 37 percent in 2008, and that seems manageable, the percentage differential of the recovery process is always more than the previous declines, and that makes recovery more difficult.

Without argument, a 58 percent return in one year is a lot to ask during even the best of times. Over a two-year period, most analysts would also consider this to be an excellent return. Therefore, immediate expectations for a full recovery needed to be moderated in 2008, and they were. Even during raging bull markets, managed accounts don't usually produce returns like that, and investors began to recognize this fact as their real wealth declined. However, the proactive strategy that I have referenced here did not have those setbacks, so it did not assume the same burden of recovery as brackish investments did. This strategy is "The Stock of the Week." Although most brackish investors remained apprehensive when the going got tough in early 2008, a select few were sheltered from the storm. Proactive strategies worked well, in most cases. And those who chose to follow this strategy also outperformed the market by a large margin. As a direct result, they were not in recovery mode as 2008 came to an end, and they were making positive headway in a down market. Growth was being realized immediately, and they were outperforming most buy and hold portfolios significantly. If this is an inherent goal embedded in the investment doctrine held by any individual or professional investor, then proactive strategies should be considered a permanent resource.

The Third Major Down Period in U.S. History

Our specific strategies are in later chapters, but this simple observation should prompt everyone to consider the difference between a brackish portfolio and a proactive one. More important, this reference should help pinpoint the potential positive impact proactive strategies can have over time. During circular down cycles evidenced by contemporary Darwinism, setbacks like this happen to the economy on a regular basis.

Although the Investment Rate tells us that the years ahead will prove that the declines in 2008 are much more serious than previous setbacks have been, we can still recognize the significance of even interim pullbacks. We can all still remember the pullback that happened after the Internet bubble because that left a mark. Most of us also recall the market crash of 1987. In addition, everyone seems to accept declines from time to time because we are trained to accept them. Accordingly, if we recognize that declines will occur from time to time, we have two choices, not just one. Either we can ride the wave lower every time and work our way out of the hole every time, or we can recognize more rewarding strategies and make use of them instead.

Meaningful setbacks will occur regularly if they are considered part of investment strategies from the beginning. Big brokers warn about these situations openly and admit that the market will capitulate from time to time as well. Their regular advice, which is usually offered preemptively, is to stay the course and let the portfolio recover from those declines on its own. However, in 2008 recovery looked questionable at best. The Investment Rate furthers that notion. Therefore, most investors should consider alternatives unless they are comfortable losing money from time to time and falling behind. If investors allow, setbacks will negatively influence brackish investment strategies as often as the economy cycles back and forth.

However, performance does not need to depend on market conditions. Proactive models have the ability to perform when buy and hold models fail. In addition, recovery is not the same between brackish and proactive models. In fact, proactive models tend to sidestep the pitfalls of recovery more often than buy and hold strategies do. If nothing more, they have the ability to do so. Nonetheless, in buy and hold portfolios, after experiencing circular losses, the next obvious question surrounds the recovery of those lost assets. Herein lies the difference. Because proactive portfolios have the ability to perform when the market declines, correlated losses may not need to be recovered at all. This defines a distinct difference between the strategies and could set the stage for a more stable portfolio for everyone who adopts proactive strategies going forward.

Arguably, the best-case scenario for brackish investors after a down market is a prompt, full recovery. Not only is that a lot to ask, but that is also relative to personal circumstances at the same time. A recovery could take one to two years. At least that was the mainstream train of thought in 2008. Prior to 2007, for the past 26 years a quick recovery occurred after every major market decline. Therefore, investors expected the same pattern to prevail after the credit crisis of 2008 as well.

For the sake of argument, let us assume that a full recovery takes place this time, too. Play the devil's advocate for a minute and assume that a break of that well-established 108-year trend, since 1900, which proves that the Investment Rate leads the market into and out of major economic cycles, occurs right now. Although this would be a major happenstance, the suppositions will also allow us to examine comparative performance ratios effectively.

Now, compare the results of a brackish portfolio that incurs those same near-term setbacks, to a proactive model, which does not. First, if the market indeed increases back to its 2007 highs quickly and returns all of the lost wealth in full, some investors may be completely satisfied. If this happens, and in a few short years, real wealth recovers again, some buy and hold investors may even gain confidence. "I told you the market would recover!" I can hear the clatter already.

Nevertheless, a full recovery is still a no-growth environment. There will be no positive headway until a portfolio has done more than simply recover. I think Maria Bartiromo put it best. While the market reeled in the middle of 2008, some analysts were touting the market's performance prior to the decline. However, she accurately pointed out that overall performance for the past 10 years was flat. Almost across the board, buy and hold investors had made nothing for the prior 10 years even though the market experienced a strong upswing between October 2002 and late 2007. In effect, there had been no growth in many equity portfolios for quite a while. There was only asset recovery. This is commonplace in brackish portfolios. Yet asset managers continued to tout period-specific performance statistics instead. They do this to influence investment dollars into their portfolios, to generate fees, and in many cases to shadow periods of weakness. This is another version of the reference I made to losing portfolios earlier. In this case, since when has making nothing been a good return?

At the same time, the relative outperformance of a proactive model is significant. First of all, in our earlier example, most people did not expect a 58 percent gain in 2009. During the best of times a 58 percent return would be too much to ask, and 2009 was not likely to be one of those times at all. Instead, as 2008 ended, even the most positive analysts called for recovery over the next few years, not just one. If that's true, and if recovery takes two to three years, then anyone holding losses and waiting for a recovery will miss net growth opportunities along the way. A return to par, like the 10-year no-growth environment Maria Bartiromo pointed out, does not constitute a positive return. Instead, that equates to zero. Therefore, while underwater portfolios struggle to get their heads above water again, proactive strategies like the one I mentioned above can continue to outperform even in the worst of times.

However, we started this comparison with a relatively strong assumption, and we should reconcile that before moving forward. We started with an assumption that the Investment Rate would coincidentally stop acting as a leading indicator for the market in 2008. Now, let us back that assumption out of this comparative analysis and re-review our subject with a more accurate lens. Instead, let's assume that the market experiences a period of extreme weakness akin to the Great Depression and the Stagflation period of the 1970s. This is, in fact, what the Investment Rate tells us to expect. With that, equity values are not expected to recover promptly, and brackish investments will remain underwater for an extended period. Instead of recovering within a few years, the recovery process for buy and hold investors could take decades. A full recovery from the Great Depression took 26 years, and assets were underwater by 75 percent along the way. A recovery from the Stagflation period of the 1970s took 10 years, with 50 percent declines respectively. Assuming a similar result during the third major down period in U.S. history, evidenced by the Investment Rate, a similar consequence is likely. After the peak in 2007, brackish portfolios could sit underwater for a very long time. Without experiencing any growth, buy and hold investors are likely to sit idle as their wealth oscillates with the market. In addition, the chance of more declines is real.

Taking Advantage of the Turmoil That Lies Ahead

As gloomy as that sounds, we all know that the market will eventually recover. Although we may have to wait 10 or 20 years to see it happen, the market trends higher over time, and lifelong investors can be assured that long-term assets in solid companies will prove worthwhile accordingly. This should comfort wealthy families who have built core businesses and passed them on through generations. However, at the same time, smaller investors may not have those luxuries. Instead, normal investors may need their money sooner than that. In any case, buy and hold investors will miss opportunities during periods of weakness; they will need to experience a full recovery before real growth is recognized, and they will be subject to market turmoil every step of the way. During that same time, proactive models will provide prospects for growth, while offering risk controls instead. Therefore, there is a clear choice for astute investors who want to protect their wealth.

Understandably, until now, most investors have not recognized this viable option. More often, most investors considered this approach desirable, but unattainable at the same time. Prior to now, proactive strategies were unmanageable for many individual investors due to associated time constraints. That has changed, and my system proves the process can work for anyone. Nevertheless, this was not a revelation for us in 2008. In fact, we have been doing this for years, but the value was widely accepted during the cheap money upswing. However, this may have been a revelation for many other investors as the market came under pressure.

Luckily, some experienced investors recognized the value of proactive trading strategies in advance of those declines. The astute nature of some investors saved them from experiencing significant losses. That was the case with us. We believe that active strategies are the best way to approach the market at all times, so the change in market conditions did not affect our approach at all. On the other side of the fence, though, others who chose not to adopt proactive strategies, or who failed to recognize them, did nothing to adapt to the changing environment either. As 2008 progressed, most of them paid the price and contemporary Darwinism caught up with them.

Understandably, most people do not remember the major down cycles evidenced by the Investment Rate, so they are not overly concerned when setbacks happened most of the time either. Reasonably, most investors were probably not fully invested during those historic declines anyway, so they are not aware of the risk associated with these major down cycles. Therefore, many investors did not have a desire to evaluate longer-term proactive strategies for use in everyday activities when the first red flags began to appear early in 2008. Everyone seemed to know that these strategies existed, but few were compelled to start using them until they were forced to. For some, the transition is taking even longer than that. Investors don't change their patterns until they are forced to do so. That put is a tough hurdle though. Some investors need to feel pain before they recognize the need for change, and sometimes that's not even enough. Investors need to have reason to change before they take action, but sometimes, perceived risk is not enough to convince some people.

Rightfully so, investors should ask questions before adopting new strategies. After all, we are discussing real wealth, and these topics are critical to our well-being. But investors cannot stare risk in the face either, and then expect their net worth to hold up while they do nothing to protect it. We are not stronger than the natural forces of the market, and I would argue that none of us is smarter than the market either. Investors must recognize undulating cycles, they must respect them, and they must adapt to the ever-changing environment that is our economy. Yet, many investors drag their heels, and this opens the door to natural selection as it relates to contemporary Darwinism.

Instead of taking action, investors often create excuses for themselves, which prevent them from moving forward. Some may consider proactive strategies too much work when they first evaluate them, and others develop unique reasons for not engaging the strategies in the first place. After all, learning something new is often a barrier to entry, so people drag their heels before taking the first step. Others may believe that integrating these strategies is beyond their means. And some might even feel as if they are not experienced enough to use them. In fact, prior to those declines most investors believed proactive investment strategies were unusable for one reason or another. Those persons interested in my strategies prior to 2008 were no exception. Most of them were more interested in the unique nature of my approach and the definition of my longer-term model than they were with the enforcement of my doctrine. Not until the pain started to impact real wealth did new investors take a serious look at my products for application. Yes, I had a loyal following that stemmed from our inception in 2000, but new subscribers had to be convinced. Prior to 2008, that took quite an effort. However, as the year came to an end, investors began to respect the ability of my strategies and they began to integrate them accordingly. Soon, they too realized that these strategies could be used to navigate the market in virtually all conditions.

Just Give Them a Chance

Unfortunately, from the beginning, most investors do not give proactive strategies a chance. This, at least, was true at the beginning of the most recent major down period in U.S. history, which began at the end of 2007. Luckily for some, shortly afterwards those closed doors began to open for the first time, and the playing field became more clear. The pain experienced in 2008 was a logical catalyst for this transition. As 2008 ended, investors began to welcome those ideas they refused to consider before. The only reason they did this is that they had to. Nothing else was working, so their hands were forced. In fact, all asset classes were declining, so there was no shelter in real estate, in business, or in traditionally secure municipal or corporate bonds. Treasuries were an alternative, but they paid nothing. The only recourse for investors who were also seeking a positive return was risk-controlled trading strategies.

Surprisingly, prior to 2008 that was a tough sell. One might surmise that risk controls would be important to investors at all times, but they are not. Instead, investors were taught that diversification equates to risk control. Clearly it doesn't, and now those same investors understand why. After 2008, a revelation seems to have hit, and everyone is recognizing the value of wealth preservation. I hope that lasts forever.

At the same time, investors are recognizing the constant equity exposure of brackish portfolios, and the lack of risk control that exists inherently in them. Now, almost everyone is looking for options that are more viable. The most obvious are proactive strategies. Transitionally, investors began to accept the weakness in the economy and the stock market as more severe than they had originally thought, and that was the driving force behind this change. As negative news continued to flow, some began to believe this period of weakness might indeed result in more severe setbacks than recent historical comparisons suggest. For those who discovered the Investment Rate, they also found out why.

In turn, they have also come to the realization that overall demand for investments within our economy is the driving force behind long-term economic cycles. The Investment Rate defines these demand cycles. If they are respected, investors, corporations, and governments can accurately plan ahead. They all can prevent contemporary Darwinism from claiming their lives, and adapt accordingly when conditions change. This could have been true for Bear Stearns, Lehman Brothers, Fannie Mae, American International Group, and all the other failed companies we know about. It could have also saved our government from incurring excessive debt that may ultimately be the demise of the dollar.

Having the Upper Hand

However, adaptation may be easier for an individual investor to do than it is for corporations and governments. Just like large money managers, corporations and governments move slowly, and their process is not predisposed to change.

More important, individual investors can incorporate models that, by themselves, adapt to changing environmental conditions, where larger institutions cannot. The most recent longer-term up cycle in the Investment Rate was an excellent case in point. Declines were short lived during that 26-year up cycle, and the market has continued to trudge ahead quickly after those setbacks. This was something Wall Street and Main Street had grown accustomed to over time. Therefore, going into 2008, everyone seemed to expect the same thing to happen again. Sure, they expected some weakness, but even the most astute economist on the street failed to recognize the longer-term declines in demand that began at the end of 2007. Instead, they talked about the supply of money, and the government did, too. The focus was on financial institutions and making sure they had money to lend. They failed to recognize that demand had simply dried up. More precisely, credit-worthy borrowers declined significantly in number. Immediately, this occurred in 2008 because lending standards changed. However, naturally, this is also a byproduct of the Investment Rate. More important, the Investment Rate tells us to expect downward trends in demand, and a lower number of credit-worthy borrowers every year for the next 16 years.

Nonetheless, lingering memories of recent pullbacks created expectations that prevented investors, governments, and corporations from acting preemptively. Instead of protecting our wealth and our country, they did nothing to control our exposure. I spoke with a few executives in 2008 who epitomized the philosophical mindset of that era. "It had to end sometime," one said. "But it was a good run!" He continued to explain how he pushed the envelope and took every opportunity that lay in front of him. The rewards were bountiful, he tried to rationalize. In fact, he seemed to have reaped rewards beyond normal measure. However, at the same time he was sacrificing risk controls for himself, his company, and the people whom he employed. After the dust settled, he paid the price, and so did everyone around him. His company was bankrupt, his employees were out of work, and he had nothing. In 2008, a man who had made in excess of $400,000 per year for the past three years had lost everything. More important, his reversal of fortune took only a few short months. Although this may seem like an abrupt change, when a blind eye is turned to risk, losses are imminent. In layman's terms, greed got the best of him. Luckily, we know there is no place for greed in this business. By definition, greed is simply another form of emotion.

Although he knew he should control his company's risk exposure, he failed to do so. In fact, this was true for most executives prior to the credit crisis as well. Unfortunately, the same held true for governments and individual investors. Very few took preliminary measures to control their risk. In most cases they didn't feel the need. The economy was booming, and "Why look gift horses in the mouth?" Instead of taking preemptive action, or conditioning their businesses to survive through both good times and bad, most executives wanted to get a bigger piece of the pie. At the same time, the government was realizing the highest tax revenues in history, so it saw no reason for change either. That is, of course, until the hammer dropped. Like most money managers, the government only reacted to these conditions after the severity of the weakness was realized. Instead of positioning themselves beforehand, all of these entities rode the economic wave as far as they could, and some were left holding the bag at the end.

In fact, most of America and the world decided against protectionist measures ahead of these declines. Inherent trading strategies used to suggest that we sell when everyone else was buying, and buy when everyone else was selling. As the most recent major up cycle in U.S. history came to an end, investors forgot this simple policy. In hindsight, we still know this to be true, but it was ignored as the market peaked.

Unfortunately, some brackish investors were still shrugging off the economic weakness at the end of 2008, and they still expected the market to recover in a short while. Better said, most of them were hoping for a recovery and far less sure that one would occur. Real wealth had dissolved, and they were feeling the pain directly in their pocketbooks. Nevertheless, they were also somewhat confident that the market always goes up, because that is what their brokers told them to expect. Surprisingly, big brokers are pretty good at this, and because some investors could not find a better option, they stayed the course, paid their fees, and watched their wealth dissolve. However, after a short while, they also expected their wealth to come back in full because their brokers told them so, so many were nervously enduring the process.

In fact, I have found that most investors expect a prompt recovery every time a setback occurs, and proving otherwise takes repetitive effort. Most do not recognize longer-term cycles in the economy as they are defined by the Investment Rate, and it takes a few reads to accept these findings as a result. However, once they do, they also recognize the difference between the declines in 2008, and the declines that took place throughout the prior 26 years. Then, from there, the path to the comfort zone becomes much clearer.

Clearly, most investors have forgotten what real weakness feels like. In fact, even long-time veterans have forgotten the pain that these major setbacks can cause. However, in 2008 those memories became conspicuous again. Unless forced to reconcile, Wall Street is extremely short-sighted. It always has been, and I expect it always will be. That is true now, it was true then, and it will be true in the future. Yesterday's news is replaced with new events immediately, and Wall Street continues looking ahead at all times. Unfortunately, investors often fail to see the forest despite the trees.

Interestingly, Wall Street looks ahead for opportunities much more often than it looks ahead to evaluate risk. That can create undulations in the system, and that is likely what caused some of the stress on our economy in 2008. Clearly, the pitfalls, which were the same ones experienced during the last major down period in the Investment Rate, the Stagflation Period of the 1970s, were forgotten many years ago. Those memories were not prominent while the economy gained momentum, and the associated warnings were not prevalent enough to influence our leaders to protect our economy as a result. Even during normal economic cycles, investors forget the opportunities that exist on a regular basis. More often than not, they are blind to sector rotation until the cycle has begun. This time, though, a failure to react had much more severe consequences.

From here, I must address inherent obstacles again. A transition to a proactive lifestyle is not only a tough hurdle for some people to accept because of its general nature, but many more have been conditioned to think the other way. In December 2008 I was listening to a CNN report that told investors that diversification was the best way to control risk. This report recommended balanced funds and proclaimed them the best place to protect wealth. I was shaking my head during that interview. Those comments were intended to help investors avoid the risk inherent in the market at the end of 2008. At the same time, I wondered if the reporter did any research on the net return of balanced funds during the credit crisis. I doubt he had; otherwise he would have understood that balance, as it is defined by current Wall Street standards, does very little to protect wealth during major down cycles. His shortsighted recommendation epitomizes Wall Street and is a catalyst to wealth deterioration instead.

Consider the American Funds as an example. This is one of the largest mutual fund companies in the world. They offer a fund that is a balanced portfolio to offer reduced volatility. This fund is called the American Balanced Fund. In December 2008, this fund was down by 23.2 percent. This fund is arguably better than all other balanced funds on the market, and it managed to outperform the S&P 500 quite handily. In hindsight, the fund lost less than the market. Nevertheless, it was a good place to be according to Wall Street measures. Still, investors lost a significant amount of wealth, so why was it being touted? The reporter, like so many others, is influenced toward unyielding standards that promote brackish investing. That mindset is ingrained in Wall Street. It is ingrained in the media. And it is ingrained in normal investors, too. However, it is also exactly what caused so many people to lose money during the credit crisis. This mindset needs to change, and investors need to adapt if they intend to survive this evolutionary economic cycle.

Fortunately, for those who are adapting to our changing environment, we have already identified an immediately actionable strategy. However, for those who are still having trouble making the transition, more consideration is required. I intend on being there. I will help facilitate a transition to a proactive lifestyle for anyone interested in this viable approach. In either case, a decision to adopt proactive trading strategies could be part of routine conditioning or trial and error. In addition, some investors may haphazardly find themselves in a unique position that allows them to benefit from adverse economic conditions, as I have said. Understandably, however, I favor conditioning to trial and error because it is a controlled environment. With proper conditioning, we are able to both adopt a proactive approach to our investments and discount pitfalls stemming from corporate or government policies at the same time. Therefore, I also offer conditioning models to my clients regularly. These are usually offered in the form of suggestions and guidelines that are intended to make their efforts easier. In any case, my purpose is to offer them an opportunity to adapt to this phase of contemporary Darwinism.

No matter what, at all times, proactive traders position themselves so as not to subject our investments to either government policy or corporate greed by embracing independence. In effect, these have no impact on our decisions, and they do not influence our assessment of risk. Instead, they are completely discounted. Arguably, we are conscious and aware of those hazards in advance, but we do not let them affect our performance. However, in most other instances, investors outside of our system have constant exposure to unnecessary risk, and that ensures occasional setbacks. Our proactive strategies naturally discourage this. In turn, that transformation separates us from the pack by first dissolving our ties with corporate bias and then preventing eventual policy changes from affecting our investment decisions. Arguably, we are one of the strongest species in contemporary Darwinism as a result. Proactive strategies can prevail in any economic or market environment, and they are protected from both corporate action and government policy. Independence is the premise for our strategies.

However, in order to adopt this approach, an underlying postulation needs to be made first. In order to accept proactive strategies, investors must admit they have no control over the market, the economy, the government, or the companies with whom they decide to invest. They must also admit that they are not smarter than the market. When that happens, doors open and investors are free to make educated decisions.

Reasonably, the same doors can open for corporate leaders and policy-makers alike. However, these may be less influenced by trading strategies and more influenced instead by the defining cycles from which we protect ourselves. In any respect, recognition promotes action, and I hope every-one recognizes the power of the Investment Rate and the circular impact of contemporary Darwinism. Unfortunately, I am not currently in a position to influence the decisions of policymakers. Eventually, I hope to help the managers of our country better understand prevailing and future economic conditions. Even so, I will make every effort to mitigate the impact of longer-term economic cycles on our economy and ultimately on our population for many years to come.

Until I am recognized, I will do it one investor at a time. For now, my purpose is to help explain how contemporary Darwinism can affect all of us on an individual basis. The same characteristics apply to individuals that apply to corporations in the face of our struggling economy. Some of us will merely survive. Some of us will experience severe financial setbacks, but other, more intelligent investors will flourish. This will depend on our individual dynamics and our ability or willingness to adapt. During these evolutionary periods only select species survive. Darwin identified this as natural selection. Contemporary Darwinism has similar characteristics. Some survivors will have the monies needed to weather the storm. Other investors may have luck on their side, or find themselves in a naturally defensive industry or niche. And others will be smart enough to see what lies ahead, and position themselves in proactive strategies.

Unfortunately, though, a larger number will remain brackish, exposed, and unwilling to adapt. Everyone must negotiate risk in order to survive the transition that has already begun, and reasonably, some will refuse. Only those contemporary investors who are willing to do so will get through it without associated wealth destruction. And only those that adapt to the en-vironment will find opportunity. Risk control is the key element to survival.

Investors who intend on surviving the potential depression that lies ahead must focus on risk control and the abatement of emotion referenced in previous chapters.

Finally, an implementation of risk controls should be true during both good times and bad. But we all know that prudent investing techniques, even if they are adopted now, won't last forever. Eventually, the stress on our economy will lift, and some investors will unfortunately be coerced back into the brackish posture that got them into trouble in the first place. Furthermore, this pattern of human nature will cycle through to our leaders again as well. Our government will eventually be prone to mismanaging risk again, and we can be assured that corporations will always be driven by greed. Unfortunately, these truths are obstinate for the broader population, and that is what concerns me immediately.

However, this does not need to be true for everyone. The circulatory mismanagement that we have been fortunate to witness in the years leading up to the credit crisis should provide us with the lessons needed to protect wealth going forward as well. The only way to do this is to recognize our faults now, and incorporate strategies that prevent those faults from coming back to haunt us. In the case of reflexivity, we should also embrace some of our faults, if we can. We all must also realize that we are prone to following the guide of government, and governments are not always the best leaders for our personal goals and objectives. We must also protect ourselves from corporate policies designed to increase revenues for those firms. Our references have been to brokerage firms, and our personal wealth has been at risk accordingly. We cannot allow their policies to impact our wealth if we intend on being one of the few left standing in the end.

Recognition is the key. Therefore, if we recognize that we are prone to pitfalls in advance, we are much more likely to avoid those mistakes in the future. However, if we do not take notice in advance, we will be subject to recurring pitfalls expectedly.

Moving forward, as the going gets tough, the strongest can survive if they are smarter. Clearly, the strongest will be those who learn from their mistakes and prevent them from happening again. From there, at least until government and corporate policies stabilize, independence will be a key ingredient to preservation. Without a combination of intelligence and independence, we will eventually be prone to the circulatory pitfalls defined by contemporary Darwinism. The trickle-down impact can affect all of us again if we allow it to happen. Instead, with a conscious understanding of our environment, we are capable of avoiding those mistakes and preserving our wealth in the process.

Unfortunately, persons who make the same financial mistakes repeatedly are not likely to survive. They will not be one of the strongest species unless they get lucky as the economy cycles. The strongest, in contemporary

Darwinism, are those entities capable of self-directing necessary mutations in order to survive and flourish during both the good times and bad. We need to adapt to our environment; otherwise, we will watch our wealth dissolve from time to time. Given the dynamic conditions that lie ahead, as policy changes are enacted and new laws are passed, adaptation may necessarily become reflexive in nature as well. The nimble, intelligent, unemotional and astute investor will survive. However, the brackish postulate that presides over Wall Street today will likely go down along with the market and the economy.

Ultimately, if reflexive adaptation is coupled with reduced emotional burden, the probability of thriving in a depressionary economic environment increases accordingly. Contemporary Darwinism is not discriminatory, but rather a natural selection based on a series of mutations and extinctions in our global economy.

Everyone is on a level playing field. In fact, individual investors may even have the upper hand. I will explain why. No matter, everyone is capable of realizing wealth even during the tough times, if investors can first embrace the circumstances, of course. In the next chapter, I will discuss that topic, so we can all embrace wealth again.

Summary

Below is a summary of the most important topics in this chapter:

- Proactive strategies can outperform significantly over time.
- The market has forced us to change our approach.
- Proactive strategies can now be used by anyone.
- Everyone has a choice.
- Our mindset needs to change.
- We can do better than our advisors.
- Taking the first step is the hardest part.
- We must admit that we have no control over the market.
- We must admit that we are not smarter than the market.
- Independence is a key to wealth preservation over time.

CHAPTER 10

Ahead of the Curve

Clearly, many investors experienced a significant loss of wealth during the credit crisis, so part of my job is to show them how to rebuild. Therefore, my objective is to provide a model that not only protects wealth, but one that provides an opportunity to restore wealth at the same time. We can accomplish that in one of two ways. Either we can try to pinpoint periods of weakness in advance, and hope we are right, or we can adopt a proactive strategy that reacts automatically to changing market conditions, and never look back. Proactive strategies allow us to move ahead in any economic condition.

However, first, the former is a strategy often used by professional money managers. They try to pinpoint ebbs and flows in the economy, and they skew the diversification models they use accordingly. Equity exposure still exists, of course, but they make every effort to stay ahead of the curve by trying to identify these cycles and modify their holdings. This creates two difficult scenarios. First, if they are wrong, the shift that has taken place within their managed funds will need to be parsed. Missed opportunity is the best-case scenario, though. If a period of weakness occurs instead, like the one experienced in 2008, the identification process and the repositioning they may have so prudently endured do not matter at all. Therefore, attempting to identify periods of weakness in advance can be futile even though intentions are good.

Obviously, some professionals are very good at predicting periods of weakness as well as periods of growth. In fact, I would argue that I am very good at doing the same. Unfortunately, though, we are all wrong on occasion. This is normal, and everyone recognizes this and accepts imperfections as a way of life. However, as they say, all it takes is one time. If we are always exposed to the market, that time will come eventually, and we will be hurt by it.

However, if our mode of operation transitions to a proactive model, those imperfections dissolve, and we are much more capable of going with the flow of the market at all times. Therefore, not only will analytical pressures be removed from the equation, but risk exposure will also be under control and prowess will improve. Both the Investment Rate and contemporary Darwinism point us in that direction. They tell us that constant exposure is risky. We all know this based on past cycles. The transition is clear. Cash is king sometimes, and that concept is integral to proactive strategies.

Reshaping and Rebuilding

After combining the Investment Rate with contemporary Darwinism, the long-term impact of the credit crisis starts to become much more apparent. Be careful not to confuse causality, though. The credit crisis did not create reduced demand ratios. Instead, reduced demand ratios forced the hand of lenders, and accelerated a trend already defined by the Investment Rate. Initially, after all, the credit crisis was a byproduct of reduced demand, not the other way around. However, after a while, the system absolutely became circular, but it did not start that way. Generally speaking, after the realization that credit-worthy borrowers no longer existed, lending practices came into question. After the going got tough, even the sparse number of credit-worthy borrowers that still existed began to pull in their reins. They did this because all asset classes were experiencing significant losses, and almost everyone was losing money. This created questions, fears, and apprehension. After turmoil like this, contemporary Darwinism is left to determine who is standing in the end. My job is to make sure that my clients are one of the strongest investors in the market. My job is to do everything in my power to make sure that they are left standing when the dust settles.

Ultimately, my objective is to help my clients remain ahead of the curve at all times. That process starts with a cleansing and a reshaping of our investment strategy. Most of the time, at least, a cleansing is required to fully integrate the process. In the previous chapters, the main goal was to offer a preliminary guide for reshaping our approach towards investments. Given the transition identified by the Investment Rate, this conversion is both timely and necessary. From here, we will be able to use the proactive tools first mentioned in the previous chapters more effectively, and with confidence. These are detailed as we move ahead. Everyone will have the ability to use these tools to sidestep the continued turmoil that will define the third major down period in U.S. history.

However, although we should all start with confidence, and an approach free from emotional burdens, free from investment-related stress, and free from doubt, we are not all likely to end up in the same place or remain on the same path I have begun to outline. Even with a re-energized approach to the market, some of us will reasonably stray from the path. Even if we all pursue these preliminary steps today, we all may not end up following through to the end. Reasonably, some will diverge from the path, and some will not reach the comfort zone as a result. The reasons for this are usually the same. The general reason is distraction. For one reason or another, many people forget the premise for this discipline while they are using it. Therefore, part of staying ahead of the curve includes staying on the path I have outlined as well.

Far too often, I have found that some of my new clients started out doing great, but then regressed after they began to do well. Eventually, they stopped using the discipline as it was intended to be used. Either they were distracted from the path for personal reasons, or they began to modify the system to better suit their needs. Either way, that problem needs to be addressed.

Although I am an unyielding proponent of structure and discipline, I find no fault in modifying the system I propose, within reason. In fact, evolution is premised on this, and I tend to discover new applications all the time as well. However, the core component of these strategies cannot be sacrificed during the mutation process. Unfortunately, I have found that risk controls indeed are sacrificed or abbreviated, or the spreads are widened in many unique derivations of my proven strategies. In my opinion, confidence turns into arrogance for many people after they start to see my system produce results. After that arrogance transgresses the process, some of them start to believe that proactive strategies can be used without proper risk controls. I discovered this tendency over time because some new clients began reporting surprising losses that seemed out of line with the results of the core model. Only after additional investigation did I discover that they stopped using the structure and discipline I had so carefully outlined.

Modification is acceptable and encouraged, but failure to put proper strategy into practice is not. Integral components must be included, or these strategies will fail. The essential elements of successful proactive trading strategies include emotional conditioning, risk controls, and all of the other workings I have been positioning us to recognize in prior chapters. They are not suggestions. More important, these steps are necessary to realizing the successful and continued implementation of proactive trading strategies. At the beginning, most of my clients appreciate this. Still, over time some investors stray from the path and disregard the defining boundaries that have allowed these systems to prosper. Instead of following the carefully established outlines I have labored to produce, some investors frustrate themselves with diverting effort.

My responsibilities therefore transcend the initial hurdles I have already referenced to include continuing education as well. The only way to ensure that we are always ahead of the curve is to remind ourselves of the obstacles that could disorient our intention all the time. I have adopted a few methods for doing this. They are simple and effective, just like my overall approach to the market. However, they are not merely suggestions either. The inclusion of this methodology into the overall process helps to ensure continued reverence for the discipline that can alleviate the strain of the economy and the market on our personal lives forever. They are tools, and we use them every day. Therefore, these will be the first part of our discussion as we transition to tools.

Thus far, the groundwork I have offered allows everyone to participate in proactive trading strategies. Everyone is able to complete his or her evolution into a proactive lifestyle using a simple defined methodology. My simplified and refined process applies to all people, regardless of age or net worth. I attempt to dispel the myths surrounding widely accepted investment practices and re-boot the mind so that surrounding noise no longer becomes an all-encompassing concern. This is not an easy task, because everyone is different, and therefore everyone requires a slightly modified translation of the process. However, similarities do exist within every unique interaction, and those make the progression to a proactive lifestyle easier to define and even easier to apply across the board.

Over time, coincidences associated with client interaction have helped me evolve a vertically integrated course of action that begins with a foundation of economic theory and ends with a source of actionable trading strategies designed to work in all economic environments. In between, the building blocks, which have been carefully put into place, allow us to engage a methodical process free from fear, greed, or other emotions. Eventually, this affords everyone an opportunity to achieve our end goal. These building blocks allow us to reach the comfort zone, a place where our investments are no longer heavy burdens on our peace of mind or general lifestyle.

Boot Camp

Thus far, we have addressed the first part of my systematic approach, and I have attempted to weed out the noise. This section will rationalize and summarize the prior chapters and point us in the direction of appropriate actionable strategies going forward. I have provided the sweeping outlay of the first steps, but I can dig deeper when my clients need me to do so. When I individualize my attention, I utilize a structure very similar to the one I have incorporated into this book. Therefore, I will introduce this added-value service and explain the process I use to accelerate the learning curve for select clients. This, in turn, will reveal the importance of the structure I am using here and open even more doors to future success. This structure is what allows my clients to remain ahead of the curve at all times.

For every client interested in going the extra mile, I also give them the option of participating in a Boot Camp. This is a personalized one-on-one interaction between my client and me. During this unique occasion, participating clients have the opportunity to learn from the founder of the Investment Rate and the architect of the integrated proactive strategies we use every day. However, more often than not, Boot Camp is more focused on the building blocks of these strategies than on the strategies themselves. The building blocks are, in fact, the most important part of the entire process. Most participants start the Camp with an excitement and exuberance, but I always stem that emotion immediately to prevent an initial diversion. That allows me to sidestep the unnecessary hurdles that usually follow oversight at the beginning.

Typical of my overall approach, I cleanse the mindset of each person I help to avoid an unraveling of discipline that might occur further along the process. Before my strategies are implemented, users must first understand why they were designed. Afterwards, after these once-excited individuals recognize both the foundation of my continued analysis and the ease of use associated with the proactive strategies themselves, their conclusion is much more grounded than it otherwise might be. In turn, they are more likely to follow through with the discipline and take advantage of the opportunities as well.

Obviously, emotions are even discouraged here. Not only do I keep it simple, but I remain consistent in all aspects of my instruction as well.

Although detailed descriptions of the progression to a proactive lifestyle are offered on my website and in this book, some clients prefer to have the personalized attention of Boot Camp to accelerate their learning curve. However, this book largely entails the same integrated components as Boot Camp, so for most readers Boot Camp is more of a luxury than a necessity. Aside from interactive questions and answers, the layout of this book is very similar to Boot Camp. Therefore, the structured sections of this book should serve as an efficient guide for all readers. Furthermore, the tools that I will introduce in conjunction with these building blocks will allow everyone to start using the system immediately.

Therefore, because the method I use in Boot Camp is so effective, I have also chosen to integrate that methodology into this book. My first objective is always to describe the Investment Rate. The Investment Rate is the foundation for all of my analysis. It accurately calculates the health of the economy in the future, and that is priceless. Furthermore, it is a leading indicator, and one of the most valuable tools available. From a longer-term perspective, the Investment Rate ensures that we will remain ahead of the curve at all times.

Narrowed down, it tells us one simple but very important fact: if the economy and the stock market will trend higher or lower over the next handful of years. From there, the Investment Rate also provides normalized demand ratios that allow us to compare current demand trends to normal demand trends at any point. That more focused comparison, in turn, allows us to identify shorter-term cycles based on perceived longer-term demand retracements or contractions as well.

The Investment Rate is the most important tool at our disposal. When making longer-term investment decisions, we all must first look at the leading indicators offered by the Investment Rate. However, this practice also applies to more active strategies. Including day trading and swing trading, the Investment Rate influences all of our investment decisions. Although longer-term trends may not initially seem meaningful to shorter-term strategies, they are. The importance of this foundation is profound because every investment decision, whether it is an active trading decision or a lifelong investment, is influenced by longer-term trends. Admittedly, the impact may be more subtle for active strategies, but it exists nonetheless. The influence of the Investment Rate propagates confidence in timely decisions. In other words, if an active trader comfortably understands the longer-term trends that currently exist, he or she is reasonably more positive in making active decisions. This free-flowing confidence, in turn, is integral to proactive strategies as well.

In one way or another, every investment decision should start with an evaluation of the Investment Rate. Decisions to invest in real estate, in the stock market, in private business, or in any other asset class dependent on the flow of money within our economy should begin with such an evaluation. Only after an understanding of longer-term trends has been made can we rightly continue with our decision-making process. Therefore, a longer-term understanding is both integral and required for every level of trader or investor.

Developing Strategy Without the Noise

However, in order to make educated investment decisions in our current environment, we must also be conscious of our immediate economic surroundings; we must identify the near-term prospects as well. While making this observation, we must not confuse the clarity of our observation. Overall sentiment and economic conditions are important, but we cannot allow the noise that we hear day in and day out to influence our decisions to invest. More often than not, noise will influence improper decisions, which in turn lead to financial loss. Our objective is to minimize that probability. This will be a focal point, especially in the next chapter.

Previously, we defined the variables that constitute noise, but a quick reminder is warranted here. Noise includes news events, economic data, and analyst opinions that cloud the broader economic landscape. Every analyst

has an opinion, and economists are renowned for taking the same information and skewing it for both a positive and negative argument. Therefore,
we might not really know what to think of a periodic release if we listen
to CNBC argue the topic. More often than not, they pit two analysts with
differing opinions against each other to avoid a one-sided discussion. Afterwards, listeners must fill in the blanks by themselves. Confusion can be
a natural byproduct for anyone looking for answers. For that reason, if our
objective is to be sure, we must also weed out the noise that transcends
opinion to include raw economic data as well. Using raw data, we are more
capable of being objective.

Instead of cluttering our mind with excess, we must encapsulate the
global economy and the intermittent economic trends to foster rational decision. This means that we need to look at the big picture, not the micro-
cosms that most economists hold dear. The only way to do that is to quell
the noise surrounding the market every day, and that means differentiating
the good news from the bad. However, unraveling economic implications
is difficult in itself, but accomplishing this task can be even more difficult
if our financial ties prevent us from making rational observations. In fact, if
we have substantial ties to the market, every piece of news carries a relative
degree of importance that might skew our otherwise objective approach.

Understandably, as my progression continues, personal barriers become
apparent. For example, some Boot Camp participants might have substantial investments in brackish portfolios, which skew their perception of good
and bad news. Others may have well-established personal ties with burdened firms that confuse their ongoing perception of risk as well. Luckily,
I have grown to expect these every time. In fact, over the past three years
every Boot Camp participant I have entertained had a barrier similar to the
ones I am describing here. In one way or another, they all had difficulty
differentiating economic news accurately on their own, and their reliable resources became sparse in 2008, coincidentally. Some were obviously better
economists than others were, but no one got it right all the time. Therefore,
as part of Boot Camp, I teach them how to do it correctly every time instead.

Noise influences everyone if allowed, and it is hard to make a distinction
between good and bad news far too often. I understand these barriers, and
I encourage my clients to embrace the rationalization that these barriers
will never go away on their own. After we accept this as fact, we can
more comfortably evaluate their real value. In the end, as every Boot Camp
participant learns, it just does not matter anyway! In effect, these barriers
are preventing us from moving forward, so I reveal a process to eliminate
them altogether. I will discuss this in detail in the following chapters.

Understandably, this elimination process is also an integral part of this
book. That is why we also must take steps to remove the ties that bind us.
This happens before we can effectively move ahead. First, we must remove
the emotional stake we have in our investments. That includes businesses

and real estate in addition to stocks and market-related instruments as well. Typically, significant exposure to either the stock market or real estate influences a bias toward progressive growth regardless of current economic conditions. In other words, investors with large stakes in the stock market have an inherent interest in seeing the market increase, and therefore a bias against market declines. This creates an unwillingness to act reflexively when trading signals present themselves. At first glance, my proposal suggests an unwinding of personal investments. In my opinion, constant exposure is not necessary. Admittedly, there are exceptions to this rule, but for most investors cash is king most of the time. More specifically, cash is an integral part of proactive trading models, and it should be embraced.

However, and understandably, select investments will not be sold regardless of economic or market-related conditions. For sake of personal reasons, I understand and accept this as part of natural discourse. However, there are limitations to my understanding. For example, I am not willing to concede that anyone should continue holding a losing investment simply because it is down significantly from his or her purchase price. In fact, in my opinion, this could be a compelling reason to sell it in the first place. Far too often investors feel as if they need to gain back all of their losses before they move forward. This is a common argument, in fact, but it references emotions again. There is no place for emotions in this business, and we do not need to win losses back in order to adopt a better strategy. Aside from unique situations, most investors who aim to protect their wealth and take advantage of opportunities for growth going forward should go to cash, integrate proactive strategies, and never look back.

Clearly, I do not expect anyone to do this without learning more about proactive strategies first. However, because cash is an integral component to wealth preservation, proactive strategies, and emotional conditioning, it is also highly recommended for almost all individual and professional investors who are serious about adopting an approach that can work in any market environment.

More specific to personal indifference, an unwillingness to revert to cash is only acceptable in certain situations. For example, a family fortune that transcends many generations may be tied to apartment buildings in San Francisco, and abandoning that exposure to real estate would probably be too much to ask regardless of current or future economic conditions. Even in that situation, though, given those pre-existing confines, a psychological separation can be made between those postulated assets and the proactive ones integral to our strategies. Effectively managing this distinction can allow a personal indifference to exist without a correlated negative impact on reflexive decisions or emotional conditioning. Therefore, this division cannot be overlooked. A difference needs to be made, and dissimilarities must be properly identified between immovable investments and assets allocated to proactive strategies in order to free emotion from future decisions. Afterwards, proactive strategies can be adopted for new investments, but an additional cleansing may need to take place before the confines of those core investments are truly lifted. These unique conditions often require an added degree of understanding before rational reflexive behavior prevails, and therefore Boot Camp could be a useful resource for persons in similar situations.

Cash Is King—Sometimes

Understandably, a recommendation to sell all longer-term investments and replace them with proactive alternatives, which revert to cash regularly, is not met with open arms at first. After all, this is a recommendation most people choose not to listen to most of the time, unless they have to. Understandably, most people think the other way, because they have been trained by traditional doctrine. In fact, almost everyone I talk to has the same general response. At first glance, most people do not consider my recommendation as a viable option until they completely understand it. Over time, I have found that most people immediately shun the proposal I offer them with a rationale riddled with personal brackish explanations. However, I am neither surprised nor discouraged by this initial response. Most of them have never known proactive strategies to be a viable option, so I do not expect anyone to embrace them until they completely understand their value.

Unfortunately, most investors only make the effort to discover strategies that are more proficient when the going gets tough. In fact, this was the case in 2008. While the market declined aggressively, investors scrambled for answers. For those who found my strategies during this turmoil, they also identified a viable alternative to the brackish investments that got them into trouble in the first place. However, arguably, distressed times like these may not be the best time to make these observations. Initially, I believed a more stable environment would provide a better place for everyone to learn. Surprisingly, though, the opposite held true, and some people seemed to learn very quickly in the face of this collapse. In fact, our learning curve was shortened from a few short weeks to a few short days because investors were forced to take action by the economic and market conditions that stood in front of them as 2008 progressed.

Without alternatives, many new clients accelerated their learning curve independently and began engaging proactive strategies immediately. Clearly, when we are forced into a corner, we all begin to fight back. This is human nature, and sometimes it is a beautiful thing.

However, regardless of the prompt reconciliation of risk-controlled strategies I witnessed in 2008, I still prefer a less emotional and a more

controlled environment in which to learn. Although this is not a requirement, I believe it is a more healthy way to engage proactive strategies for
the first time. However, as noted, when we are backed against a wall, our
abilities transcend these suggestions, and we are able to handle much more
than we might otherwise believe. As a result, in 2008, many people accepted
my advice to move to cash and adopt the proactive strategies I proposed.
For some of them, they have become much more comfortable with their
decisions because of it.

However, I did not begin making a recommendation to revert to cash
in 2008. Instead, I began doing this in the first quarter of 2007. I issued
a report titled "Top of the Market to You," which described my position
in advance. This report was actually offered in 2006, anticipating the 2007
peak in the market. My advice at that time was clear. I advised all of my
clients to sell all of their excess real estate and all of their long-term equity
positions, and I told them to strongly consider selling any businesses that
would not flourish in a depressionary environment. This included professionally managed accounts, mutual funds, IRAs, 401ks, and any investment
properties that they owned. I also advised them to adopt proactive strategies from that point forward. Understandably, for the most part, my initial
advice fell on deaf ears. After all, the market was still roaring higher, and
greed-stricken investors saw no end in sight. More important, though, they
were also blind to the risks associated with their ventures because they were
being led through the muck by our federal government. Most investors unconsciously adopted a follow-the-leader approach, most willingly accepted
large amounts of personal debt, and most believed that borrowing from
Peter to pay Paul would work forever.

Uniquely, these micro periods of circular contemporary Darwinism appear most prominent when the economy approaches a longer-term peak.
The oscillation channels in the chart of the Investment Rate clearly define
these. In 2007, our economy experienced exactly that, and the reverber-
ations circled the globe. Risk was assumed with excess and without embedded control. This was true in every aspect of the economy, throughout
all walks of life, and within all asset classes defined by current theory.
Nothing was sheltered from the euphoria in 2007, and everyone wanted a
piece of the pie. That is typical of longer-term peaks in the economy and it
should be remembered. Eventually, this will happen again at some point in
future history.

Unfortunately, Wall Street forgets fast, and the executives at many large
financial institutions, for the sake of windfall profits, discounted those
associated risks. These were learned previously and well documented in
financial journals, but they still were forgotten. These executives, like many
individuals and the government at that time, ignored risk and allowed their
emotions to control their decisions. For most, that emotion was greed. Others simply did not recognize the warning signs.

However, some of my original clients, individuals and institutions who had been with me for years, took my advice in 2007 and placed their otherwise core holdings up for sale. In hindsight, I assume that those were tough decisions. This was probably true for clients who had already believed in the Investment Rate as well. However, because the overall structure of my discipline promotes emotionless decisions from time to time, a seamless transition to proactive strategies was much more manageable than it otherwise would have been. The rationale, provided by the Investment Rate, offered clarity and support for the risks that existed in the economy as the third major up period in U.S. history came to an end.

However, convincing new clients that proactive strategies were the best place to be in 2007 was not nearly as effortless as this rationale to grandfathered clients was. In fact, this explanation was much more difficult for new clients to accept in 2007 than it was in 2008. Initially, when my observations began to unfold in the early part of 2007, the market was still heading higher. Private equity was taking advantage of cheap money, and there was a break above the longer-term channel that we follow. This caused some investors to shun the findings of the Investment Rate altogether. They did not recognize the core value of the analysis, and they were not interested in learning more about it either. After all, everything they were investing in was working well, for the most part, so they did not care. Stocks, real estate, businesses, everything seemed fine in the early part of 2007.

Therefore, because most investment choices seemed to be providing ample return, normal investors did not see any reason for changing their approach. Admittedly, from the standpoint of unfamiliar observers, my recommendation to control risk at that time seemed aggressive and bold. In addition, it was also relatively out of touch with the current environment.

Almost everyone was willing to assume risk without discourse, and everyone who did expected it to pay off no matter what. Even Erin Burnett mocked me as the Grim Reaper in the middle of 2007 when I offered the Investment Rate to her audience on CNBC. Those who were not already familiar with my abilities questioned my aptitude, and many opted to stay exposed to the market without pursuing the opportunities to control risk that I placed in front of them. Unfortunately, the dark side of human nature is that we usually do not act until we are forced to. In the early part of 2007, most investors saw no reason to consider my proactive strategies. Furthermore, many new clients even refused to evaluate the models. Eventually, we all know that the resulting declines hit almost everyone hard. Therefore, as it is with each one, in hindsight everyone wishes they took action. To those who did, I salute you!

Although it seemed bold, my reason was well grounded. The purpose of my recommendation was twofold. First, I did not want my clients exposed to the risk I saw in the market. The Investment Rate told us that normalized demand ratios would peak in 2007, regardless of current trends, and I wanted to protect my clients from the resulting decline. Second, I believed that proactive trading strategies would be the only way to make money in the stock market given the expected declines evidenced by my analysis. Therefore, because the best way of approaching proactive strategies is free from emotional burden, I took steps to help free my clients from that added stress as well. This was a natural course of action, and it helped reduce their exposure to risk and allowed them to approach the market free from concern or bias accordingly. I was successful by helping them manage their exposure to all asset classes.

Opportunities Abound

To thwart the anticipated brackish influence that goes hand in hand with excess ownership, I made recommendations that leveled the playing field for my clients. Afterwards, I attempted to categorize economic weakness and a declining stock market with constructive opportunity instead. This required a disposition free from emotional ties and without upward bias, of course. Although my proposition seems resolute now, this shift in mindset was not easy for me to pass along in 2007. Reasonably, my clients had questions, and they were apprehensive even though they may have trusted my models before. The proposition I was making this time was life changing, and it would likely impact wealth ratios forever.

Deservedly, my clients were asking questions, and responsively, I was also providing answers. My longer-term model was proven, we had already used it convincingly from the bottom in 2002, and we were positioned to do it again. This time, though, the signals pointed the other way. The opportunity was virtually the same, we were still able to remain ahead of the curve, but there was just a shift in direction. The only difference this time was that the signal was to sell. Instead of having opportunity on the upside, the opportunities were on market declines instead.

Therefore, when I introduced this shift I was only able to encourage efficient actionable strategies after first changing the mindset that sat re-soundingly with so many market participants. They were not accustomed to anticipating market declines, and they were even less accustomed to profiting from them. This held true for individual investors, and it was true for institutional clients. Many institutions failed to distinguish periods of decline properly, and in turn, their clients lost money. I was initially surprised by this, because I too had held these professionals in high regard at first. However, institutions are even less willing to make fundamental changes in their approach, and that was discouraging.

As it turned out, I was only able to induce recognition and influence a proactive approach by first proving that opportunities exist when the market declines. Furthermore, the arrogance of many institutions prevented them from seeing the light altogether, but individuals who recognized that their wealth was at risk were much more nimble and uniquely willing. Therefore, they became my focus. Eventually, the brackish nature of many institutions put them at more risk than they should have otherwise been exposed to.

However, given the existence of retirement plans and the restrictions most of them impose, my position was a tough sell prior to 2007 for these individual clients as well. Many of my clients took advantage of my 2002 recommendation within their retirement plans. Now that the market was positioned to decline instead, opportunities seemed to dry up for many of them. Retirement accounts do not allow short selling in most cases, and that was the logical option during periods of weakness. However, some clients found short selling counterintuitive as well, and frowned upon the practice because they were not familiar with it. At the same time, there was a coincidental development in the financial markets that changed the playing field completely. Given the anticipated declines identified by the Investment Rate, that addition made all the difference for opportunities within retirement plans going forward.

Specifically, these were market-based ETFs, and particularly those designed to short the market. In fact, ETFs, which are designed to short the market, were not largely available until 2007 anyway, so direct short selling was the only way to approach opportunities during periods of severe weakness before that. However, because retirement plans are not allowed to short stocks, this prevented retirement plans from taking advantage of market declines prior to 2007 by rule, and their only available option was cash. Although cash does protect wealth, cash is not a growth instrument, and it was not very attractive for growth-oriented investors. Thankfully, the invention of those short-based ETFs provided my clients with opportunities they did not have before, and that opened doors for them to profit from market weakness accordingly. For others, it gave them a confidence they did not have before because it made short selling as easy as buying a stock. Either way, the invention of these market-based ETFs paved the way for a proactive approach within both qualified and unqualified accounts, and we have integrated them into our proactive strategies accordingly.

Clearly, the premise for our transition to proactive strategies in 2007 was the peak in the longer-term up cycle, which we identified in the Investment Rate. In 2007, identifying the top was easy. Better said, we knew that overall consumer demand for investments within the U.S. economy would peak, and we understood that a multiyear down trend would begin. For anyone capable of stepping back, weeding out the noise, and looking at the broader picture, this was relatively easy to understand. The Investment Rate told us that a longer-term transition would take place in advance, and it defined actionable strategies based on simple slope variances. Selling near the top did not require rocket science in 2007 because the Investment Rate painted the picture clearly.

However, the economic conditions that developed immediately after 2007 brought unique situational variables into play that prompted further review. This is where the tools we apply to the Investment Rate make a difference. Indeed, the Investment Rate pinpoints longer-term trends accurately, and we are able to take advantage of them when they occur. However, these longer-term turning points do not happen every day, or every year, for that matter. Therefore, unless the market is at a cusp, continued analysis is vague if the Investment Rate is used as a standalone instrument. Without the inclusion of our tools, the Investment Rate only provides periodic trading signals and longer-term direction. Coincidentally, 2007 was one of those longer-term turning points. Going forward, now that 2007 has passed, our proactive tools come into play. These tell us what to do during the in-between times, and that is important to us today.

After the longer-term health of our economy is defined using the broad strokes of the Investment Rate, our tools provide the actionable strategies that drive our model from there. In fact, these tools are integrated in the overall thesis of the Investment Rate as well, and they play an integral role in the timing models we propose. In essence, our timing tools help us identify cyclical shifts in economic and market cycles in advance. This is true during the years in which the Investment Rate defines a turning point, and this is true during the oscillation cycles that result afterwards as well. In turn, our tools work seamlessly at all times.

In addition, they adjust to the market automatically as well. Therefore, anyone who incorporates this method can rest assured that the proper implementation of the resulting strategies will afford them the luxury of going with the flow of the market if it transitions most of the time. In turn, this will hold true during both good times and bad, and in up markets and down. These tools have helped me recommend profitable trading ideas to my clients over time, and they are critically important to successful proactive strategies going forward. More important, they can also be used independently to achieve the same results. My observations, therefore, are building blocks for individual application.

However, achieving this goal can be complicated if investors are not already free from the emotional ties and burdens that prevent reflexive shifts to correlated market trends. That is why I have spent so much time on this topic. Clearly, this is where emotional conditioning starts to become important. With burdens and emotional apprehension, investors often find themselves contemplating action, instead of making the right decisions. This, and prior chapters, were aimed at accomplishing the goal of cleansing, a process integral to moving ahead of the curve.

Without emotional cleansing, investors are more apt to remain on a course prone to pitfalls and major setbacks. The same holds true for institutional investors who define one strategy and never adjust to changing market conditions either. However, with emotional conditioning, that brackish posture can change, and it should. Nevertheless, that is not traditional thinking yet, though it is starting to be recognized again now that risk levels are so high.

In the late days of 2000, I listened to many pundits comment on the problems inherent in the mutual fund industry. The resounding theme was that they refuse to adapt. Although we might consider these comments rather futile after severe market declines, those pundits were right. Institutions should not be one-sided. Instead, they should prepare for setbacks from time to time, and move to cash in advance. More important, they should also be able to benefit from that professional knowledge. Brokerage firms warn of occasional capitulation anyway, so that foresight should be attuned for opportunity as well.

During upward-sloping cycles in the Investment Rate, like the one between 1981 and 2007, brackish investment techniques can provide ample returns to passive investors, and institutions can stare risk in the face with minor concern. However, when the tides turn, those investors must also be willing to adapt to current market conditions or they may be left behind. Currently, individual investors cannot count on their brokerage firm or investment advisor or their money manager or mutual fund to protect their wealth. An inherent bias toward corporate profitability and a propensity for recurring circulatory mismanagement prevent that from being true.

Interestingly, though, eventually they come to realize that this mismanaged standard coincidentally affects their revenue streams. Unfortunately, for most investors, that is too late. When big brokers finally come to realize that a substantial reduction in client wealth directly impacts the fees generated for their firm as well, those accounts are usually already down substantially. Big brokers are usually behind the curve with managed client accounts, but, interestingly, they are ahead of the curve quite often with in-house trading accounts at the same time. They were behind the curve with client accounts during the Internet debacle, and they were behind the curve during the credit crisis of 2008. They cannot be trusted to provide wealth protection as a result. Therefore, investors must accept the onus of wealth preservation themselves. This means they also need to understand the dichotomy that exists within the broker-client relationship in order to facilitate an orderly transition.

Further, investors must realize that the government cannot be expected to protect them from predatory banking, predatory lending, or financial mismanagement either. In fact, government policy has allowed bucket shop operations to exist again, and therefore government policy has also played a major role in the financial crisis experienced in 2008. Again, the onus is on the individual investor.

In fact, in every instance, regardless of situational variances, the onus of wealth preservation is always on the individual investor. Investors cannot rely on anyone other than themselves to protect their wealth and properly manage their accounts. Yes, third parties can provide integral tools, and some of those tools should be used diligently in the fundamental development of diversification models, but expecting third parties to react preemptively to changing conditions is foolhardy. Individual investors must make these observations themselves, and therefore an orderly transition is necessary.

For reasons already described, my recommended transition is to move from a brackish posture, which only works in upward-sloping market environments, to a proactive strategy that works regardless of market direction. Importantly, the proactive strategies, which will be revealed from this point forward, are capable of working in any market environment. Therefore, even when the market trends higher, these strategies will control risk and provide opportunity for growth.

However, when the market declines, these strategies will still have the ability to keep us ahead of the curve. This will be true regardless of corporate action or newly enacted government policy. In addition, it protects us from exposure to contemporary Darwinism over time as well. In all instances, the proactive strategies I am recommending, and the integrated tools I will reveal from here, allow us to remain ahead of the curve at all times.

In the next chapter, we will introduce the first of these. It is the Return to Parity.

Summary

Below is a summary of the most important topics in this chapter:

- Proactive strategies incorporate a structure that should be respected.
- The structure allows us to stay ahead of the curve.
- We must break the financial ties we have with the market.
- We must dispel personal barriers and restrictions.
- We must look at the big picture at all times.
- We should separate any assets that cannot be sold from proactive assets.
- We can stay ahead of the curve by maintaining this approach.
- From here, additional tools will follow.

CHAPTER 11

2009: Return to Parity

The next step in our overall process is an exposé of the tools we use to leverage our proactive abilities over time. Specifically, these tools are the next set of building blocks as we progress toward the comfort zone. Reasonably, in order for us to incorporate proactive models we must first understand the foundation on which they were built. Accordingly, this is the first step in that process.

Until now, our longer-term assessment of the Investment Rate has acted as the foundation for all of our analysis. That will always be true. However, reasonably, our longer-term evaluation of the Investment Rate usually leaves behind a void in our current analysis. In turn, that needs to be addressed. The Investment Rate itself is the longest longer-term analysis available. Stemming from 1900, the average duration of the up cycles is 26 years and the average duration of the down cycles is 11 years. Reasonably, opportunity exists in between those peaks and valleys as well. However, the sweeping guide of the Investment Rate, as a standalone observation, fails to identify the tighter frequency oscillation patterns in between those extended durations with precision. However, our return to parity analysis does. Our return to parity analysis satisfies that void. It can be used to determine current demand ratios and therefore it can be used to project more immediate economic conditions as well.

Going into 2009, our return to parity analysis can help us determine the most probable economic environment in the year ahead. It can also be used to do the same in future years, too. Again, our premise is the Investment Rate, so nothing has really changed. However, this process has been refined, and that could make the difference between good decisions and bad ones as the year progresses. In fact, we will be able to conduct this same analysis every year and adopt rational expectations accordingly. Instead of measuring the overall direction of the demand cycle as the Investment Rate does, our return to parity analysis is measuring immediate demand ratios instead. From there, with an accurate assessment of today's demand, we can compare that to normalized demand trends from the Investment Rate. For example, if today's demand ratio is much higher or measurably lower than the normalized demand ratios offered by the Investment Rate, an accurate assessment of future economic conditions can be made. My observation suggests that demand tends toward equilibrium over time, and this opens the door for scrutiny.

However, in this case, a return to parity is always true. Other economic models might erroneously suggest a return to equilibrium from time to time, but this model is different. It is based on normalized trends and human nature. Because demand is a natural occurrence, we can be sure that normalized demand ratios exist, and we can be sure that current demand ratios will trend toward equilibrium over time.

Although my original analysis was based on the premise of keeping it simple, the return to parity analysis I am offering here is a little more complicated. Reasonably, this also satisfies the interest of modern-day economists. Most econometric models include dozens of added variables, which, on a broad scale, create more harm than good. We have already discounted the majority of these, and in doing so we have also weeded out the noise that might otherwise cloud our clear understanding of the progression of our economy over time.

However, as we become more focused on these relative demand ratios, additional variables need to be included in our model. Therefore, the return to parity analysis, which will be described here, requires an added degree of insight. Thankfully, though, for those of us who have adopted proactive trading models, this return to parity analysis just does not matter. Even if it is complicated, it will not have any bearing on our proactive activities.

In other words, our proactive trading models dispel the need for this type of economic evaluation. Proactive trading models adjust by themselves, so we do not need to pinpoint interim direction. However, this return to parity can add value. More specifically, the conclusions it draws help us improve our efficiency. The conclusions should also help us increase our confidence. In every unique situation, if we have an understanding of the broad picture, we are more capable of acting reflexively, and the return to parity helps with that.

Measuring Immediate Demand Ratios

Reasonably, this is a second step in our longer-term analysis. First, we painted the broad strokes with the Investment Rate. That gives us an overall evaluation of future economic conditions and market direction and prompts the need for emotional conditioning. Now we will be more precise. Although that will not affect our proactive models, that will give us additional insight into immediate trends, and in turn that will also help us stay on the path to the comfort zone.

Arguably, though, the return to parity analysis will be extremely important to other investors. This is especially true for new clients and brackish investors. For those people who are continuously exposed to longer-term equity positions in the stock market, in real estate, in private business, or in any other asset class that will be affected by the current down cycle I have already defined, this return to parity analysis carries significant weight. More precisely, it tells us if we can expect equity prices to improve over the next interim cycle. My demonstration focuses on 2009, and therefore the conclusion provides an understanding of current demand trends and their immediate impact on equity prices as well.

That brings us to the root of this analysis, and the added variables that will be included in this equation. In order to further our evaluation we must correlate demand ratios from all asset classes. We need to know what the current level of demand is within the real estate market, for example. We also need to know what the current demand ratios are for stocks. Moreover, the same study needs to be conducted for every asset class that requires a steady inflow of money to grow. Without question, this also includes bonds. Reasonably, though, as I will concede later, given the zero yields of 2008, Treasury bonds could be considered a detriment to the demand for other equity investments over time.

After carefully evaluating the demand trends that exist within each of these specific equity classes, we are then able to combine that analysis. Over time, I have learned that a combined analysis is much more efficient than unique observations because it paints a more accurate picture of immediate demand ratios. For those economists who are interested in going to work, an evaluation of these demand cycles will pave the way to a lengthy study. In fact, I will also gladly offer a detailed study of the return to parity at some point in the future, and that should support third-party research, which might be conducted today.

However, this chapter offers a broad understanding of that concept. Based on recent economic conditions, the findings should also be very easy to understand.

First, this return to parity analysis does not affect the overall trend in demand evidenced by the Investment Rate. Demand ratios peaked in 2007 and a decline lasts for the next 16 years. Nothing will change that. However, during that 16-year span, there will be occasions when demand ratios are lower or higher than the normalized trend of the Investment Rate. The years leading up to the peak in the market were a great example.

Prior to the end of 2007, cheap money defined our economic landscape. The most obvious reference is private equity. Private equity was able to buy companies for virtually nothing. With the issuance of debt at very low levels, private equity was able to step in and buy some of the most well-known names on Wall Street, where otherwise they would not have been able.

However, the influence of cheap money did not stop there. Of course, we all know that cheap money influenced investments into real estate that should not have been made. Low mortgage rates and unregulated standards in the mortgage industry influenced monies that would not have otherwise been invested. In other words, monies, which would have otherwise been allocated to the market in 2008 or 2009, were allocated to the market prematurely. The influence of cheap money increased the demand ratios prior to 2007 as a result, and current demand ratios at that time were far higher than the Investment Rate suggested they should be.

This anomaly broke the longer-term oscillation cycles defined by Fibonacci and the golden sequence. Investments were influenced into the economy that should not have been there. That created an overshoot above the normalized demand trends offered by the Investment Rate, and in 2007, a clear return to parity setup existed.

After the fact, we all know that demand ratios were still relatively high in 2007. Arguably, growth fostered by debt assumption was commonplace. However, with all arguments aside, everyone has accepted that the universal demand for investments in real estate, in the stock market, and in private business was extremely high. The influence of cheap money on the flow of dollars was the obvious reason. That overshoot suggested that a return to parity would come as the economy continued to cycle. In other words, when normalized demand ratios broke higher, the overshoot told us that those demand ratios would ebb down eventually. In turn, that suggested that equity levels would also fall. This time, though, unlike 2002, those declining demand ratios affected all equity classes.

Eventually, the economic conditions developed as I expected them to develop. No one seemed to want to admit it in the middle of 2007, but a return to parity was necessary.

However, immediately afterwards another unique phenomenon took place. Again, this was a direct result of the cheap money environment that existed in years past. The misguided investments, which were influenced into the economy prematurely, eventually caused a reverse anomaly. Immediately following the 2007 peak in the market, the economy was hit with a surprise void in demand. This time, instead of abnormally high demand ratios, in 2008 demand ratios were abnormally low.

The Return to a Declining Curve

Quite clearly, an overshoot to the downside occurred in 2008. But let us step back for a minute. According to the normalized demand ratios offered by the Investment Rate, demand indeed peaked in 2007, but it only trickles lower until about 2010. Then, from there severe declines in normalized demand ratios continue through 2023. Barring abnormal circumstance, real demand should also trickle down until about 2010 and then fall off a cliff. However, instead of trickling down along with normalized demand trends, our economy experienced an absolute void in demand in 2008 instead.

Arguably, tightening credit standards were one of the main reasons. Credit-worthy borrowers simply did not exist. Still, our government was more concerned with the supply of money than it was with the demand for investments. Our government continued to satisfy financial institutions with hard money, and until 2009, they failed to address the root of the problem. The root of the problem in 2008 was demand.

Unfortunately, there was nothing anyone could do to change the economic landscape that existed. A void in demand was real and true. That was a direct byproduct of the premature investments made in 2004, 2005, and 2006. Even if prices dropped significantly, demand just was not there. Clearly, immediate demand for investments in all asset classes had been completely exhausted because of the cheap money environment with which everyone is now so familiar.

Therefore, instead of recognizing this and engaging prudent fiscal policy appropriately, our government spent trillions of dollars trying to support the economy. This indebtedness will come back to haunt everyone. As time goes by, we will need to repay all of the monies we are borrowing today. Therefore, one of two things is going to happen. Either our government is going to tighten the reins and engage prudent fiscal policy, or Treasury will decide to print money and the value of our dollar will plummet instead. Or, of course, a combination of these is reasonable.

Reasonably, this scenario will not pan out for a number of years, but when it does, Social Security and Medicare are likely to be front and center as well. Therefore, the irresponsible fiscal policy that we witnessed in 2008 and that seemed to be developing in 2009 will paint a picture for what will likely be a Greater Depression in the next handful of years.

However, with those longer-term projections put aside for the moment, our immediate observation concerns the return to parity that may exist in the years ahead. More specifically, what is going to happen to the market and the economy in 2009?

Because current demand ratios have overshot to the downside, my return to parity analysis offers a bright picture for the immediate future. Although nervous tension will almost surely still exist, and although immediate economic concerns may surface from time to time, overall demand trends should improve for a while. In turn, that should help our economy stabilize, and equity markets should increase as a result.

Nevertheless, that does not give everyone the green light to go out and start buying and holding all over again. Instead, that gives brackish investors and those persons nervously holding longer-term equity positions a final chance to get out.

As 2009 progresses, the recovery in demand will only return to parity within a downward-sloping curve. In effect, the Investment Rate tells us to expect declining demand ratios for an extended period. Therefore, although a return to parity is a bullish indicator for the near future, 2009 may also turn out to be one of the biggest head fakes of all time. Investors have been accustomed to immediate recovery because longer-term demand ratios were increasing precipitously between 1981 and 2007.

Now, demand ratios are declining, and they continue to decline every year until 2023. Therefore, the return to parity that I project will only be a return to declining demand ratios. Reasonably, though, this process may last through 2009 and slightly into 2010. From there, however, the normalized demand ratios offered by the Investment Rate should prevail and substantial market declines should continue accordingly.

However, with this relatively positive immediate economic outlook understood, an additional caveat also needs to be recognized. The flight to safety, which drew big money into U.S. Treasury bonds in 2008, has also created a circular trap, which is likely to impede the progress of our economy during this projected recovery.

More specifically, large amounts of money, which would have otherwise been investable back into either the stock market or the real estate market at some point during the recovery, are now tied up in U.S. Treasury bonds instead. Now, that is where they are going to stay, and reinvestments are unlikely to materialize with the same aggression as that which existed when those monies exited the market during the credit crisis.

Early in 2009, I recommended that all of my clients strongly consider shorting U.S. Treasuries. Yields were effectively zero, and there was little risk in taking this position, in my opinion. In addition, though, if demand ratios do improve and if economic conditions stabilize accordingly, I also expect the flight to safety to dry up at the same time. Based on Adam Smith's resounding theory, if demand subsides and supply remains the same, prices will decline. Therein lies the circular trap I expect in U.S. Treasuries.

If prices of U.S. Treasuries begin to decline and the yields start to increase from near zero, those monies that have been invested in U.S. Treasuries will have lost value. In turn, the expected safe haven from big money coupled with U.S. Treasury bonds may indeed turn out to be one of the worst investments imaginable.

Not only will those investments offer meaningless returns, but the circular trap and U.S. Treasury will also dampen economic recovery. Investors will not have access to those monies, and they will not have the ability to repatriate them into the stock market or into real estate until maturity is realized. By that time, it may be too late to make a meaningful difference.

Interestingly, we were already beginning to see signs of this in early 2009. In January the volume of activity in the stock market dried up. I believe this was a direct result of the circular trap in U.S. Treasuries. From there, I expected volume levels to remain low for the near future. Big money has opted for safety rather than allowing money managers and hedge funds to control their wealth. Reasonably so, smart money has also identified the beginning of the third major down period in U.S. history.

With that understood, my advice to my clients at the beginning of 2009 was as follows:

- Expect economic stability after the first quarter, expect the stock market to begin to improve, and expect real estate prices to react accordingly. However, do not expect a prolonged recovery, because it is not going to happen this time.
- Do not engage in any long-term investments.
- Instead, use the anticipated strength associated with this return to parity to liquidate all longer-term investments and revert to cash. For example, selling real estate or longer-term equity positions in the third or fourth quarter of 2009 might be smart. We will not be sure until the year progresses.
- Begin using proactive strategies immediately if that has not been done already, and start learning how to control risk at all times. Use these strategies to manage current investment accounts, and create a game plan for emotional conditioning going forward as well.

After some early turmoil, I expect a good year in 2009. However, I also believe this will be one of the most significant catch-and-shoot scenarios in our lifetime. Those caught up in it may not survive. Some investors will be bitten by the bug, and they will not respect the economic weakness evidenced by the Investment Rate. For those investors who fail to see the risks, they will still be prone to wealth destruction.

However, for those persons who continue to control their risk every step of the way, a much more rewarding life is achievable instead. My objective is to provide that opportunity, and that is a function of our proactive strategies.

My 2009 return to parity analysis lays the groundwork for some action strategies, but for most of us, it does not affect our proactive decisions at all. This interim analysis is important, but more for those investors who still find themselves behind the curve. Anyone who is still struggling with losing positions and anyone who is still hoping for a recovery will find a greater benefit from this analysis than those who are already prepared for the third major down period in history.

Last, proactive traders should also find solace in knowing that the market often flows higher for period durations within longer-term down cycles. However, eventually major setbacks will happen again. Because proactive strategies are best for this environment, we continue to be in the right place at the right time.

This return to parity analysis is the first of a series of tools that will be revealed from this point forward. Our next chapter will solidify the conditioning standards we have referenced and provide an outline for incorporating our tools accordingly.

So far, our first tool was the Investment Rate. It is our longest longer-term analysis. The second was the return to parity. It is our next longest analysis. Now, from here I will work our way down to active disciplines and reveal a series of strategies with a defined methodology that anyone can use to take advantage of market cycles in any economic or market environment.

Summary

Below is a summary of the most important topics in this chapter:

- The Investment Rate defines normalized demand ratios.
- Current demand ratios can be compared to normalized demand ratios to identify intermittent cycles.
- If current ratios are above the IR, the analysis suggests an eventual economic slowdown.
- If demand ratios are lower than the IR, our analysis suggests an eventual increase in demand.
- This return to parity can be used to guide brackish investors.
- The return to parity does not directly influence proactive strategies.
- Instead, it increases the confidence of proactive investors.
- The return to parity is our second tool.
- More tools follow.

CHAPTER 12

Personal Balance Sheet

In the preceding chapters I attempted to dispel widespread misconceptions, deeply rooted idealism, and in many cases doubts about the stock market, financial institutions, and our global economy. In doing so, important steps had to be taken. The most important step is emotional conditioning. The only way we can move forward productively within a proactive model is to be able to react to timing signals, and that requires a stranglehold, of sorts, on emotional burdens. These and other subtle suggestions were critical to moving forward. Now we are freer to progress. The chapters that follow will transition the conditioning that took place in prior chapters and offer tools that will allow us to achieve our goal. These additional tools will build upon the first two tools we have already introduced.

However, lingering concerns almost surely still exist. The preceding chapters did not cover all bases, although we covered the general concerns well. Admittedly, the suggestions, revelations, and conflict offered in previous chapters do not detail the spectrum of burden that might otherwise prevent would-be investors from reacting appropriately. Everyone has unique circumstances within this broad array, and those may or may not restrict their decision-making process. Therefore, everyone needs to evaluate his or her own unique conditions carefully to determine the potential hazards that might pre-exist within his or her individual approach. Sometimes we may even have a hazard we are not aware of, and this process will help reveal those as well. This, in turn, opens the door to routine conditioning accordingly.

Thankfully, we can continue to keep this simple, too. The identification process is virtually the same as we have already discussed, so this incorporation should not be too hard to do. Similarly, after recognizing problems in our routine, and after taking steps to eradicate them immediately, traders must also reconcile them so they do not impede forward progress at any time in the future. This is the only way we can effectively reach our end goal and the comfort zone.

Identify Personal Hazards

Therefore, hazards are both emotional ties and routine mistakes that prevent us from moving forward. Some might argue that these are one and the same, but they are different. We have already tackled the emotional side of this two-part conditioning model. From here, we will eradicate routine impediments.

In any case, neither of these is binding if they are respected as potential impediments at the onset. The need for observance and subsequent realignment is clear in almost every unique circumstance. None of us is perfect, and we all need to be continuously reminded of our personal hazards so we do not let them affect our portfolios. The process I am recommending and that I will detail here allows us to reduce or expunge those weaknesses altogether. Once we are able to minimize the impact of potential hazards, we will be even freer to integrate proactive strategies. For some, identifying personal hazards will be a logical progression with a clear corresponding course of action, but others may not find it so easy. For those readers who are unsure how to identify and manage their potential hazards, I can offer an appropriate correlation.

Correcting problems that exist in our routine incorporates the same procedure as correcting problems that might exist within our bodies as well. We touched on this earlier. Most of us can readily identify personal health conditions because we can feel them inside. The same process works for personal hazards that may adversely influence our investment decisions. In fact, for some of us these two might be congruous. Most people can also indentify problems that may flare up in their investment decisions as well, if they step back and observe objectively. In order to heal we must first recognize the problem. This is required. For example, if our intention is to cure a shoulder pain that prevents us from exercising properly, we first need to understand why the pain exists. We can do that by identifying the angles that cause the pain or the exercises that make it flare up. If that does not work, we can summon the help of a personal trainer or a doctor. Eventually, we will find the root of the problem and the cure because we first identified that one existed. These same steps can be applied to our investment practice regularly. Once we recognize causality, we can take steps to alleviate the strain. However, if we fail to identify problems, they will repeat continuously. Therefore, this is a critical step.

Admittedly, everyone has unique tendencies, inclinations, predispositions, and restrictions that might otherwise prevent them from pursuing a proactive lifestyle. Here is a great example. Most people have retirement accounts, and some of those impose limitations by definition. Interestingly, the rules and restrictions associated with many retirement accounts curb the process we are evolving even further. More so, these accounts typically house a significant amount of wealth for aging contributors as well. Here is a more precise case in point. 401ks, a retirement plan commonly used by most major corporations, are restrictive in nature. They could be a thorny impediment all by themselves.

Anyone with an active 401k plan should pay careful attention to the predefined restrictions within those plans. Akin to the purpose of brokerage firms, the money managers who handle the investments of a 401k plan also want to encourage investors to stay the course so they can manage the accounts easily. By definition, 401k plans influence brackish investment decisions much more forcefully than brokerage firms do. 401ks should be looked at carefully as a result. They may not be the best place for money, if we can help it. I will explain why.

Situations involving corporate retirement plans, and other accounts that are also restrictive in nature, should be addressed individually. Financial advisors could help identify a way around certain restrictions, but the process is often difficult. In fact, brick walls exist in many cases. Fortunately, most IRAs do not have the same restrictions and therefore they do not prevent our forward progress like other restricted retirement accounts do. Therefore, our models can be used in individual retirement accounts much more readily. Please consult advisors or plan administrators for details about specific plan limitations. These plans could add significant and avoidable market-related stress if their limitations are not observed in advance. Alternatively, a 401k rollover into an IRA could afford many investors the freedom to control their risk instead.

Unless recognized beforehand, every emotional variance including but not limited to the reference above could prevent some people from reaching the comfort zone if they are not careful. Therefore, for persons facing unique conditions, repostulating and reconditioning are required. Wealthy families might be the best example of a specific limitation yet again. Most wealthy families I know have retained investments for generations, and therefore emotional ties exist that cannot be broken. The family business might be a bearing emotional tie, but long-term equity positions in the stock market may be more precise to our example. Although neither of these is ideal, the potential hazard can be overcome with alternative conditioning. It all starts with recognition. Inherited wealth simply needs to be categorized as such, and allocation needs to be made to separate proactive models alternatively. From there acknowledgment can be paid to each account separately, and the burdens will be lifted, or at least offset. I mentioned this before, but it also has bearing on routine conditioning, so it is important again. Not everyone has inherited wealth like this, but many people have investments that may need to be separated from their proactive strategies. These all need to be evaluated and addressed separately, but with equal consideration.

Regardless of the specific restrictions facing us individually, we can all hurdle these obstacles if we try. The first step is admitting that a situation exists and identifying the root cause of that problem thereafter. The process of identification is not rocket science, but it does require conditioning, and that is what we are all about. We must recognize and accept the process in order for it to become effective. Reasonably, as effortless as that sounds, it will work only if it is also easy to follow. Complex systems will be forgotten after a while, and investors will start to make mistakes again.

Make a List and Check More Than Twice

Therefore, when devising a method of operation I reverted to my KISS theory. The result is user friendly, as we might expect by now. All investors should start the process of routine conditioning by making a list of the potential hazards facing their proactive decisions. I call it a *personal balance sheet*, and that is how I will refer to it from here. First, include every potential emotional burden that might influence our future decision-making process and all restrictions that might otherwise impede our progress.

Without a doubt, the list should be comprehensive. At the onset, consider this a brainstorming exercise, and once the inventory has been compiled, reorganize it. This adjustment should be based on priority as it relates to the potential impact associated with each entry. The most burdensome potential hazard should go on top, and the rest of the list should be determined by order of importance. This personal balance sheet will first be used to help us recognize the potential problems that exist within ourselves, and that should help to ensure that they do not affect our decision-making abilities in the future. However, it can do more.

Not only will this process allow us to identify and isolate our individual fallibilities, but it will also permeate our growth process. A carefully designed balance sheet can be very powerful. In fact, most professionals use this approach to further growth within their own line of work. Salespersons often put a goal on the bulletin board near their desk so they see it every day. Immediately, when they enter their office, they are reminded that they have something to achieve.

Accordingly, a developing proactive investor who wants to go the extra mile could tag his list with a growth target in a similar manner. In other words, if an investor wants to achieve an annual rate of return of 40 percent, he should write that down near the top of the list so he always remembers why he takes the steps to recognize his potential pitfalls. Although the process seems the same, the purpose of my developmental model extends beyond a simple goal. In this case, we not only set a target, but ultimately we define a process. This slight difference is meaningful.

Continually, by using the list concept we can see our personal hazards in advance and prevent them from affecting our decision-making process dynamically. This is an integral step to unbinding the unique ties that exist within the broad spectrum I have already defined, and a tool that can be used over time.

If that were not enough, this process can do more. In fact, most people will eventually understand that a cognitive and recurring recognition of potential hazards can often be enough to avoid their related ailments altogether. This requires constant recognition, though, not occasional observance. As long as those hazards are continually observed, the resulting impact can be minimized. However, that is not all. Arguably, recognition leads much further than these preventive measures. Yes, recognition will help us avoid brackish indiscipline, but it could also be a cure in itself. We are all creatures of habit, so this plays right back into our observance of human nature. Most often, the problems that are facing our personal lives, our health, and our portfolios are routine—and ingrained. Therefore, those can also be changed.

Correctively, treatment centers for health concerns focus first on breaking destructive routine and that facilitates productive treatment. The same process is used here, but our process is not as recognizable. Because of its unobvious consequence, personal balance sheets may work more effectively than traditional remedies. Over time, our list, and the change of routine that accompanies recognition, could cure the ailments we have recognized without any additional effort. Over time, our habits will change because of the record, and the inventory of hazards we identified will become more obscure. Of course, new additions will be made over time, but the dynamic process furthers our mission and is capable of eradicating misalignment altogether. In itself, this will eventually be considered a routine, but a constructive one, of course.

Therefore, once we adopt this simple process, we should expect to use it forever. Over time, the benefits of this process will materialize. Although certain ailments will not be cured, they can be overcome by simple inclusion. When new potential pitfalls arise, they too can be quelled with an insertion into the fundamental process we have adopted. It is a lifestyle and a choice. The objective is to make sure that our known conditions do not resurface or manifest to impair our decision-making process.

The Things We Do Wrong Correct Themselves

With that in mind, another component is required to complete our personal balance sheet. We must also try to recognize the things we do right. Using the same brainstorming process, we should compile a second list of topics.

Personal Balance Sheet

Wrong	Right
I am emotional	I watch the market carefully every day
I overthink all the time	
I make errors when I process trades	I identify support and resistance levels well
ADD MORE	ADD MORE

FIGURE 12.1   Personal Balance Sheet.

As if we were personal accountants, we should create a T chart. On the left side, we should list our potential hazards. On the right side, we should list the things we do well. (See Figure 12.1.) Over time, we will be able to move entries from the left side of our ledger to the right. Therefore, over time, our personal balance sheet should also become dynamic. In turn, that makes it motivating, and that keeps us in touch with the process at all times as well.

Although we all can successfully incorporate this simple model into our routine, some investors may want to complicate it, as some try to do to everything else as well. My advice is to refrain from such action. Like my proactive strategies, this does not need to be reconfigured.

Unfortunately, like the widespread peer-based apprehension to the simple science that produced the Investment Rate, investors are bound to complicate their personal balance sheets. Overcomplicating the system will detract from its potency. Doing so may also allow the perceived potential hazards, which are clear and evident now, to resurface later. All we need to do is make the list and look at it every day. The power of our balance sheet will do the rest.

Potentially, our identification of golden handcuffs is a great example. Big brokerage firms were able to bind investors with golden handcuffs successfully because investors did not recognize the ties that were being made. Then, once the handcuffs were in place, they were tough to get off. With cognitive recognition, though, we were much more capable of picking the lock. That ability only lasts as long as our conscious understanding of the persuasion lasts. Once we forget the underlying objective of fee-based management, and once we stop recognizing the revenue mandates of big brokerage firms, those same golden handcuffs can re-bind us to brackish investments.

If our objective is to avoid this latency, then we must remain aware of the potential hazards we face at all times. This means we should maintain our personal balance sheets accordingly. However, if the list we strive to maintain becomes overcomplicated, or if we push ourselves too hard, we eventually will stop using it efficiently. We may even stop using it altogether. If we do, we will almost surely succumb to the same pitfalls again. Although we might strive vigorously to dispel them today, the moment we stop respecting them is the moment we start descending back into the edifice of contemporary Darwinism.

Unfortunately, investors do this all the time. They forget what got them in trouble in the first place, and they repeat mistakes unwittingly. Do not let this happen. Develop a personal balance sheet today, and maintain it. The process is almost effortless. More important, it is extremely rewarding at the same time.

Recognition, as I have shown, not only plays an integral role in healing, but it may indeed be a cure-all in itself. Therefore, from this point forward, cognitive function includes a personal balance sheet. This might also be considered the most important part of the function because it is tangible. Once we are able to recognize that problems exist, we can take immediate action to lessen their impact.

Ultimately, the goal would be to eradicate these problems altogether, but unique circumstances obviously prevent that from happening in all cases. We should try to do this as much as possible, but the path to the comfort zone does not require us to be perfect. Instead, as long as we remain on the path, and as long as we recognize and embody personal emotional conditioning as an integral part of the process, we are probably doing enough to be successful. We just need to define perfection and position ourselves to take advantage of it occasionally. Therein lies the scope of the proactive strategies I will soon begin to outline.

If our objective is clear, and if we recognize hazards before they affect our emotional state, we can react appropriately to shifts in the market, we can efficiently adapt to changes in the economy, and we can easily incorporate the reflexive tools that I will introduce shortly. The personal balance sheet I have offered is a tool that acts as a means toward further progression. From here, we are able to incorporate more traditional tools into our model efficiently.

Always, our incorporation or strategy begins with an initial understanding. Therefore, once again, before I explain the more traditional tools I use, I will first explain how I use them. Using the same process I used to introduce the Investment Rate, I will first show how I use the tools that devise our proactive models, and then I will describe how those tools are integrated. I believe this is a better process, especially for persons who are being introduced to proactive strategies for the first time. In turn, I will also offer a concise understanding of each one as well. In the next chapter, I will complete the next phase of this process accordingly.

Summary

Below is a summary of the most important topics in this chapter:

- Keep a personal balance sheet.
- List the negatives on the left.
- List the positives on the right.
- Look at the list every day.
- Update the list on occasion.
- This list will help correct recurring mistakes.
- A personal balance sheet is the third tool in our development.

CHAPTER 13

Every Day Is a Tuesday

Officially, our tools section has begun. We have already defined emotional conditioning, and we have already begun to dispel common misperceptions. Appropriately, we have also introduced a longer-term tool in our return to parity analysis as well. We always start with a broad understanding of current and future economic conditions because it helps further our purpose. By initial observation, the next logical step in our process might seem to be to introduce the traditional tools I use every day. However, there is a better approach. In fact, I have already used this approach once in this book. When I first introduced the Investment Rate, I also revealed the concept by first explaining how it was used. Afterwards, I detailed the underpinnings of the strategy. More often, this is the most effective method of introducing new strategies. Therefore, with the assumption that proactive strategies will be a relatively new resource for many investors, I will use the same approach here.

Before I detail our traditional tools, an outline is warranted first. Patterned discipline recurs throughout my daily routine. Whether it is my daily analysis, Boot Camp, or articles and media relationships, I always start the same way, and I always end the same way. More specifically, my form is internally dynamic, with Chaos-like boundaries instead. The consistency is proven, productive, and results driven, so I will pass it along here. The result will provide a structure for routine conditioning within individual circumstance accordingly.

Every day I use a machine-like approach to produce my daily market analysis. The result is an objective point of view with concise trading recommendations. These recommendations are simple and straightforward. More important, they are also the driving force behind the performance of my models. The methodology is mechanical, because it has to be. Without a mechanical approach, the results would be haphazard, instead of consistent. However, consistency is not the same thing as perfection. My approach is not perfect, but it strives to be, and that is the most important part. Most of the time striving to be perfect is enough. Anything more would push the envelope and could degrade the model by pressuring the constructor more than he or she is already. That could be anyone who chooses to adopt this approach. I do not expect to be perfect; if I did, the pressure on me would be immeasurable, and I would make mistakes in my analysis as I tweaked it to fit my needs.

Our Model Works Effectively Every Day

Instead, my model was developed with a flawless goal in mind, and managed expectations bringing up the rear. Careful consideration and years of experience have given rise to this process. I have worked through bear markets and bull markets alike. I have seen investors throw in the towel when the going gets tough, and mortgage their homes to buy a stock in the midst of trading bubbles. I have made personal mistakes during the discovery process, too, and I have learned from them and reconciled my process accordingly. Every step of the way I have made slight changes to my model with the intention of improving it and edging closer to my goal of perfection.

When I first began, major changes were made regularly until I found something that worked. This was a trial-and-error period, and I was doing it in a real-world environment. I was not in a lab, and the variables were not controlled. Therefore, my initial hurdles were difficult. My goal was to produce a model to make money in any market environment. Initially, this required plenty of revision. After that lengthy course of development, those changes have all been implemented. Now, changes are extremely subtle in nature. Nevertheless, variance still exists, and admittedly, change will always play an important role in the system. Just like the dynamic personal balance sheet we should use regularly to keep us on the path to the comfort zone, my defined process needs to shift with the market from time to time as well. I have designed the process to adjust gracefully on its own, and the result-driven purpose is effective. The end product is an innovative proprietary model, which is not founded on modern theory or pre-existing text, but rather on real-world application.

This modern approach to investing can be used in any market environment. The applied theory of the Investment Rate is in itself an advanced understanding of otherwise flawed conventional attempts at defining long-term economic cycles. The structure I use throughout my daily routine is not different. By offering an unconventional approach, I also am able to avoid major pitfalls. Combined, these provide both a means for protecting wealth and a structure for making money at all times. This will be the way of the future for many investors. In the end, our refined approach should keep everyone ahead of the curve as well, but it starts with routine conditioning.

More important, though, our execution techniques are extremely efficient as well, and they surprise some new subscribers to Stock Traders

Daily. Their first exposure is always to the Investment Rate, of course. However, new members try to jump right to performance and execution while skipping the most important part. Unfortunately, a transition to proactive strategies cannot be effective without first understanding the process. Impatience could cause unnerving setbacks, so we will not make that mistake here. Those investors who might choose the immediate route often find themselves floundering. Until they focus again, they continue to flounder as well. Therefore, a gap must be bridged between their mistakes and the correct application of our models. That delay can be avoided, though. Assumptive, but based on observed experience, this takes even more time than understanding the procedure at the beginning. More often than not, this fast-forward method is a waste of time. That is why we will focus on the outline first, and then move forward. In turn, the outline provides the guide for all the strategies that we use.

Fortunately, the process for all of our models is similar in structure, and therefore the learning curve is finite. We start from the same place and work toward a defined goal in each instance. After understanding the underpinnings of one, it can be applied to all. I offer an array of models using this derivation. We will discuss six unique strategies in Chapter 17, which is dedicated to Rule Based Trading. These include our longer-term model, also known as our Strategic Plan. In one way or another the Strategic Plan is part of all other observations, too. Then we will discuss our Swing Trading and Day Trading models. Coupled with those will be our Lock and Walk Strategy. That is used in the first hour of the day only. Finally, we will reveal the Stock of the Week and Featured Stock of the Day applications. These will all be related to automated strategies accordingly, and that will bring us to the action plans we have been looking for.

Although each one of these has a uniquely defined purpose and varying risk associations, they all have one thing in common. These are all proactive models, and none of them incorporates buy-and-hold strategies. Defined plans come in advance and strict risk controls are associated with all of them. There are no exceptions.

This machine-like approach allows us to make money in any market environment. It also controls our emotions because it prevents us from thinking too much or at inopportune times. Instead, the process restores our daily trading practice or occasional investment decisions to a state of permanent rational perception. It also offers ample preparation time and affords early anticipation of trading directives.

Plan in Advance and Never Diverge from the Plan

Instead of attempting to calculate news on the fly and making rash decisions in light of market circumstance, our actions are predefined. That makes every day the same. I have coined a phrase for my clients: "Every Day Is a Tuesday." This suggests that our approach today will be the same as to-morrow, the next day, and the day after that. In real time, our technique transitions from evaluation to reflexivity. This is where my positive deriva-tion of reflexivity comes into play. Because we know we are reflexive by nature, we can prepare in advance and use that to our benefit accordingly.

In fact, I advise all of my clients to evaluate the decisions they will make in advance, always. For example, on Sunday night I evaluate Monday's trad-ing session. Then, during Monday's trading session, reaction to predefined circumstance is all that is necessary. Accordingly, we will prepare for Tues-day's trading session on Monday night, and so on. After a while, we all discover that our reaction time improves and our prowess increases mea-surably if we take the time to predefine our decisions outside of market hours. This alleviates real-time market-related stress and promotes rational decisions. I evaluate the market for my clients every night accordingly. For some, my analysis saves them time, but for others it supports or refutes their independent observations as well. However, anyone with ample time can do the same thing I do every day. My purpose here is to demonstrate how this process can work for everyone.

First, one of the main objectives of my daily analysis is to lift the bur-den that real-time evaluation may have on emotional conditioning. This is done by predefining strategy. Therefore, so as not to falter, I use the same approach day after day. In turn, I advise my clients to do the same in their exercises, whether those drills are analysis or execution, or a combination of them both. Until now, I have explained the foundation of the analysis I provide to my clients, and I have suggested that my clients follow this analy-sis with machine-like precision during their trading schedule. That suggests a reliance on my analysis, though, and that might be contrary to some indi-vidual objectives. Therefore, I would like to break that mold for a moment if possible. In doing so, everyone should develop an aptitude for achieving the same results independently. This is one of the most important parts of the mission statement offered at the beginning of the book. Independence promotes freedoms and luxuries that otherwise could not be realized. It is routine, and it is conditioned.

Every day, my labors commence at the same time, and my structure is well defined. Although I watch CNBC from time to time and although I listen to the abundance of news and opinion that come through the media more often than I probably should, I do not let the noise that I hear on a daily basis affect my evaluation of the market. This may be the hardest thing for investors to do. Assuredly, I have already proven that this dismissal has positive results. This same tactic helped us identify longer-term economic cycles in the Investment Rate, but this situation is a little different. Almost everyone hears the clutter of economic data on a regular basis, and most of us are directly impacted by some of it. That presents obstacles, and sometimes it is hard not to listen as a result.

Therefore, I encourage occasional listening, with a caveat. In fact, one of the requirements referenced in earlier chapters calls for an attention to current economic conditions. However, that can be pressed too far if we allow it to be. Clearly, I want everyone to be aware of economic happenstance. However, I do not want the noise to influence our decision-making process. We can achieve this goal if we try.

Once more, this is contrary to popular belief. Most professional investors react to news for a living. Although professional traders can impose leverage and balance using sophisticated instruments to help them make money regardless of the market's interpretation of news events, it is not necessary for us to complicate the process like that. In fact, one of the most popular models that I offer trades two stocks and two stocks only. Risk controls are integrated, and sophisticated tools are not needed. As a result, the noise has no bearing on our decisions, and that adds significantly to our prowess. This is our automated and correlated market timing and stock selection tool, and that is part of our alerts viewers. Maintaining our defined standard, this is a simple and effective model, not a complex one. Redundantly, complexity often results in missed opportunity or large losses. Indirectly, listening to the noise can result in confusion and therefore should be discounted as well, but without being discontinued altogether.

Arguably, the noise that we eschewed when making our longer-term observations may actually be extremely important to short-term cycles. In fact, I would argue in favor of exactly that. Therefore, a dichotomy presents itself. If noise slows reflexive action and causes missed opportunity, but it is also important to short-term cycles, then how can we incorporate important news events and economic data into our model without being adversely impacted? I will explain. Interest rates, housing data, oil prices, employment figures, they all are important to near-term economic cycles. They may also have a direct impact on investor sentiment.

Uniquely, this may also be the only instance where emotions play a role in our strategy. That does not mean that we are emotional ourselves, but rather we should be conscious of the emotions of the market as a whole and the people around us who might be market participants as well. We must treat the market as an independent entity, with unique characteristics, habits, and emotions that could cause superfluous cases of elation and concern over time. When we are able to do that, we will define strategy with confidence and respond to our line of attack with ease.

However, interpreting the market's reaction to news is a difficult chore. For some, interpreting news comes easy. However, even the good ones are faced with a market that moves contrary to current headlines sometimes. Here is a real-life example: The day before I wrote this paragraph, the employment figures for November 2008 were released to the public. The economy had lost 533,000 jobs, the worst in 34 years, and the unemployment rate was skyrocketing. First response assumes an extremely weak market, and an abundance of sellers with the potential for additional downside momentum as investors run for the exits as fast as they can. Instead, the Dow Jones Industrial Average ended higher by 259 points, or 3.09 percent. This surprised many on the street. Before that, though, the market was lower by 258 points during the same trading session, and then it experienced a complete 180-degree turn. In effect, the market reacted contrary to the news.

Interpreting News Events Is Not Necessary

Obviously, astute investors also have trouble identifying market direction even though they are quite capable of interpreting news events. This is why professional traders use assessment models, sophisticated products, and a high degree of leverage to make money. Professional traders realize the nature of the market, and the sometimes-unexpected reactions that the market has to otherwise obvious events. Scaling into and out of investments is an integral component for most professional investors as a result. Professional traders maintain a go-with-the-flow approach because they scale in or out once the market makes up its mind on direction, not because they can interpret news better than others can. This proves the notion that we are not smarter than the market.

Truly we are not; none of us are. Therefore, we must work with the market, not against it. If instead we fight the market, we will be fighting a war we cannot win. Nevertheless, once we accept the market as an independent entity with internal emotions, which are identifiable, and once we realize how to identify those emotions, we can facilitate strategy appropriate to both up and down cycles respectively. We do not need to use excessive leverage or the sophisticated trading instruments that professional traders do. Nevertheless, we should recognize their assessment models, because they are important.

My swing trading model for December 5, 2008, was a great example of predefined strategy. It also explains advanced market-based emotional interpretation and the effectiveness of our models in the face of otherwise surprising conditions. This was the day the employment news for November was released to the public. My model did not interpret the news on the fly because my analysis was made the night before. Instead, my analysis interpreted the sentiment of the market in advance and formulated strategy accordingly. As we move forward, we will learn that this is always more effective than disseminating the news itself or any personal interpretation that may be associated with it as well. My December 5 strategy was based on derived data, which includes sentiment indicators. I will explain them in detail in Chapter 15, "Oscillation Cycles."

For now, the raw data and the comparative market action listed below demonstrate the effectiveness of this process. It shows that the preemptive efforts we made helped us define shifts in the market before they actually occurred. In this case, those shifts were also aggressive in nature.

Figure 13.1 shows my exact analysis on Thursday, December 4, 2008. This analysis was made at night and intended for use on December 5, 2008. Therefore, my clients had ample time to prepare for Friday's trading session. With clear inflection data in hand, they had the opportunity to prepare in advance, and that allowed them to be ahead of the curve. My structured approach was almost exact, as demonstrated in Figures 13.1 and 13.2.

As the graphs reveal, being close is close enough in most cases. On the surface, the objective of my daily analysis is to provide my clients with opportunities. Actually, though, the process offers much more. After reviewing the graphs in Figure 13.2, I will demonstrate not only the process that allows us to achieve accurate trading results, but I will also demonstrate the reach of my daily analysis as it relates to an accurate understanding of the economy and longer-term cycles as well. Figure 13.2 depicts the corresponding oscillation cycles of the market on Friday as it relates to the concise data offered on Thursday night.

Figures 13.1 and 13.2 show that the market came very close to an official test of 1400, our stated support level, and then turned higher. This reversal provided my clients with an opportunity to profit because buy signals fired when 1400 was tested. These alerts fire on a regular basis, and they are not dependent on market news or economic conditions. Over time, my clients have grown to understand that my analysis works in any market environment. Overall direction is less important than successful or unsuccessful tests of support or resistance levels as well. Therefore, the results of my structured efforts are actionable strategies that virtually anyone can use.

In any case, over time we have learned that the market reacts in advance, so we are less capable of reacting proactively after news events occur. In fact, proactive and afterwards are contrary by nature anyway, so the aforementioned statement is obvious. Instead, our prowess is better served by anticipating market action ahead of news events instead. In fact, this process allows us to embrace reflexivity during market hours. This rationalizes the surprising reaction to the unemployment data referenced above, and our ability to react to it. This can also explain other surprising events that happen on a regular basis, too. In this example, the market seemed to have already built in the negative news.

In addition, and more important to my purpose here, this example has shown that we are indeed capable of advance preparation. In our example, the identification of support was almost exact, yet it was produced the day

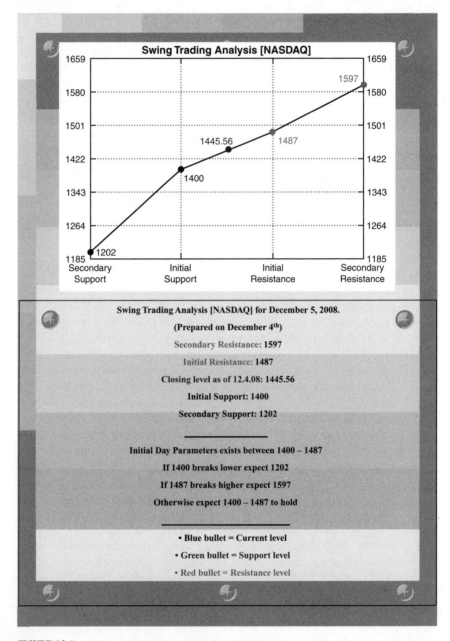

FIGURE 13.1   Advance trading analysis for 12.5.08.

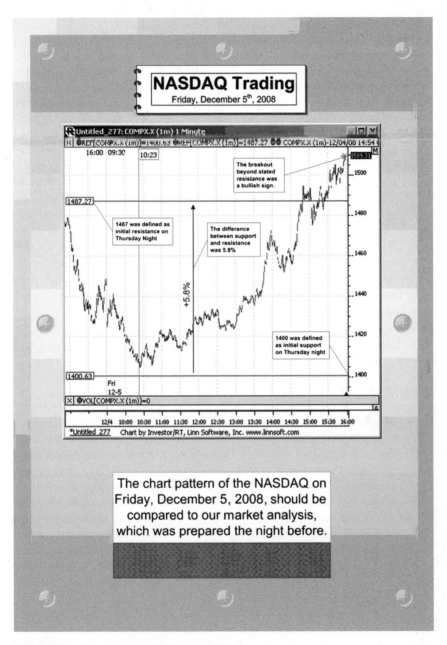

FIGURE 13.2 Intraday market cycle on 12.5.08.

Chart by Investor/RT, Linn Software, Inc. www.linnsoft.com

before. Specifically, in many cases we are able to identify when investors are likely to step into the market, as well as when they are likely to get out. More important, we can do this before those decisions are actually made. The above reference was an excellent example, but an alternative proof might be more intelligible. We can offer further evidence of the same paradigm by reviewing action in individual stocks, and that might be easier for some to understand.

More traditionally, we can identify buyers or sellers in an individual stock quite easily because price changes reflect buy and sell decisions in only one security (not thousands as in the broad market), and that makes it easier for some of us to rationalize. In addition, this same principle applies to the broad market as well. Price movements before important news releases are often eye opening, and most people are able to identify additional volume, while isolating where buyers or sellers step into the stock at the same time. Some would argue insider information at times, but others suggest that the activity is due to risk aversion instead. Smart money, mutual funds, hedge funds, and other closely tied investors can readily identify the risks associated with upcoming news, and they are more able to gauge the impact that news could have on the company and the stock itself. This prompts them to react in advance, and that allows us to also identify opportunities if we take notice.

Turn Missed Opportunities into Realized Gains

Interestingly, though, risk aversion is not always what it seems to be. In fact, risk aversion sometimes includes the risk of missed opportunity. Better said, prospects of future gain are often catalysts for buying decisions ahead of anticipated news releases. In either case, the obvious trends of both sellers and buyers are identifiable in advance, if we pay attention. If we look carefully, we can clearly see where buyers begin to enter a stock and also where the sellers step in. In fact, we can do this with any stock, at virtually any time, before news events occur, but more important, sometimes when no scheduled news is on the agenda as well. This process, in turn, tells us where buying opportunities exist, where we should lock in gains, and where we should turn short. These observations help us develop actionable trading plans for the stocks we watch.

Accordingly, this process also holds true on a broader scale. Although perception might lean the other way, sector and rotation analysis are not necessary in association with broad market observations either. Instead, the same technical shifts can be identified using the same simple observation techniques as those used to identify buyers and sellers in individual stocks. The market in itself is an entity, and we should evaluate it in the same manner as we evaluate the stocks we watch. By looking at the market, we can see where buyers or sellers make important decisions that affect its value as well. In fact, these are much more meaningful observations because the market cannot be manipulated with ease, unlike an individual stock.

Although exceptions to the rule exist, the direction of the broad market accurately represents the underlying sentiment of Wall Street most of the time. In addition, the oscillations we observe are real money decisions. In nonprofessional terms, in order to move the market, investors need to put their money where their mouth is. In many instances, though, their money acts before their mouths do, so the method we use can be extremely effective as a leading indicator. Consequently, the same process used to identify buyers and sellers in an individual stock can be more effectively used to determine future market direction based on the investment decisions of big money over time.

Like individual investors with emotions in tow, if the market feels as if the environment will worsen, it will decline, and sellers will step in. If it feels as if the environment will improve, the market will increase accordingly. Again, anticipation drives decisions well before the public recognizes those prospects, so this evaluation gives us an edge. In addition, in normal market environments those emotions are also coupled with educated investment decisions. That makes them extremely powerful by nature. As a result, if we are able to identify them, we can also capture a tool that is much more powerful than analyst observations or opinions could ever be.

More so, the market is short sighted, it rarely looks back, and always anticipates future cycles. Amazingly, the market is usually right as well. In fact, the market usually moves much faster than general opinion anyway. Therefore, the market will usually react negatively before troubling economic data is released or positively before good economic data surfaces. Built-in perception drives decisions prior to events most of the time. This is where the phrase "buy the rumor, sell the news" comes from. Sometimes, when news is finally released, the wave of buying or selling that was once driving the market becomes exhausted, and the market moves the other way instead. The reference to the employment data above is a good example of this on a near-term basis, but market action often leads opinion on a longer-term basis, too.

Unfortunately, most analysts are taught to react to news after it comes; they are not taught to be proactive ahead of it. Therefore, their models often include variables based on current data, not future data. That is why analysts appear to be behind the curve most of the time.

I have already offered two examples of this. The first was the strong buy ratings during the Internet debacle in 2002, and the second was the failed identification of the credit crisis in 2008. In addition, I will offer a third. Here's another great example related to that same crisis. This one

might eventually be a contrarian indicator, though, but only time will tell.
On December 1, 2008, a panel of renowned economists made a formal
statement regarding the recession that everyone believed was taking place
at the time. The market was already down approximately 35 percent year to
date, and everyone was worried about future growth. However, a recession
had not yet been declared. Still, the fear of a recession existed, and the
possibility that a depression would follow continued to worry the street.

Investors had already lost significant amounts of money by the time the
recession was declared official. The market was already down significantly
and many investors were nervous, to put it lightly. Clearly, the market declines occurred before this formal reconciliation. Nonetheless, on December
1, 2008, this renowned panel concluded that the market had indeed been
in a recession since December 2007. They were a little late to the game, but
then analysts usually are, as I have grown to expect. If investors were waiting
for the news, they were well behind the curve, too. However, if they were
paying attention to market signals, and to the preemptive decisions of smart
money, they were probably saved from those resulting declines instead.

The market is intelligent, and if we respect it, we can act intelligently,
too. The often-used phrase "put your money where your mouth is" should
not be taken lightly. Investors make important buy and sell decisions based
on perceived risk, so money is the driving force behind the oscillation cycles
we observe. In addition, smart money does this in advance, and that is more
important to us.

Therefore, our job is to know when intelligent investors make decisions
so that we can anticipate future moves accordingly. Interestingly, though,
an integral component to this process is conditioning. More often than not,
individual investors want to know why decisions are being made, when the
answer does not matter in the first place. They want to know why buyers
exist or why sellers are driving a stock lower. Nevertheless, the answers to
why are usually less important than the answer to when. Why is debatable,
futile, and often linked to already dispelled noise. When, on the other hand,
is precise.

Once we realize that most of the noise we listen to on a daily basis has
nothing to do with future market cycles anyway, the opinions we hear can
be completely discounted. Our personal opinions can also be discounted.
We can avoid the personal temptation to rationalize market moves, and we
can refocus on reacting to them accordingly. Reflexive action, therefore,
becomes a requirement for proactive strategies.

Anticipate Market Reactions and Be Right Most of the Time

Although near-term economic data and commentary may be interesting, and
although those may help us formulate opinions about the market over time,

they do very little to impact immediate decisions within proactive models. Instead, that noise dampens the prowess embodied with those models and often reduces performance ratios accordingly. To use proactive models effectively we must focus on their central components. The important criteria are the emotional bias of the market itself and the definitions derived from the flow of money into and out of the market over time. An evaluation of these variables will structure our proactive models to be immediately actionable.

Admittedly, this requires a level of trust. Before we can completely discount the opinions of analysts, the noise of economic data, or the fear and greed, which drive individual trading decisions over time, we must first accept the market as intelligent. Although it can be emotionally driven from time to time, there are defined boundaries within the oscillation cycles of market patterns.

A frightened investor, for example, cannot drive the market down all by himself. Therefore, if the market appears to be in free fall, we can reasonably assume that most intelligent investors are on the sell side, too. The perception of market intelligence is important because it lends credence to the root of our analysis. Preemptively, if we respect the market, we can more accurately determine future cycles by using associated analysis that corresponds to intelligent reaction to news and related events. An unintelligent or unsophisticated investor might otherwise make poor decisions, where the market itself typically makes educated decisions. Therefore, by accepting the market as intelligent, and discounting the "why" variable, we are able to focus on when investors make important trading decisions instead. That is the root of our analysis.

The same principle applies here that applied in the development process of the Investment Rate. I wanted to know the rate of change in the amount of new money available for investment into the economy when I developed the Investment Rate in early 2002. Near-term cycles are not so different. Interestingly, we are still interested in the flow of money. Within these defined shorter-term trends, we want to incorporate comparable evaluations objectively. In our proactive strategies, we want to know when buyers or sellers will enter the market in advance, so we can position ourselves ahead of the curve to realize gains. Instead of using a long-term measure that weeds out the noise, though, we actually use a more precise account, which takes all of that noise into consideration instead. Interestingly, many investors do not realize this until after they have been using the system for a while.

Surprising as this may sound, my construct includes noise variables on a short-term basis without requiring an evaluation of the same. The process that I use incorporates the perceived emotions of the market and the opinions of all the pundits in advance so that I do not have to do it myself. If these opinions, feelings, and decisions are truly driving the flow of money into and out of the market, they will also be important to my model and therefore they are considered when anticipating future market cycles. However, if they are not important, they will not be included at all. This determination happens automatically. In either case, I am not required to make these decisions on my own, and I can continue discounting the noise as before. Instead, the process is automated for me. I do not need to evaluate the pundits, the economic data, or any other noise variables, because my model does it on its own. Let us talk about how that works.

Every step of the way, we have been keeping it simple. This is no different, and just as effective as our prior utilization of KISS theory. News, which is important to near-term sentiment, is incorporated automatically in our models, and therefore it becomes less of a burden to us. Negotiating news events independently could take forever. Instead, with the help of the market itself, I am able to determine which news events are good, which are bad, and which ones will have no impact at all. In addition to being the most accurate indicator available, the market is also the most trustworthy source of information and analysis that I know of. Not only is it objective, but investors are also making their opinions heard with real money. This ameliorates the process in a few important ways. First, this adds a significant measure of confidence to the conclusion. In addition, it removes associated stress from the recognition process along the way. Therefore, this should also be considered a key element on the path to the comfort zone, and another facet of emotional conditioning as well. The emotional stress associated with deciphering news individually is cumbersome at best, and fallible to boot.

Uncertainty surrounds every aspect of individual dissemination. As we all know, sometimes it is impossible to reconcile the interpretation of news events properly. Individual reconciliation of news and events is therefore prone to error and should be avoided. Both sophisticated traders and in-dividual investors face similar problems, and therefore they should adopt a more effective method. Instead, most investors try to formulate opinions themselves by using an inconclusive means. Unfortunately, attempts at pre-dicting market direction based on news dissemination are futile because everyone will make mistakes from time to time. Eventually, those mistakes could manifest as well.

Many investors who attempt to do this are surprised by reverse market action as a result, they are unprepared or unwilling to react, and this cre-ates apprehension toward future conclusions. Slowly but surely, confidence levels decline and emotional insecurities escalate. This demise usually starts when an initial determination was drawn contrary to market action, and after losses are realized consequently. Specifically, when the market moves contrary to news, or when seemingly obvious response is met with resis-tance, once rationalized dissemination breaks down. This, in turn, happens because investors fail to observe market signals clearly when they search for answers in the first place. From there, a displacement occurs, and investors can stop being proactive.

Instead of using a disciplined structure, most investors confuse the process with noise, and a snowball of uncertainty begins to build as a result. However, for those that are on the path I have outlined, this potentially growing problem can be avoided altogether. I was an athlete in my early life, and I have an excellent analogy in view of that. I liken this to sidestepping the punter during a kickoff return. Usually, if a punt returner can avoid the last tackler during the runback, his path to the end zone is free from any other obstacles. Coincidentally, the last tackler is usually the punter, too. The same fundamental premise is true here. All investors need to do is step back and read the signals that stem from the charts of the market itself without disseminating each news item individually. By doing so, we are sidestepping a major pitfall and avoiding the last tackler on our path to the comfort zone in the process.

Successful traders will find that those undulations, which would otherwise pervade their objective, begin to smooth out as a result. In the end, an unbiased market analysis offers conclusions that are more accurate than news dissemination and easier to navigate. Further, this process reduces the element of surprise to a fraction of what it otherwise could be, and it encourages proper reaction. This positions investors to profit in any market cycle or economic conditions that may exist, and over time, this increases confidence levels accordingly.

The process I use is Technical Analysis. It does everything for us, and I will explain how. Clearly, the charts that I use to evaluate the market on a daily basis weed out the noise. This is a refined approach to strategic investing. The process offers conclusions based on money flows, and these are the most important indicators of them all. More important, though, Technical Analysis also discounts information that is not important to the market, while seamlessly including information that is also important to the market at the same time. I will explain more about this soon. With that, though, I do not have to do anything more than evaluate money flows because the decisions to buy and sell, which I am observing already, incorporate an evaluation of current news itself. In effect, if I did take steps to evaluate news on my own, I would also be doing the same thing twice. That could be a double negative, so to speak. If nothing more, it adds burden to our process, and that burden should be avoided. Keep it simple. By doing so, my refined process allows us to focus on the things that are most important to proactive strategies.

Incorporated within every chart that I review are all of the important factors that affect the market at any given time. This happens automatically, every day, and all I need to do is observe and reconcile those trends. This, in turn, produces the foundation for my near-term, midterm, and long-term proactive strategies. With that understood, I do not need to listen to the pundits that appear on CNBC anymore. I do not need to impatiently wait for economic news to be released either. In addition, I do not need to confuse my analysis with the interjection of redundant clatter. If I did, I would only be adding to my own potential emotional burdens as I try to differentiate one piece of news from another. My efforts would only become more complicated because I would need to understand which news events were more important than others were, and which were less important, and why. I would also need to evaluate which analysts have more impact and which have less aptitude for current conditions as well. Then I would have to evaluate the market itself to determine where I thought the market would go afterwards. As a result, market analysis would become burdensome and extremely complicated.

However, we do not need to do this because smart money does it for us already. Every time institutional investors make a decision, they do it after carefully disseminating news and market-related events first. One might be better than another might be, but as a group, they are smarter than everyone is. As a group, smart money is the market. Therefore, when we identify the flow of smart money by watching technical trends, we are also identifying their reaction to market-related events. We have already differentiated market moves from the moves in individual stocks, but this warrants repeating now. It is much more difficult to manipulate the market itself, so the ebbs and flows we identify in the market are much more reliable than they might be in individual stocks. Therefore, because smart money makes decisions based on events that are important to the market, and because they are smarter than all of us, identifying the money flows that result from their decisions is the best way of anticipating future market reactions. This is a leading indicator, and an integral component designed to keep us ahead of the curve.

Without a doubt, the alternative to keeping our analysis simple requires a tremendous amount of time, a multitude of skill sets, and acute dissemination of all variables every time. Unfortunately, that is hard to do consistently, especially because accuracy is so important to us. Therefore, instead of focusing on every measure individually, I encapsulate all of them using my charts, and the indicators, which stem from those charts, of course. I incorporate this tool in every duration analysis I conduct. Technical Analysis is integral to the timing arm of the Investment Rate model; it is used in our active trading strategies, and everywhere in between as well. The process is redundant, but proven and effective.

Technical Analysis is also used every day in my daily recurring analysis. In fact, everything stems from it. From there we update the Investment Rate, the Strategic Plan, our Alerts Viewers, and our Automated Strategies. I offer dissemination through my daily analysis, and the value is embraced by my clients. Therefore, a discussion of my daily process is the next logical step on our path to the comfort zone. Accordingly, I will provide a formula that can be used by anyone to develop strategy and manage wealth over time. In the next chapter, I will outline my daily routine and provide that guidance accordingly.

Summary

Below is a summary of the most important topics in this chapter:

- Every day should be approached the same way.
- Technical Analysis is a key component of our strategies.
- News is automatically incorporated in Technical Analysis.
- Opinions are automatically built into Technical Analysis.
- Expectations are automatically built into Technical Analysis.
- We do not need to conduct individual evaluations.
- Technical Analysis tells us when to buy and sell.
- We should let our reflexive nature work for us.
- We should identify strategy in advance.
- We do not have to be perfect.
- We can control risk and react to market shifts faster than large institutions.

CHAPTER 14

The Game Plan

Thus far, I have introduced disciplines and strategies that did not require anything more than recognition and insight. These were important, though, as the building blocks of the objective. Because they were introduced first, and because we have been conditioned to embrace proactive strategies, the following section should naturally fall in line with our forward progress. However, I never said this would be easy, and for some the next three chapters may be difficult. However, for others this logical continuation will also facilitate their further progression to independence as well. This is the meat of the tools section. In addition, though, it is also a direct catalyst to our actionable proactive trading strategies and actionable systems. Therefore, this section is extremely valuable. That should be all the reason we need to try our best to absorb the tools I will describe here. Eventually, they will lead us to the comfort zone, which is where we all want to be.

Reasonably, though, even after reading the following chapters some are going to have questions. This is where technology comes in. Ten years ago, I would have never been able to offer this, but then we would probably all still be relying on our brokers for information. The Internet is a fabulous tool, and through my website I will offer everyone continued assistance with all of this. In fact, although the workings of our tools are described here, the daily updates I provide on my website provide the result, too. Therefore, anyone who begins to use these tools can use my daily analysis to corroborate theirs as well. After a while, with practice and real-world experience, these tools will be second nature as well. Therefore, after reviewing this section, you are also welcome to evaluate these tools in a real-world environment.

Everything is included in the daily analysis I offer my clients. That is where we left the discussion in the last chapter, so that is where we will begin this one. With a thorough review of my daily analysis, an outline becomes apparent, and we are able to create a Game Plan for our personal daily routine accordingly. Reasonably, this process should take between one and two hours every day. This assumes an understanding of the methodology, of course, and that is what I will describe here. The learning curve may seem steep after this chapter, but it also plateaus. Once we reach that level, it becomes simple, and we can revert to the KISS theory, which I embrace wholeheartedly. In addition, however, one of the added values of my services is that my clients can also reduce their independent analysis to minutes by reviewing the analysis I have already conducted for them. In any case, this tools section and my daily analysis are extremely important, and we will all benefit from it accordingly.

Starting the Analysis

Every day my analysis begins at the same time. Immediately after the market closes, I begin to evaluate strategy relevant to the next trading session. For example, when the market closes on Monday I begin my analysis for Tuesday. Then, when the market closes on Tuesday, I begin my analysis for Wednesday, and so on. Every day I produce analyses using the same methodology, and that results in strategy designed to be used in the same structured manner every day. This happens without deviation. After getting used to the practice, this becomes routine.

However, actual application comes during market hours. I recommend a strict adherence to our predefined strategy as well. I recommend that everyone respect this discipline. Unconditionally, my clients do not need to use my data points. They can produce an independent analysis if they choose and still use the structure of my proactive models. The models I will introduce do not require an incorporation of my analysis. Instead, they can also be used independently. However, they do require everyone to act like a machine. This requires a willingness to react, of course, but more important, an ability to act reflexively as well. Our prior discussions have laid the groundwork for these conditions appropriately. That ability is a byproduct of our emotional conditioning and our preliminary tools.

Importantly, intraday analysis is avoided in almost all instances as well. Instead, reconciliation is limited to after-market hours purposefully. We never produce strategies during the trading session because that causes confusion, it delays our reaction time, and it increases emotional burdens in the process. Equally as important, though, an intraday analysis is not usually any better than our nightly analysis either. Unfortunately, for many new traders, they quickly realize that intraday analysis can actually be worse.

More often than not, when investors permit themselves to make intraday changes to their strategies, they do so because they have already incurred a small loss, and they want to win it back. I have already analogized the Vegas correlation to this mindset. It is a losing proposition. From there, with Murphy's Law close behind, they change their position to try to win back that loss. Instead of accepting a small loss from time to time as part of the business, many investors feel that they need to make money every day. From there, almost always after an intraday reconciliation takes place, they lose a little more all over again. In this position, undisciplined investors are left holding two small losses, when they should only have had one. Not only does this reduce return ratios significantly, but it also prompts them to try again, and again, and again. Illogically, they reconcile once more, and Murphy's Law comes back into play a third time. After that, emotions are high, confidence is low, and investors give up on strategy altogether. This causes new investors to fail. But it doesn't need to be that way. If instead they accept occasional losses as part of the practice, and if they are willing to adhere to our predefined disciplines, this will not have a material impact. Therefore, given the drawbacks of intraday analysis, and the lack of added value therein, I advise all of my clients to refrain from evaluating strategy during market hours.

The Tortoise versus the Hare

Admittedly, my recommendation is to follow risk-controlled strategies mechanically every day. That means free from emotion and free from hesitation. However, that also requires an initial level of confidence in my system, so confidence is something I need to provide to new members regularly. For the most part, after being exposed to the process using simulators and paper trading techniques, new members draw the same conclusions as my existing clients do. For patient and disciplined traders, the process I will outline works wonderfully. We do the same thing every day, without fail. Some days we lose a little, some days we make money, but every day we are consistent, and that is the most important part. This applies to active trading strategies and long-term proactive strategies, too. Economic news, analyst opinions, and market analysis do not matter to us during market hours. We approach every day with the same mechanical strategy that we did the last, and we will use that same strategy during the next trading session, too. That does not imply that our entry and exit levels will be the same; those are dynamic, of course. However, it does mean that we incorporate the same structure always. As a result, our approach is free from emotion, free from burden, and free from doubt. We recognize that risk controls are used every step of the way, so even if we are wrong we only lose a little. In the end, the outcome is productive because we minimize losses and maximize gains. We are the tortoise in the race with the hare. We are patient, unyielding, and we are rewarded because of it.

This is how it starts. Every day when the market closes I go to work. My first step is to review the closing level of the market. This is always important to my analysis. Then I update my charts to make sure that the data is correct. From there, I verify my data with a second source just to be sure. Never trust the data from your chart provider without confirming the data with a second source. From time to time, I have found discrepancies in closing data, and I have had to update my charts manually to match correct market levels. Although data is correct most of the time, there are occasional errors that stem from the technological aspects of data feeds, and this catch helps sidestep that potential problem. Small discrepancies could result in misinformation, which in turn could result in poor strategy and material losses. Therefore, confirmation is an important step and it should be routine as well. After a while, just like our conditioning efforts, our developing system of checks and balances begins to pay off by improving performance meaningfully. In addition, over time successful traders discover that the little things really do make a difference to performance ratios as well.

After confirming the closing levels of the market, I populate my charts for the three major market indexes. I focus on the S&P 500, the Dow Jones industrial average, and the NASDAQ. My analysis encompasses all of these markets by examining each one individually first and concluding a summary observation afterwards. Doing this produces data points essential to our formation of strategy. In essence, the beginning process of my daily routine is a combined analysis that evaluates all markets with consideration to multiple directions and durations. Wordy as that may be, both the result of that effort and the process of obtaining that result are not complicated. I use the same approach, every day, and I recommend that everyone do the same as well. Repetition is an exceptional tool for perfecting this system. Using the same method, repeatedly, helps us improve our routine, and that should have a direct impact on performance, too.

Eventually, these steps become second nature, but never discount their importance. Many people are apt to start diverging from their discipline if they find the underlying process mundane. Some might even start diverging from the discipline because it works so well, and they become overconfident. Although repetition is burgeoning, this could be a hazard for some that use my system. Patience is a virtue, and so is discipline. Unfortunately, these two are easier to recognize than they are to implement for many people. Fortunately, that is where my automated strategies come into play. I will introduce these after the tools section, but they strive to eradicate the burden of human nature from this routine activity, and that goes a long way.

Unfortunately, most traders feel as if they should be doing something all the time. They feel as if they need to be in a trade, always. For some, this is a thrill. Nevertheless, emotions have no place in this business, so that thrill is a double-edged sword capable of inflicting mortal wounds. Instead, cash is integral to my strategies and a valuable part of the discipline. In fact, most of my strategies are in cash most of the time. Those that follow these strategies start to appreciate this, too. If the market imposes stress from time to time, cash reasonably does the exact opposite. With calming and stable qualities, cash is often king. For those that might otherwise have an apprehension to cash initially, consider this. Sometimes doing nothing is actually doing something. Therefore, consider cash a trade if needed. In most cases, otherwise impatient traders get anxious when they are in cash, even though they are usually doing the right thing. Instead, all they need to do is embrace the process. Understandably, that comes from experience, and that in turn comes from repetition. Uniquely, if most traders step back and embrace the process instead of trying to redefine it, their results could improve measurably.

Admittedly, the system I am explaining here will probably be used as a foundation for individual derivative strategies with the same objective. Traders will probably take these guidelines and refine them even further to work with their own systems. However, that will not dispel the recurring cash position integral to all of my models. Therefore, if anyone perceives cash as a potential hazard to his or her stability, an entry may be well deserved on our recently created personal balance sheet. The entry might read something like this: I always feel as if I need to trade. I hope that if this is a hazard now, it will no longer be after this inclusion. However, remember to look at the personal balance sheet every day because recognition makes it effective and results driven without any additional effort.

It Is Not Rocket Science

After a while, everyone begins to recognize that there is nothing exciting about what I do. Instead, my system produces results without fanfare. The gains are not immediately impressive, but they are not meant to be either. We offer building blocks, not rocket ships. However, over time our models produce results because they are based on risk control and opportunity, not just one or the other. The process is critical, resourceful, and effective, but it could also be construed as monotonous.

Recognition can be the best solution to this hazard, too, as it was with golden handcuffs. Therefore, be aware of this admonition and consider another entry on your personal balance sheet if one is so required. Without a doubt, we are the tortoise, and we embrace small gains all the time. We realize both wealth preservation and opportunity from our daily analysis, and the strategies associated with it. With that objective in mind, our harmonized daily analysis measures our assessment of current and future market conditions aptly. That should be thoroughly understood. From here, the outline begins.

Keeping It Simple: The Daily Routine

Every day I start by making three separate pages on my computer. One is titled Dow Analysis, the second is titled NASDAQ Analysis, and the third is titled S&P Analysis. Obviously, these represent the three markets integral to my work. From there I separate each page into three separate parts as well. Those specific parts are near-term analysis, midterm analysis, and long-term analysis respectively. After I am finished with this initial phase of the outline, I am left with three pages, each of which has three sub-sections. As a result, I have nine sections altogether, and each one is important to my analysis.

Figures 14.1 through 14.3 depict a good example. In the next chapter I will offer the three-page layout in a more descriptive form, but for now imagine Figures 14.1 through 14.3 side by side. This is the horizontal analysis that allows me to compare the near-term charts of the Dow, NASDAQ, and S&P 500, to conclude a summary observation. This is near-term specific, but the same procedures guide my midterm and long-term analyses, too. This layout is important to the outline I am disclosing. The derivation of the charts will come later, after the format is clear.

After evaluating each market individually, I combine that analysis to formulate conclusions. In Figures 14.1 through 14.3, I offered the near-term charts as an example. I review the near-term charts for the NASDAQ (Figure 14.1), Dow (Figure 14.2), and S&P (Figure 14.3) individually first. Then I combine that analysis horizontally and write a summary paragraph describing the group of three near-term charts that comprise my initial step appropriately. Accordingly, I do the same thing for my midterm and long-term chart analysis as well. Constructively, this is a horizontal analysis because I evaluate all near-term charts first, then all midterm charts second, and then all longer-term charts last. However, when I am finished, a vertical analysis is conducted as well. My vertical analysis combines my near-term, midterm, and longer-term analysis into one complete combined analysis (see Figure 14.4). The vertical step is the conclusion. That is usually most important.

In doing so, this brings up a predictable concern. Occasionally, new subscribers to this process wonder how my combined evaluation can apply to all markets. More often than not, this question surfaces because market similarities have not yet been observed. Typically, the markets move in tandem. They may diverge here and there, but the charts I use encapsulate the dynamics of all of them most of the time. Therefore, one combined observation can usually serve all markets sufficiently. However, this attribute does not mean than an evaluation of one market applies to all markets all the time. Our combined analysis is therefore important. Reasonably, although one market can provide insight to all, we must always conduct the same multi-tier analysis for all markets and look for idiosyncrasies, too. Sometimes, one of the markets may offer insights that another does not. Occasional

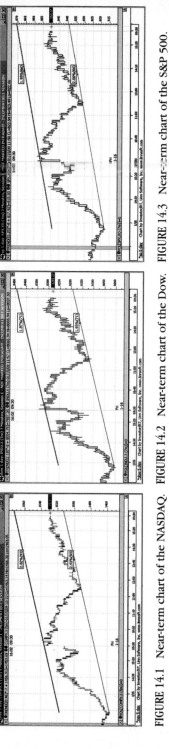

FIGURE 14.1 Near-term chart of the NASDAQ. Chart by Investor/RT, Linn Software, Inc. www.linnsoft.com

FIGURE 14.2 Near-term chart of the Dow. Chart by Investor/RT, Linn Software, Inc. www.linnsoft.com

FIGURE 14.3 Near-term chart of the S&P 500. Chart by Investor/RT, Linn Software, Inc. www.linnsoft.com

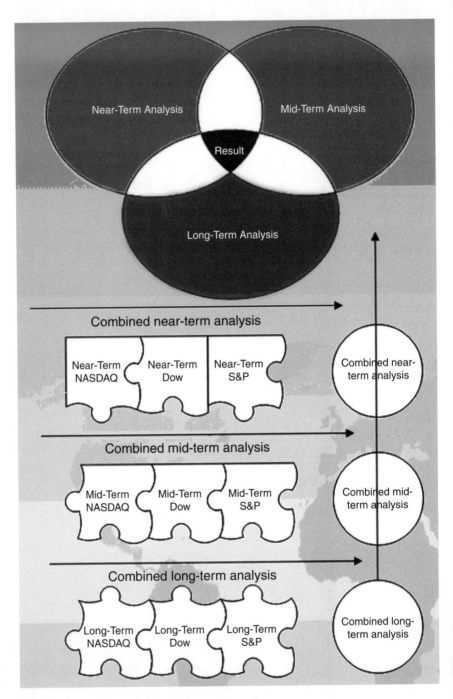

FIGURE 14.4   Horizontal and vertical analyses.

divergence occurs, but a return to synchronicity usually follows shortly thereafter as well. Therefore, I can almost always assume that the markets will begin moving in tandem again if they diverge slightly along the way, and that could offer opportunity. One may need to catch up with another, but normalized congruent patterns typically prevail over time. As a result, my combined analysis is most useful because it weeds out anomalies and occasional chart variance, while focusing on broadly defined patterns instead.

As a result, my combined approach allows me to identify advance signals more accurately than I might otherwise be able to. That keeps us ahead of the curve. Signals may stem from one market that may eventually affect another, and my approach allows us to identify those leading indicators during my evaluation process accordingly. For example, the NASDAQ could be breaking support while the Dow and S&P 500 may simply be testing their own respective support levels at the same time. Although some might unknowingly overlook this forward signal, it could also be the first sign that breaks of support might occur in all markets eventually as well, so it deserves to be recognized. Here, too, recognition is critical, and this time it is being used to produce strategy.

Therefore, knowledge and foresight are incorporated into the summary analysis I offer every night as well. Although I write these summaries for my clients to review, this process also helps me rationalize the conclusions I draw for myself. As a result, this attribute can help individual investors instill confidence in their efforts as well. Therefore, because this promotes confidence, and because confidence improves reflexivity, it also supports our proactive decisions, and that is what is most important to us. A similar course of action can help everyone solidify personal understandings of current conditions over time, and I highly recommend it. My process is reliable, and it offers a tangible rationalization for our decisions. Anyone can conduct this analysis independently and then use my analysis as a confirmation until they are good at it.

Appropriately, the next logical question in the line of processing is how we evaluate the market. In the next chapter, I will address technical analysis in detail, and I will offer methods for identifying critical support and resistance levels within defined oscillation cycles. However, the outline I am producing now will serve our immediate purpose well. Just as I did when I introduced the Investment Rate, I am discussing application first. The broad steps are important to address initially, and perfecting the procedure comes later.

Using Data Points to Make Trading Plans

As we move ahead with the outline, after reviewing each chart, I am able to determine accurate support and resistance levels, and I record them for future use. This includes all nine of the durations I review every day and the combined summary. Specifically, I conduct an analysis nine times every day, and each time I get a support and resistance level specific to the chart I am reviewing. Therefore, I produce 18 data points every day. With that, I integrate the data into trading models to formulate precise conclusions. Doing so produces the strategies we use for day trading, swing trading, and long-term proactive models appropriately.

Although our application includes all three markets, we formulate our day trading and swing trading strategies based on the data derived from the NASDAQ. However, our combined analysis includes signals from the Dow and S&P, too, so they are subtly included nonetheless. Seamlessly, I could use data from the S&P 500 or the Dow Jones Industrial Average for the same purpose if I wanted to. In fact, I may eventually incorporate automated models that are based on these markets as well. However, I launched our service during the Internet bubble, and we have been using the NASDAQ as a guide ever since. More important, we have been good at it. This applies to our short-term and active trading strategies only, though. The NASDAQ serves as our market timing guide, and when tests of support or resistance occur in the NASDAQ, our timing models fire alerts. From there, we take action according to predefined rules. Those will come when we discuss specific actionable strategies.

However, our longer-term models focus on the Dow Jones Industrial Average instead. Admittedly, the NASDAQ is less of a focus for long-term investors. The Dow has been in existence much longer, and it is better suited as a barometer for the longer-term health of the economy because of its constituents. Reasonably, because of its broader constituency the S&P is also widely used for longer-term investments. Even so, I prefer the Dow to the S&P for this purpose. Consider it a coin flip and recognize that either the Dow or the S&P 500 is good for longer-term assessments. Therefore, I provide analysis for both while focusing my longer-term strategies on the Dow specifically.

Again, some investors might suggest that these markets are not the same, and I agree completely. That is why it is important to review all three every day. We can never leave anything out, and we cannot skip a step either. After a while, this becomes second nature. Clearly, the NASDAQ is heavily weighted in technology and biotechnology, the S&P 500 is broadly diversified, and the Dow Jones industrial average is focused on large cap companies, which have significant international footprints, too. However, over time I have also found that these markets trade in relative tandem. The near-term charts above show this distinctly for reference. They do this, even though internal differences exist between them all, and that makes the combined analysis even more valuable than any stand alone market analysis could ever be. Over many years, one market may indeed outperform another decisively, but that divergence is usually diminutive within the durations that are most important to us.

For example, if technology is suffering, the NASDAQ may experience a prolonged period of weakness, as it did after the Internet bubble. In fact, most investors realize that the Dow managed to make new highs again in 2007, but the NASDAQ did not come close to doing the same. The NASDAQ underperformed the Dow significantly between 2000 and 2007. Although longer term divergence is reasonable, intraday divergence is less likely. Opening levels may vary based on news associated with specific stocks, but after the initial open, the intraday patterns of the Dow, S&P 500, and the NASDAQ tend to be identical. This correlation allows us to focus on one market, the NASDAQ, to guide our trading decisions exclusively. That does not preclude an analysis of the others, though. Because the data from all three markets has bearing on our review of the NASDAQ, it is encapsulating. In conclusion, our analysis of the NASDAQ subtly includes all of the technical analysis we have conducted for all markets and all tiers, and it satisfies our purpose accordingly.

After my near-term analysis is finished, I move ahead to my midterm analysis. The same process is used when I evaluate the midterm charts of these markets as well. Using a side-by-side analysis, I look for coincidences in my midterm charts, and I aim to exploit them for opportunity. The result provides sentiment indicators on a midterm basis accordingly. Then, I evaluate the longer-term charts using the same methodology. The end result is a similar combined sentiment evaluation based on the longer-term duration appropriately. Again, I will offer a comprehensive analysis at the beginning of the next chapter.

With these three unique observations in tow, we are almost ready to define strategy. However, definitions are important before we move forward officially. Different signals stem from varying durations, so in order to achieve dependable results, methodical observations need to be respected and reused continuously. This does not influence my chart analysis, though. My charts are always the same. I use the same intervals every day for my near-term analysis, for my midterm observations, and for my longer-term conclusions as well. Over time, I have determined that specific boundaries should be applied to each one. Near-term charts should be 5-minute charts and limited to 5 days. Midterm charts should be 30-minute charts and limited to 15 days. In addition, although longer-term charts may need to be extended on occasion, a daily chart spanning 6 months is usually sufficient.

However, when longer-term support or resistance levels break, and when no clear support or resistance levels exist in the longer-term charts that are currently in use, extending that duration is required. For example, in 2008, longer-term support broke numerous times, and I was forced to extend the boundaries of my longer-term charts to 10 years instead of 6 months.

Fortunately, this adaptation only applies to the longer-term charts, and not to the near-term or midterm charts in any way. Those remain constant over time, regardless of market action, capitulation, or exuberance.

Constructively, I consider my longer-term analysis more important than the others because longer-term market moves are usually decisive and more important to long-term wealth ratios over time. Accordingly, my midterm analysis carries more weight than my near-term analysis. In effect, my near-term analysis is less important than the other two, but it should not be ignored for any reason. After all, our near-term analysis is more responsive to immediate news and events that could shape current sentiment indicators more obviously. When smart money reacts to news, it shows up in the near-term charts, and we need to recognize it. In the next chapter, I point out how this is done.

In any case, the result of our multi-tiered analysis of all three markets leaves us with an array of data for each market. Unique to each one, this data is presented in a summary table because I consider that an easy-to-use format. I recommend this method because it keeps the process simple. The summary table is a derivative of the array we produce. I will explain how it works in detail.

In Figures 14.5 through 14.7, I have provided an example of our NASDAQ analysis, data array, and summary table. This is my actual analysis

FIGURE 14.5   Near-term chart. (Near Term Chart: Data points = 1514, 1574)

Chart by Investor/RT, Linn Software, Inc. www.linnsoft.com

FIGURE 14.6   Midterm chart. (Mid Term Chart: Data Points = 1460, 1530)
Chart by Investor/RT, Linn Software, Inc. www.linnsoft.com

for Tuesday, January 20, 2009. Of course, this analysis was produced the day before so my clients had plenty of time to prepare. Figure 14.5 is our near-term chart. Figure 14.6 is our midterm chart. Figure 14.7 is our long-term chart analysis. Each of these includes data points that are critical to our array. Those are described as well.

Of particular interest, our midterm chart (see Figure 14.6) actually offers three data points, but only two are relevant to this initial analysis. If the market begins to move aggressively, a repatriation of this third data point may be necessary as well. That data point is 1622. In fact, when I introduce our swing trading strategies, we will also see that 1622 will play an integral role there. However, for now, and in most cases, two data points are all that is needed from any one chart. This situation is not unique, and it should be recognized as a dynamic of real-world strategies. We are not in a lab, and I have not constructed a model to reference. Instead, this is the actual analysis I provided to my clients, and it includes all of the nuances of real-world strategies accordingly. Not only does this help us learn, but it also proves that the model works in the real world.

FIGURE 14.7   Long-term analysis. (Longer Term Chart: Data points = 1137, 1756)
Chart by Investor/RT, Linn Software, Inc. www.linnsoft.com

The longer-term chart (see Figure 14.7) of the NASDAQ is unique for many reasons. In the next chapter, I will explain why the NASDAQ is on an island of its own when longer-term observations are being made. That does not discount the importance of these data points, though. They are still relevant to our model.

Developing an Actionable Array

Now that we have the data, we are in position to develop the array. Each chart offered two data points, and therefore our array includes six data points plus the current market level. If my example included all markets, we would have 18 data points instead. The current market level is shown in each of the preceding charts. Therefore, our array is organized from lowest to highest, with seven data points in total. The current market level is in bold below:

NASDAQ Array: 1137 − 1460 − 1514 − **1529** − 1530 − 1574 − 1756

Admittedly, I have probably lost a few people during this explanation. Charts and graphs are embraced by some and seen as hurdles by others. Technical analysis comes very clear to me, and I hope to pass that along to everyone in the next chapter as well. For now, all we are concerned with is how to use the data once we know it. This is a compelling reason to learn the science. Therefore, even if this chapter has been cumbersome so far, understand that it also produces actionable trading strategies. The array, which is produced using our combined technical analysis, is the tool we need to engage proactive strategies particularly.

Reasonably, given the array above, 1514 is the first level of support, and 1530 is the first level of resistance. These prompt a simple understanding of some associated rules. There are two distinct buying signals, and two distinct short signals for every technical analysis. These are set in stone, and only need to be learned once.

Buy signals:
- Buy when support is tested or
- Buy when resistance breaks higher

Short signals:
- Short when resistance is tested or
- Short when support breaks lower

Given the combination of the array and these simple rules offered above, the following summary illustrates associated actionable strategies:

- Initial intraday trading parameters: 1514–1530
- If 1514 breaks lower, expect 1460.
- If 1530 breaks higher, expect 1574.
- Otherwise expect 1514–1530 to hold.

Incorporated in our analysis are critical events and news that are already defined as important to the market. This is one of the characteristics of technical analysis. However, another very important feature exists as well. These data points, because they were derived using an analysis that already incorporates the sentiment of smart money from three different durations, also allows us to approach the trading signals that stem from our array without monitoring current events along the way. Because the market acts in advance, and because we conduct an analysis every day, we do not need to re-evaluate our conclusions during market hours. In effect, we can shut off CNBC altogether, or listen selectively instead.

This added benefit eradicates the need for intraday analysis, and that allows us to react reflexively to our predefined trading signals. Because we have prepared in advance, we are able to act like a machine. Without distraction, we can approach the market the same way every day and take advantage of our predefined cycles along the way.

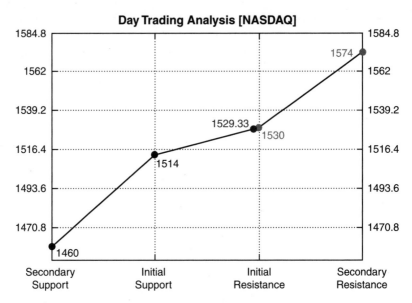

FIGURE 14.8   Our actionable strategy.

However, this can also be taken a step further. Figure 14.8 is the same model we use in our Automated Day Trading Alerts Viewer. This is one of six strategies I will outline in Chapter 17. However, this is also an excellent example of how our process weeds out the noise every day. When reviewing this chart, also imagine a day when news is driving the market and investors are frantic for one reason or another. Many investors would become emotional along with the market in that environment, but a select few would still be able to remain balanced instead. Our process furthers that goal. Instead of reacting to the news, all we do every day is react to the successful tests or breaks of our data points. In effect, every day is the same. Every day is a Tuesday. We do not care about the news, and we do not care about the emotions driving the market. We do not need to listen to any of it, and therefore none of it influences our decisions. We only care about the data points and how they guide our decisions, of course.

Clearly, there is a set of rules associated with this model, and those will be detailed in the actionable trading strategies section. This illustration shows the effectiveness of the process. Although the steps may seem complicated at first glance, the result is extremely easy to use, straightforward, and effective. This is a results-driven model free from noise, with integrated risk controls, of course.

Starting a Personal Journal

Constructively, I have outlined an important process here, but there is more to the successful implementation of our strategies. This part is directly tied to lingering concerns and addresses the need for ongoing emotional conditioning. It is a critical part of the outline. After these data points have been determined and after technical trading strategies have been developed, I am free to express opinion. However, until my data analysis is complete and the strategies have been integrated, I refrain from offering any opinions or personal observations whatsoever. The initial phase is purely technical. The second part is my opportunity to shoot from the hip, and it is the only time we are permitted to express emotions. Luckily, for some, we get to do it every day.

After my data analysis is done, I express feelings, beliefs, and opinions in a one- to two-paragraph review. This is used to condition my audience and myself. The text summary is important for confidence, and it fosters proactive decisions during live market conditions because it rationalizes the associated technical indicators in advance. I never skip this important step. If nothing more, this provides a vent for my emotions, and that can be priceless.

However, the text section of my analysis is also discounted completely. My opinions are moot. In fact, opinions, beliefs, and rationalization have no bearing on anything that we do. In essence, these are either already automatically built into our technical analysis or they are noise. Given that admonition, my effort to produce opinion is seemingly futile. However, with a second glance we can also see that it is not completely useless. Although our strategies are based on specific data points exclusively, a textual rationalization of the combined chart analysis can increase confidence levels. Usually, we are able to find correlations between news, events, and the chart patterns if we try. Reasonably, most investors react warmly to jargon, but I have conditioned my clients to take it with a grain of salt. Anyone following these steps independently will find that developing an opinion once a day helps centralize the findings from our unique arrays, and that adds value.

Appropriately, I also produce a nightly newsletter, which combines all of this data in an easy-to-use format. This is also where I take the opportunity to shoot from the hip. In that newsletter, I usually reference the Investment Rate. Ultimately, the Investment Rate affects all of our trading decisions. Therefore, every day, religiously, after my initial analysis has been produced and the first phase of operation has been complete, I revert to an evaluation of the Investment Rate to find coincidences. If I find them, I exploit them. If I do not find them, I simply pass on the information I have derived through my multi-tiered technical analysis. Every day, as a result, my clients stay aware of the longer-term health of the market, as well as the near-term opportunities that await them. They also get an added opinion to disregard at their leisure.

Clearly, if an individual investor integrates this process into his or her daily routine, he or she will not be producing a nightly newsletter for the same purposes. However, I still encourage a similar process. Comfortably, we all need to express our individual opinions on a regular basis. That, unwittingly, provides support to reflexivity. In my newsletter, I might express my opinions about the economy, government policy, recent economic data, or daily news events. Individual investors should do the same. Reasonably, we cannot bottle up our feelings or they will eventually impair our proactive approach to the market. Everyone has opinions, and they need to be expressed.

On an individual level, conducting routine analysis produces actionable strategies that allow us to make money regardless of market direction. Those strategies should also free emotional burdens that might otherwise impede decisions. Although they are effective, actionable strategies do not offer a release. Therefore, individual investors should also start keeping a journal that acts like my nightly newsletters. This is a place when we are all able to shoot from the hip as well. I call this a personal journal. It should be used in conjunction with the personal balance sheet introduced earlier.

In lieu of writing a newsletter, individual investors who incorporate this practice should express their feelings about the market, the economy, and the rest of the noise they might hear every day in a constructive method. Therefore, after the mechanical process of technical analysis has been complete, summarize the findings, incorporate opinions, and release that energy. Consciously or unconsciously, this will become a healthy exercise. It should be done every day.

Soon, just like the list we created and have on our wall already, this journal will help distill burdens that might otherwise exist. If nothing more, we will discover that our opinions are not always right, and therefore our opinions should not be trusted to make trading decisions either. That is another important reason we use technical analysis. We do it so our opinions do not get in the way of our decision-making process. What we write in our journals, or what I write in my newsletter, may not have any influence on market direction whatsoever. More important, our feelings, opinions, and beliefs have no influence over our proactive trading models. Better said, personal feelings dampen the performance of proactive trading models over time, and they should not play a role in the process at all. The implementation of a journal could help most of us realize this without forcing us to learn the hard way.

Unfortunately, most investors have already learned the hard way in one way or another. Most investors regularly incorporate their feelings and their emotions into their investment decisions with the hope that their opinions will move them ahead of the curve. That needs to stop immediately. The exact opposite is usually true. A personal journal will support that cause, and it should help relieve personal emotional burdens accordingly.

The last phase of my outline comes before the market opens. During this phase of my analysis I am not interested in re-reviewing my data points, I am not interested in knowing what the morning news is, I am not interested in seeing which stocks are gapping higher or lower, and I am not interested in economic data. All that concerns me during this last phase of my analysis is the function of my proactive strategies as that relates to the opening level of the market. For example, if the market is gapping higher or lower at the onset, I may need to adjust my parameters to include secondary support or resistance levels. In fact, I could possibly be forced to add a third support or resistance level if needed. However, these data points were also generated the night before, so I am not required to re-evaluate the market. Therefore, the sole purpose of the last phase of my analysis is to determine if I need to include an additional level of support or resistance into my automated market timing and correlated stock selection tools. From there, my systems work mechanically, and I can follow my game plan as outlined.

Although I pay attention to news every day, and although I listen to analysts on occasion, none of it is really important to me. Just like my opinion, the noise I hear every day is moot. Admittedly, because I am an economist and a market strategist, it is hard for me not to listen sometimes. Often, I envy people who are not tied to their computers or exposed to the television throughout the day. More often than not, they do not hear the excess jargon. However, they still need to pay attention to our indicators, and to general economic concerns, but they are sheltered from the noise most of the time. In fact, one of the most important qualities of our model is its ability to function regardless of immediate opinion, current news, or excess jargon. Regardless of most intraday restrictions, almost everyone can use our tools effectively as a result.

Although my personal routine may seem rigid, it is proven, and it can work for everyone. The layout of my daily routine as noted above references strategies, which allow us to achieve our end goal. Obviously, in order to incorporate the routine, we must understand how to use the tools. In the section that follows, I will discuss technical analysis more specifically. I will explain how to use it, and satisfy any existing trepidation so it can be incorporated seamlessly into our normal routine every day. I will detail the layout of my multi-tier analysis as well, and offer associated summary evaluations for reference.

Summary

Below is a summary of the most important topics in this chapter:

- A combined technical analysis of all markets is required.
- Repeat the same method of analysis every day.
- Repetition helps us improve performance.
- Avoid intraday analysis.
- The little things matter.
- We are the tortoise in the race with the hare.
- Cash is an integral component to our strategies.
- Create a personal journal to vent feelings and emotions every day.
- Cash is our fourth tool.
- Our personal journal is our fifth tool.

CHAPTER 15

Oscillation Cycles

Technical analysis is a study of money flows into and out of the market. By definition, technical analysis already incorporates news and associated expectations, which are driving the decisions of smart money. Therefore, reasonably, technical analysis is all-encompassing as a standalone observation. However, it requires regular updates because support and resistance levels change over time as smart money makes conscious decisions to buy and sell.

In addition, many investors argue that fundamental analysis is more important. I too regard fundamental analysis as an important part of the overall process, but there are limitations. Specifically, fundamental analysis has no bearing on trading decisions at all. Therefore, technical analysis is the driving force behind all of our proactive strategies, not fundamental analysis. Appropriately, I will explain why and dispel all arguments before we move ahead.

With that said, fundamental analysis does play a role in our overall process, so I need to be clear. However, it does not play the same role as traditional doctrine might have some readers believe. I first encountered the traditional approach to stock market investing when I was a registered investment advisor for large brokerage firms. Aside from their relative ability or inability to assess the underlying strength of any specific company accurately, the analysts I saw followed the same directive. Their stock ratings—buy, sell, or hold—were all recommendations based on the fundamental observations made by the analysts. In other words, they evaluated each company based on the business it was in, the quality of its balance sheet, and the competitive nature of that particular entity in relation to its peers. In essence, that only provided a broad analysis of the company itself and had nothing to do with the stock price. However, that fundamental analysis can be a benefit if the assessment is correct, so it should not be completely discounted. An accurate evaluation tells us if the company is good or bad relative to its peers.

However, this fundamental approach fails to tell us if the current price of the stock warrants an investment. Absolutely, an analyst could consider a company a good company based on its fundamentals, but the price of that stock could still decline measurably due to the associated trading patterns that might currently exist. Therefore, fundamental analysis must be separated from technical analysis. Reasonably, a fundamental analysis of a stock should come first. This is where I agree with traditional doctrine. Therefore, before any trading decisions are made, an investor should evaluate the fundamental condition of the company he or she is considering. This process separates good companies from the others. Afterwards, a technical analysis of that company should be made as well. This will tell us exactly where to buy it and how to set our risk controls appropriately. That is where my divergence from traditional doctrine comes in. For example, once we identify the companies that appear to be the relative leaders in their industries, we then conduct a technical analysis of the stocks we identify to determine which of those companies are offering buy signals at the same time. Only when technical analysis and buy ratings coincide do buy signals really surface.

Reasonably, if our technical review of these stocks tells us that they are trading near their respective resistance levels, we should not be buying them quite yet. This would be true regardless of their position in the industry. On the other hand, if the stocks we are interested in are trading near their relative support levels, an investment with risk controls might be a good idea. Therefore, with fundamental analysis acting as the foundation, an investor can implement technical analysis to pinpoint the timing of his or her decisions. This is contrary to the recommendations of most big brokerage firms, unfortunately. Most of them offer their clients the fundamental observations of their analysts without consideration to the associated technicals at all. During my tenure, I found this to be troubling. Brokers were instructed by the firm to recommend stocks based on fundamentals, not on technical indicators. This would be true even when the technical analysis of that same stock was offering conflicting evidence that could negatively affect the price of the stock, and therefore real wealth. Therefore, I believe technical analysis is both essential and all encompassing.

In effect, offering technical analysis is exactly what I do every day. Nevertheless, that seemingly leaves the void of fundamental analysis to be resolved. Fortunately, I have already addressed this important issue. In this case, though, instead of addressing an individual stock, I conduct a fundamental analysis of the market and the economy instead. The Investment Rate is that fundamental analysis. The Investment Rate tells us if the market and the economy will be healthy or if they will deteriorate in the years that follow. That fundamental analysis is the same in principle as the fundamental analysis that analysts make for specific companies. In turn, the Investment Rate tells us if we should buy, sell, or hold. Uniquely, in down markets like the one we are in now, proactive trading strategies are the best option. Those, in turn, are based on technical analysis. Therefore, appropriately, we start with a fundamental analysis using the Investment Rate and incorporate Technical Analysis afterwards to define actionable strategy.

Technical Analysis Defines Trading Strategies

Using our defined methodology, technical analysis is a study of the flow of money into and out of the market. As I mentioned in the last chapter, this definition is powerful. We want to know when smart money is coming into the market, and when it is going out. More specifically, we want to identify technical trends so that we can react in advance the next time an oscillation cycle completes itself. Properly identifying oscillation cycles is the root of successful technical analysis. Our primary objective in defining these cycles is to determine our entry and exit strategies. In addition, because we are interested in the market as a whole, diversification strategies are not needed in this unique approach.

Uniquely, Warren Buffett was quoted as saying, "Wide diversification is only required when investors do not understand what they are doing." In our strategies, not only do we have a defined objective, but also our instrument is already pre-diversified too, if we are using market-based ETFs.

Therefore, we are free to evaluate the market without incorporating traditional doctrine. Our fundamental analysis has already been done, we know what to expect from the market in the years ahead, and now we are free to incorporate technical analysis accordingly.

Therefore, the next phase of our operation is to offer guidelines that will help everyone pinpoint accurate support and resistance levels over time. Every day I offer my analysis to my audience. Specifically, I display all nine of the charts I write every day for everyone to see. Uniquely, these charts do not include Bollinger bands, stochastics, or moving averages. Instead, I base my chart analysis on the traditional line method. Over time, I have found that the traditional method of technical analysis is much more effective than anything else. Derivations and shortcuts simply do not work as effectively, in my opinion. As a result, anyone attempting to engage in the practice of taking shortcuts might also be prone to unnecessary pitfalls.

However, do not misconstrue this observation. I am not claiming that my technical analysis will be perfect every day. In fact, I will be wrong on occasion. Given that reconciliation, some investors may be better equipped than I am at defining support and resistance levels from time to time. I welcome skilled traders because my disciplines work for them as well. Individual investors can use their own analyses in the same general manner, as I will describe going forward. As long as the structure and discipline are still intact, the strategies will continue to be effective. In this chapter, I am describing my method for evaluating support and resistance levels. However, if another predefined method has already been proven accurate, that data can be incorporated instead.

In view of that, the discipline of technical analysis that I use is a simple process of connecting the dots. I use this process always, but especially when I conduct technical analysis, I try to keep it simple. This can only be done if we eradicate the why variable first, of course, and then use the straight-line approach. Instead, if we ask ourselves why in the middle of this evaluation, the process itself will eventually fail. Never ask why. Why is a derivative of fundamental analysis and it has no place in this phase of our process. The Investment Rate answers that question on a broad scale, and we answer the questions that may come up daily by using our personal journals every day.

The Architect of Strategy

In this section, I will provide examples of connecting the dots. This same methodology can be incorporated into everyone's routine on a daily basis. We are also looking for identifiable trends when we take these steps. With the exception of extreme peaks or valleys, two distinctive data points define a trend at least. Sometimes trends slope higher, sometimes trends slope lower, and sometimes trends move sideways. In all cases though, a definable relationships usually exist within our chart patterns. Our objective is to define those relationships. (The figures in this chapter come from the same charts I introduced in the last chapter.)

Predictably, the analysis shown below also follows a defined set of rules. Therefore, when reviewing the systematic process below, also recognize the following three points:

1. Always determine direction first.
2. Define peaks and troughs afterwards.
3. Conclude the analysis with an identification of oscillation cycles.

Reasonably, the following is only a static real-life example. It was actionable at the time it was offered only, and updates were required afterwards. Specifically, if support or resistance levels break, updates are needed, so this static analysis should be used for reference only. Almost surely, anyone reading this will see that certain support and resistance levels have already broken. Since then, of course, updates have been made. I publish updates every day through www.stocktradersdaily.com.

Although it provides specific reference to my methodology, this summary is not a complete lesson in technical analysis, either. My depiction is meant to show the simplicity of my approach, which helps demonstrate the effectiveness of the model.

First, as outlined, my analysis starts with a review of the near-term charts. Accordingly, Figure 15.1 shows the near-term chart of the NASDAQ. Step one is to determine direction. From the beginning of the period to the end, the slope is up. That should be relatively clear. Next, we need to define the peaks and troughs of this upward trend. I have combined both of these observations in Figure 15.1.

Next, we need to connect the dots once we take these steps. In this case, data points one and two are functional. Together, they form a trend line, and the support line of our developing channel is revealed by drawing a line between them. If that is true, data point three will act as the initial indicator of the developing resistance line within the same upward-sloping channel as well. Appropriately, Figure 15.2 shows the trend lines from this review.

In Figure 15.2, I connected points one and two. This provided us with a straight line and defined the support line of this oscillation cycle

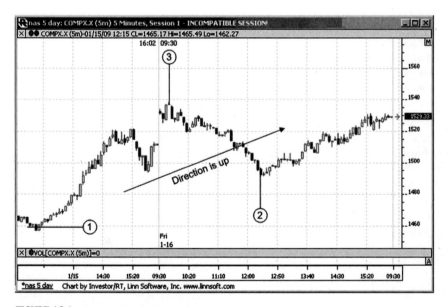

FIGURE 15.1   Data points—near term.

Chart by Investor/RT, Linn Software, Inc. www.linnsoft.com

FIGURE 15.2   The trend lines—near term.

Chart by Investor/RT, Linn Software, Inc. www.linnsoft.com

accordingly. Then, using charting software, I drew a parallel resistance line, which crossed at point three. The result is a parallel oscillation cycle, and that provides the two data points we used in our analysis from the last chapter. The first data point is the support level, which is where the support line crosses the y-axis. The second data point is the resistance level, which is where the resistance line crosses the y-axis. When this same analysis is conducted for the Dow and S&P 500, the combined analysis completes our near-term review. Therefore, I will combine this analysis at the end of the chapter to demonstrate this process in detail.

Next, we move on to our midterm analysis. However, the first step in this process requires a unique derivation that did not exist in the near-term charts. This is an excellent example. Although the direction of the overall pattern seems to be down, the pattern itself is not. Clearly, it was down at first, but the resistance line of the down channel has also been broken. When resistance levels break, neutral channels develop thereafter. This is a rule. Appropriately, this rule applies in the opposite direction, too, so it is not one sided. When the support level of a defined up channels breaks, lower neutral channels develop, and the new channels should be respected.

FIGURE 15.3   Midterm chart—NASDAQ.

Chart by Investor/RT, Linn Software, Inc. www.linnsoft.com

In any case, Figure 15.3 shows that the established down channel was not only broken, but a subsequent confirmation occurred, too. In turn, the midterm pattern that we are observing in this phase of our analysis is actually a neutral midterm trading pattern because the down channel was already broken.

With direction in hand, we are free to move ahead with our second step and define peaks and troughs associated with this duration. There are three definable data points in the midterm chart shown in Figure 15.4. The first is a recent peak. The second is a recent trough. In addition, the third is an intermediate level of resistance. In almost all cases, when neutral channels exist, intra channel support or resistance levels exist as well. In the natural growth sequence offered by Fibonacci, intra channel parameters are an expected occurrence.

In this specific instance, that intra channel level of resistance, defined by data point three, could also turn out to be the most important data point in this sequence.

FIGURE 15.4   Data points—midterm.
Chart by Investor/RT, Linn Software, Inc. www.linnsoft.com

From the data set shown in Figure 15.4, we are free to draw our trend lines and define our oscillation cycles as well. Because the chart pattern is neutral, our trend lines are also horizontal. Each one crosses the y-axis at a level that is parallel to the data points we have already identified. This creates a neutral channel.

In addition, because support was tested most recently, this pattern also suggests that higher levels are likely if intra channel resistance breaks higher. Reasonably, after oscillation cycles are drawn and trading patterns are visualized, a rationalization of those patterns can be made accurately. In effect, that is exactly what I do when I combined the analysis of all three markets. I will demonstrate this in more detail when I reveal the combined analysis. Until then, Figure 15.5 completes this phase of our midterm analysis, and after a similar review of the Dow and S&P 500, a summary conclusion will also be drawn.

In the third phase, I conduct the same basic analysis to evaluate longer-term patterns. However, because I focus my longer-term observations on the Dow, I have appropriately outlined the technical indicators stemming from the Dow Jones Industrial Average in Figure 15.6, and not the NASDAQ.

FIGURE 15.5   The trend lines—midterm.
Chart by Investor/RT, Linn Software, Inc. www.linnsoft.com

In Figure 15.6, I have first defined the direction as neutral, and then I have identified peaks and troughs appropriately.

However, one of these data points deserves an added explanation. Data points one, two, and four should be logical. If data point four is not logical, please recognize that it also correlates with a prior peak in the market, and this offers confirmation for that data point accordingly. However, data point three is relatively unique. This is a peak associated with a past head-and-shoulders formation. Typically, I have found that the head within this formation is usually an important level of resistance after the formation itself has been broken. Specific to Figure 15.6, the market completed the head-and-shoulders formation, and after a while, that pattern was broken. Now the market appears to be oscillating between data points two and three, respectively. Furthermore, data point one confirms data point two and tells us that this identified longer-term support level is also very important to the longer-term health of the market.

Appropriately, the chart pattern depicted in Figure 15.7 shows us that the market is in the lower tier of a neutral longer-term pattern. If it is capable of breaking above longer-term intra channel resistance, point three,

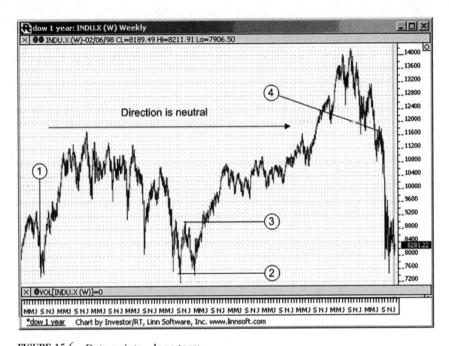

FIGURE 15.6   Data points—long-term.
Chart by Investor/RT, Linn Software, Inc. www.linnsoft.com

an aggressive increase should follow. Otherwise, a retest of established support levels is likely to occur again at some point instead.

Combining the Patterns

Obviously, the technical analysis derived from these chart patterns is an excellent start, and this lesson should point everyone in the right direction. However, this is hardly a detailed review of technical analysis, and it is not updated with current channels, but the same technique can be used now to draw conclusions about today's environment. The art of technical analysis is much more involved than this simple association suggests, but this is a great starting point nonetheless. For anyone who is already well-versed in this discipline, conducting a thorough technical analysis of all three markets in accordance with our structured discipline will also be second nature.

Nonetheless, as promised I will now provide an example of my combined analysis. Included within every phase of my review is a textual summary. With a simple one-paragraph explanation, I summarize all of the near-term charts, for example. Then, using the same summarized method,

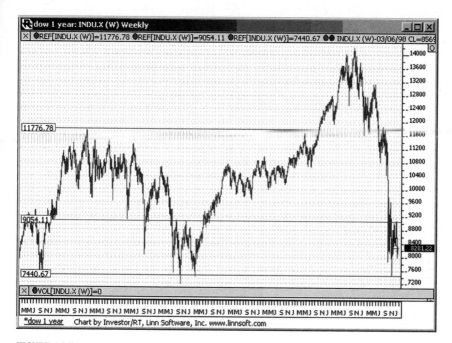

FIGURE 15.7   Trend lines—long-term.

Chart by Investor/RT, Linn Software, Inc. www.linnsoft.com

I offer an analysis for all the midterm charts. Then, finally, I comment on the longer-term charts in the same relative fashion. Once this horizontal analysis is done, I integrate those three paragraphs into a concise summary. That is my overall analysis and my conclusion restively. All of these are in the outline that follows. I start with the Dow, then the NASDAQ, and finally the S&P 500. This is a real-life example, based on the same charts we have already been looking at.

Before I begin, I will point out one more subtle hint that will increase the efficiency of technical analysis for everyone. Specifically, when two data points within an array are too close together, combine them and divide by two. This scenario plays out in the analysis of the Dow below, so I can appropriately use that as an example. 8445 and 8385 are too close together, and therefore I combined them to offer 8415 as initial resistance instead. In reviewing the Dow analysis below, consider this appropriately.

Once more, this is a real-life example, and not a laboratory event. In real life, adjustments like this are required on a regular basis. Only experience helps everyone jump these hurdles over time, and sometimes we all have to learn as we go anyway. After all, the market is dynamic, and it requires us to be proactive accordingly.

Summary Technical Analysis for January 20, 2009

(This takes into account the near term, midterm, and longer term charts)

Normally my combined analysis goes here, but I have reserved this for the end of the outline.

Initial intraday trading parameters for the DOW exist between 8200 and 8415

If 8200 breaks lower expect 8026

If 8415 breaks higher expect 9054

Otherwise expect 8200 - 8415

Initial intraday trading parameters for the NASDAQ exist between 1514 - 1530

If 1514 breaks lower expect 1460

If 1530 breaks higher expect 1574

Otherwise expect 1514 - 1530 to hold

Initial intraday trading parameters for the S&P 500 exist between 840 - 858

If 840 breaks lower expect 821

If 858 breaks higher expect 871

Otherwise, expect 840 - 858 to hold.

Now, I will show how these data points were derived using combined analysis

Combined Near Term Analysis – 1.20.09

Our combined near-term analysis tells us that the market is in a near-term up channel and it suggests that the market is also in the process of oscillating higher towards resistance levels again. Recently, according to the chart, a test of initial support was made, and since that successful test, the market has already begun to trend higher. Therefore, according to our combined near-term analysis the market is likely to begin the day Tuesday with a bias to increase. From there, we should expect a test of resistance relatively soon thereafter.

Near Term Chart Analysis for all markets

Near Term Support for the DOW exists at 8200

Near Term Resistance for the DOW exists at 8445

******

Near Term Support for the NASDAQ exists at 1514

Near Term Resistance for the NASDAQ exists at 1574

******

Near Term Support for the S&P 500 exists at 840

Near Term Resistance for the SP 500 exists at 871

Combined Mid Term Analysis - 1.20.09

Our combined midterm analysis tells us that the market is trying to confirm a bottom. Clearly, the downtrend, which had been in place since January 6, has been broken. Now, our combined midterm analysis tells us that the market is oscillating within a neutral trading channel while it makes up its mind. From this point forward, the relatively tight neutral channel represented by support and intra channel resistance should be respected as an inflection channel. If either midterm support breaks lower or midterm intra-channel resistance breaks higher aggressive market moves are likely to follow. Further, the aggressive moves should be in the direction of the break. In other words, if midterm intra-channel resistance breaks higher the momentum move will likely be up, and vice versa. In addition, our combined midterm analysis also tells us to expect a test of midterm resistance again soon, so that adds to its importance. With that understood midterm intra-channel resistance should also be treated as inflection for swing trades going forward.

Mid Term Support for the DOW exists at 8026

Mid Term Resistance for the DOW exists at 8385

******

Mid Term Support for the NASDAQ exists at 1460

Mid Term Resistance for the NASDAQ exists at 1530

******

Mid Term Support for the SP 500 exists at 821

Mid Term Resistance for the SP 500 exists at 858

Combined Long Term Analysis – 1.20.09

Our combined longer-term analysis tells us that the market is floundering within the lower tier of its longer-term neutral trading channel at this time. Although all three markets are important to us, our focus for our longer-term analysis is always on the Dow. Therefore, with extra attention paid to the longer-term chart of the Dow Jones Industrial Average, our longer-term analysis tells us to expect the market to continue to flounder with in the lower tier of its longer-term neutral channel for the time being. Until either neutral support or neutral resistance breaks lower or higher respectively, the market should trade back and forth within this established pattern. The array below depicts the inflection points for the Dow on a longer-term basis

7440 - 9054 - 11776

******

Longer Term Support for the NASDAQ exists at 1137

Longer Term Resistance for the NASDAQ exists at 1756

******

Long Term Support for the SP 500 exists at 771

Long Term Resistance for the SP exists at 951

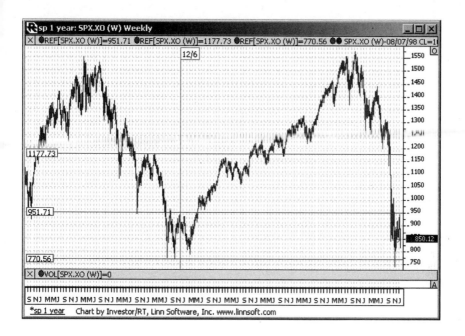

Finally, after each of these nine charts has been drawn and evaluated, I combine the text summaries vertically to produce a combined analysis that encompasses all tiers. Normally this would be at the beginning of the combined analysis because it is most important to my clients. However, I have offered it at the end in this circumstance to help demonstrate the process I use to come to this conclusion every day. This is the associated combined analysis for Tuesday, January 20, 2009 accordingly.

Overall Combined analysis for January 20, 2009

Our combined analysis tells us to expect the market to begin the day Tuesday with a bias to increase, while continuing to oscillate higher towards near term resistance. According to our analysis, the market is now within a near-term up channel and it is trying to develop direction on a midterm basis as well. Clearly, the midterm down channel, which had been in place since January 6, has already been broken. The market is now looking for direction within the lower tier of its midterm neutral channel as we might expect. Currently, the market is oscillating back and forth within this lower tier, and that opens the door to moves in both directions as well. Without a doubt, this lack of direction has already been felt and traders and investors appear confused. In any case, coincidentally near-term resistance and midterm resistance are both important. Therefore, when initial resistance is tested treat that as inflection as well. Because the market has recently identified a midterm support level and because it has already begun to turn higher, the risk is still waited to the upside too. Specifically, if initial resistance begins to break higher aggressive upward market moves are likely to follow as well. However, the catch is that initial resistance will have to break higher in order for that to happen. That is why initial resistance is inflection for Tuesday's trading session. It could also be inflection for swing trades. If it remains intact, instead the market is likely to continue to oscillate within a confusing neutral lower tier midterm channel instead.

Here is our simplified combined analysis for the NASDAQ on Tuesday, January 30, 2009: treat 1530 as inflection. If it holds, expect the market to decline to 1514. However, if 1530 breaks higher an aggressive market increase could follow. Our upside target would eventually be 1574 if resistance breaks.

Clearly, this is a NASDAQ-based observation, and for good reason. We use the NASDAQ for trading purposes, so it is more important to us. The NASDAQ is usually more volatile, too, so when we are right, we get a better bang for our buck.

With reference to the example above, the near-term charts are almost identical for all markets, and the midterm charts are, too. This is normal. In addition, the longer-term charts of the Dow and S&P are congruent as well, but the longer-term chart of the NASDAQ appears skewed when compared to the others. Again, this is normal. The NASDAQ is not a good indicator of longer-term conditions, but it is an excellent for trading. Anyone can use the process I have outlined. It can be used every day to produce profitable trading strategies. Like everything, a learning curve exists, but the result is worth the effort because it leads us further along our path. Even those persons who decide to use my proactive strategies or automated system without taking the time to conduct an independent daily analysis should have a general understanding of the process I use to generate the proactive disciplines. If nothing more, that adds confidence and promotes reflexivity.

With that understood, the next step is to introduce traditional tools, complete our arsenal, and incorporate them all into our proactive trading models. In the next chapter, I will disclose the final tools that I use, and then I will introduce the strategies themselves.

Summary

Below is a summary of the most important topics in this chapter:

- Technical analysis is powerful.
- Technical analysis is the study of money flows. Technical analysis determines rule-based strategies.
- Developmental instruction has been provided.
- Real-life examples were used for reference.

CHAPTER 16

The Golden Sequence

Without a doubt, technical analysis is one of the most important tools that we use to develop our strategies. However, it is not the only one. In this chapter, I will introduce a handful of additional tools that also play an integral role in the development of our strategies. These will be most important to stock investors. Then, in the next chapter, I will officially introduce all six of our proactive trading strategies. Continuing with the same format I used in the last chapter, I will also include a series of graphical references to help me explain each one of my tools. Of course, included with every image will be a detailed explanation. However, I expect that my textual review will not come close to the visual explanations associated with them. From here, as we continue with our tools section, imagine using these in the open market every step of the way. This is where the conditioning we have worked so hard to achieve starts to pay off. With these tools, we can begin to protect our wealth and realize opportunity. Accordingly, when I detail the strategies in the next chapter, I will also be using real-life examples to demonstrate the effectiveness of these models.

Added Value

Herein are four specific tools that add value to our efforts. Each of these is integral to one or more of our proactive trading strategies, so they are all important to our learning curve. I will discuss these in the same order outlined below, because they build on each other.

- Stock Reports
- Stock Filters
- Sentiment Table
- Fibonacci Calculator

Stock Reports

Our individual *stock reports* are a unique assessment of specific companies. These reports are a technical analysis of individual stocks. Understandably, our individual stock reports are not a fundamental analysis of the company, but smart money is making decisions to buy and sell that stock based on fundamentals, so they do play a role. Further, in similar reference to the example described in the last chapter, after a fundamental review of a stock has been made, our technical analysis could also be used to pinpoint specific trading strategy for that stock as well. In other words, our individual stock reports tell us exactly how to trade the stock in question.

I am going to explain the process I use to develop these reports, so everyone will be able to produce these independently as well. These reports are a powerful tool, and they are an integral part of proactively trading individual stocks. I start by conducting a technical analysis of a stock on a near-term basis and generate data points. Then I do the same on a midterm and long-term basis to generate the same information. This gives me the data required to produce the trading plans that drive our decisions to buy, sell, or hold. I use a proprietary regression analysis to produce these reports electronically, but anyone can use simple technical analysis to achieve the same result. In total, I cover 1,300 stocks using this automated method.

Real-time examples of these reports are online, on my website, through Reuters Research or Yahoo Finance. On my website, all a user needs to do is type in the stock symbol, as shown in Figure 16.1, and the real-time report appears as requested.

FIGURE 16.1   Download a stock report.

Source: Stock Traders Daily

Appropriately, and in line with our defined structure, we use the same multi-tier analysis to develop trading plans for individual stocks as we did to develop trading plans for the market itself. First, we evaluate the stock on a near-term basis, then on a midterm basis, and finally on a longer-term basis, as I have outlined already. In addition, we also determine if the stock is strong, weak, or neutral in each of these durations. Finally, we offer data points for each and use those to formulate specific trading plans for the stock in review

Therefore, in the same manner used to develop market strategy, we also develop arrays appropriate to the stock we are considering. The summary table in the image below provides the data to develop the array for this example. Find the summary table for RIMM in Figure 16.2.

Similar to our combined market analysis, the day trading plans encompass all of the data points associated with our analysis. Specifically, when

FIGURE 16.2   Review the summary table.

Source: Stock Traders Daily

we review individual stocks, we have nine potential data points to work with. There are three data points from each term. Therefore, for day trading plans, all nine data points are included in the array. From there, we organize them from lowest to highest, yet again. Then, we incorporate the current level of the stock into the array and develop strategy. In the arrays below, the current level of the stock is in bold. For swing trading, only the midterm and long-term data form the array. The longer-term arrays are exclusive to long-term data as well. This too is the same as the market analysis from prior chapters. The only difference is that we use three data points for every term in our regression analysis for stocks, instead of two, which are for the market. This is just an intra-channel level, nothing more.

This is the day trading array associated with the trading report:

Day Trading Array: 0, 29.19, 32.17, 41.37, 45.44, 50.09, 50.76, **51.78**, 51.81, 60.47

This is the swing trading array associated with the trading report:

Swing Trading Array: 0, 29.19, 32.17, 41.37, 50.76, **51.78**, 60.47

This is the longer-term trading array associated with the trading report:

Long-Term Trading Array: 0, 29.19, **51.78**, 60.47

Once we establish the array for the duration we are interested in, all a user needs to do is incorporate the same process we used in the last chapter. Specifically, the first data point below the current stock price is the first level of support, the first data point above the current stock price is the first level of resistance, and so on. At the onset, investors may need some practice. Therefore, for reference, anyone can go to our real-time reports and click on the plan choices above the summary table to confirm findings as well.

To reveal strategy specifically, in Figure 16.3 I have offered an example of the swing trading plans for RIMM. The rules associated with the array are the same as the rules associated with the array we used to formulate market strategy. Purposefully, I will repeat these to make sure everyone takes notice, because they are an important part of our analysis. By rule, there are only two times to buy and only two times to short any instrument. This is true for the market and for individual stocks.

Buy signals:
- Buy when resistance breaks higher or
- Buy when support is tested

Short signals:
- Short when resistance is tested or
- Short when support breaks lower

With those rules, and with every array, come four associated trading plans. Two of those plans are to buy the stock, and two of those are to short it. As a result, there are four trading plans for every duration we review. This applies to day trading, swing trading, and long-term strategies. Therefore, there are 12 trading plans for every stock. Although they may look similar sometimes, day trading plans are not the same as swing trading plans, and swing trading plans are not the same as long-term trading plans, and vice versa. Please make this distinction to avoid future problems. All of these plans are unique.

Following with our example, the specific Swing Trading Plans for RIMM, derived from the summary table and the associated array, are in Figure 16.3.

This is an excellent assessment of RIMM, but we can do this for any stock we follow. However, it leaves a lingering concern. Logically, the follow-up question is which plan to choose. The next tool I will introduce will provide

FIGURE 16.3   Capture the trading plan.
Source: Stock Traders Daily

that answer. However, before I introduce our stock filters, I would also like to point out unique aspects of the trading plans above. First, notice there is no target for the long resistance plan illustrated. That is because longer-term resistance for RIMM is 60.47, and there is no resistance level above that yet, according to our current array. In simple terms, a break above this resistance level would be rather bullish. More important, though, because our trading reports are dynamic, if a break above 60.47 takes place, the next update of this report will almost surely have a new longer-term resistance target for us to work with. Therefore, if 60.47 broke higher, there would be no target for a short while. Be aware of this when breaks of extreme support and resistance levels occur.

In addition, these trading plans incorporate strict risk controls, and those should also be addressed before we move forward. Although they help identify opportunity, these structured plans must also incorporate stop losses. Once risk controls are relinquished, these plans become ineffective. With that understood, I also incorporate two additional rules into these strategies. The first references tests of support or resistance, and the second references the stop loss.

- Tests occur when the stock is within 0.05 of support or resistance.
- Stop losses are 0.21 for every trade.

These numbers are at the discretion of the end user. However, because we adhere to strict disciplines, and because I have been relatively good at pinpointing accurate support and resistance levels over time, I keep stops tight. Using these disciplines, losses are also minimized.

Reasonably, the first time anyone reviews my strict discipline, questions arise. Most people are not used to tight stop losses. In fact, many brokers that I know use 10 percent as a stop loss instead. Reasonably, that is because they also charge their clients $500 or more per trade and cannot rationalize selling when support breaks. Regardless, a loss like that would be detrimental, so I am amazed that they could ever allow it to happen in the first place. I have asked it before, and I will ask it again: Where is the risk control?

My alternative reconciliation is they are not capable technicians, so they listen to the fundamental analysts of their firm and are conditioned by corporate structure not to recognize technical indicators. But we recognize these indicators, so we all know that keeping losses small also keeps us in a position to realize opportunities when they surface along the way. Instead of having to make up the 10 percent losses before growth is realized, we position ourselves for opportunity immediately instead.

Instead of relinquishing our control, we are in the business of producing results using proactive strategies. We must draw the line when support or resistance breaks against us. In simple terms, either we are right and we let that trade ride to profitability, or we are wrong and we pull the plug immediately. There is no middle ground, and if losses occur, they will be minimal as a result. Using this method, we stay in control of our wealth. That is our first goal, and a requirement.

These trading plans are focused, disciplined, and effective, and the real-time reports are actionable. However, the reports do not tell us which plans to use. That brings us to the second tool in this section.

Stock Filters

Although I am a technical analyst, in the last chapter I conceded that fundamental analysis also plays an integral role in some decision making. To a certain extent, fundamental analysis offers a broad understanding of the market, and it helps us evaluate the longer-term health of the economy. That works for individual stocks as well. Therefore, in an effort to pinpoint the best trading plan for any specific stock, I have also developed a tool that provides a broad dissemination of the stocks we follow. That tool is our *stock filters*. They do not provide a fundamental analysis, but they do offer the broad dissemination needed to satisfy our objective.

Cohesively, our stock filters are used in conjunction with our market analysis, and therefore an underlying fundamental analysis is included. Specifically, our stock filters are tools that tell us which stocks are closest to their respective support levels at the time we initiate a filter. They will filter the stocks for resistance, too. More precisely, if the market is testing support and we are looking for stocks to buy, identifying those stocks, which are also testing support at the same time, is usually the most rewarding option. Appropriately, our filters allow us to determine which stocks are testing their respective support levels at the same time as the market, and that improves our efficiency, which, in turn, accelerates our performance ratios over time. On the same note, if the market is testing a resistance level and we want to find stocks to short, we can also filter the list for short resistance plans as well. In accordance with our rules, the stock filters work for the two buy strategies, and the two short strategies referenced in the last chapter, and referred to again above.

Reasonably, I do not include all of the 1,300 stocks we cover in this filter. Instead, I have narrowed down the list to about 100 stocks. These stocks comprise our focus list. Our focus list includes stocks that trade actively with the market. After all, this is a market timing tool, and correlation is important. Therefore, we want to find stocks that move with the market so we can take advantage of the signals stemming from our market analysis seamlessly. There are four ways to do that, the four quadrants that comprise our stock filters:

- Long Support Plans
- Long Resistance Plans
- Short Support Plans
- Short Resistance Plans

Long support plans are filters that show the stocks that are trading closest to their respective support levels at the time of the filter. Long resistance plans are filters that show the stocks that are poised to break above resistance at the time of the filter, too. Timing is important to this process.

Conversely, short support plans are filters that show the stocks that are poised to break below their support levels at the time of the filter. In addition, short resistance plans show the stocks that are trading near their respective resistance levels when the filter was made. Appropriately, I offer filters for day trading, swing trading, and long-term trading plans. This allows everyone to find a stock to buy or a stock to short that fits his or her general interest. In Figure 16.4, I have illustrated the use of our day trading filters. After selecting day trading filters from the main menu, a quadrant box appears representing the four types of plans referenced above.

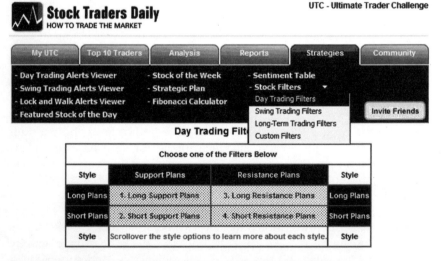

FIGURE 16.4   The quadrants.

Source: Stock Traders Daily

In this Figure 16.4, assume that the market is testing support, and we want to find a stock to buy that is also testing support. By rule, we should therefore choose long support plans. In doing so, the result will look similar to the upshot below. The outcome is a list of stocks that are trading nearest to their respective support levels at the time the filter was requested. If the filter happened when the market was testing support, this filter also turns into a correlated market timing and stock selection tool automatically. That increases the value immensely. After requesting the filter, a user would then review the list to determine if any of those stocks were particularly attractive. I have highlighted QCOM in Figure 16.5 for this reference.

Assuming that QCOM met the desired criteria of the user, an actionable trading strategy would be at hand. However, this filter also takes this process a step further. We have the option to trade the plan, too, according to predefined disciplines. That option is in the far right column. If a user clicks that link, the displayed strategy will be executed according to plan. However, unless this feature is also tied to the automating trading APIs of a brokerage account, this process will execute a simulated trade according to the predefined structure and discipline integral to our stock reports instead. Usually, all of my users start with this simulator. This is real-life experience,

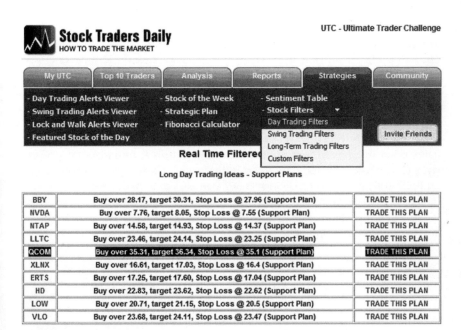

FIGURE 16.5   Select a plan.
Source: Stock Traders Daily

and it helps them understand the circumstances that may affect the controlled disciplines I recommend to everyone. If we select "trade this plan," a summary analysis appears, and we have the option to confirm the strategy. Integrated into that summary are a few exceptional features.

The features of trading plans:
- Profit stops are included.
- Trailing profit stops are included.
- Stop losses are included.
- An entry range is used (not a limit order).
- Target prices are included.
- The orders are hidden from market makers.
- The trade is repeated if so chosen.

Obviously, risk controls are an integral part of the operation. In the simulator, we learn how those risk controls affect the strategy, then the strategies can be applied in the real world. Here are several examples of that. First, the entry range is important to differentiate. When we incorporate technical analysis, we only want to buy near (and slightly over) a support level, for example. However, using a limit order often pervades this objective. Instead of buying above support, a limit order tells our broker to buy at our entry price or better. In many cases, if an entry level is equal to stated support, and a limit order is used, the entry could effectively turn out to be under support instead. In turn, that dilutes the effectiveness of our technical analysis considerably. After all, if support breaks, a sell signal occurs. Therefore, we use an entry range instead, and that keeps us on the right side of technical indicators at all times.

Next, trailing profit stops are important. These kick in automatically. A user can modify these as he or she sees fit, but the objective is to secure gains when we have them. Before a trading plan is summarized, our users have the option to modify the stops if they want. These include profit stops, trailing profit stops, and stop losses. We can also modify the entry range and the target price if we so choose. In any case, these risk controls are important to the overall performance of our simulator and the associated strategy.

Finally, hiding orders from market makers can be a very useful tool as well. More often than not, market makers recognize open orders and can effectively force a trade to take us out of the position as a result. Most usually, we might place a stop loss to protect our position, and then walk away. However, that stop is visible to all market makers, and market makers could easily stop us out if they so choose. However, if they cannot see the order, they do not have this option at all. Our orders are hidden from market makers because the program itself reads the stock, and it does not rely on the discount brokerage firm to do this. In turn, it does not execute an order until the condition is met. This is also a very valuable feature.

Trade Plan Summary

Please Read the Trading Plan Summary below to verify that this is the plan you have chosen. If it is not you may edit it. Click the Accept Button if this plan is correct. This trading plan will not execute unless you accept the plan.

YOU MUST CLICK THE ACCEPT BUTTON BELOW.

Your Stock: Qualcomm Inc (QCOM)

Buy QCOM between 35.31 and 35.36. Target 36.34. If it is triggered set a stop loss at 0.21 away from the entry price in case the stock moves against the trade to protect the position. If the stock triggers as indicated above and then moves into the money by $0.35 set a $0.1 trailing profit stop to secure a gain from the trade in case it reverses. Using this approach will maximize the value of the trade and it will protect the position too. If it is stopped re-enter the trade. Limit # number of trades to 3 though. Don't trade it more than 3 times with both stops and profit stops included. No matter what end the day in cash to avoid the risk of holding the position overnight.

☑ Notify me when this plan trades

[Accept] [Edit] [Cancel]

FIGURE 16.6   Trade plan summary.

Source: Stock Traders Daily

The summary shown in Figure 16.6 is an excellent example of this at work.

Afterwards, if we click the accept button, this plan will execute for us according to the risk-controlled strategy outlined in the summary. From there, as performance records build, users compare their results to their peers' and begin to perfect their own strategy in a real-world environment. Once they are comfortable with the simulators, they are free to move on to live trading.

Anyone well versed in programming could integrate code into the trading platform at his or her brokerage firm to do exactly this. Everyone should take the time to evaluate these.

Sentiment Table

Next, I will introduce the third of the four tools included in this chapter. Our *sentiment table* is an excellent resource for identifying relative strength, and I will offer a guide to help everyone use it. Once more, the sentiment table is in conjunction with our focus list and tied to our individual stock reports as well. Our sentiment table is a simple derivation of the strength of each one of the stocks that we follow as that relates to the durations we review respectively. Specifically, every stock is strong, weak, or neutral on a near-term, midterm, and long-term basis. Therefore, each stock will have a designation, which represents the trend of the stock in each duration.

Although there are approximately 100 stocks in the focus list, and although each one of those has three durations and therefore three strength indicators, our sentiment table makes those numerous observations concise. By automatically evaluating them and then combining them into a usable structure, this table makes our evaluation of sentiment both swift and accurate at the same time.

Accordingly, our sentiment table tells us which stocks are strong, which are weak, and which are trading sideways for every duration. Obviously, it does this for near-term, midterm and long-term durations, but we will focus on the near-term for explanation.

Primarily, I use the sentiment table as a contrarian indicator. Furthermore, in my opinion the near-term row is the best contrarian indicator in the table. For example, if all the stocks are strong near term, I can reasonably determine that the market has been strong recently, and that is a contrarian indicator most often. In fact, associated skew is often obvious in the stock filters when the market is extended as well, so that supports the findings of the sentiment table accordingly. In this case, if almost all of the stocks are strong on a near-term basis, we can reasonably surmise that the market may be approaching an overbought condition. Therefore, we could reasonably expect a pullback at some point soon as well. The opposite happens as well. When the market experiences a period of excessive pessimism, all of these stocks will be weak, and an oversold condition might exist instead. This contrarian indicator has been very valuable, and we use it regularly to confirm extremes in the market more accurately.

Interestingly, though, when I requested the sentiment table for this reference, there were no compelling observations to be made, but that is okay. We cannot force the issue. Either we can identify indicators or we cannot. They cannot be fabricated, and we cannot make the market do what we want it to do. As a result, there is nothing revealing about the sentiment table shown in Figure 16.7. However, it too was a real-world observation, and the real world is where we make our money. Therefore, I still consider this an excellent example even though there is not a concise read.

Obviously, I use the sentiment table to identify contrarian indicators. Over time, I have found that to be extremely useful. However, many of my clients use it in a different manner. For example, if their market analysis tells them that the market might be strong during the next trading session, they might go to the sentiment table and look for stocks that are also strong

FIGURE 16.7   The sentiment table.

Source: Stock Traders Daily

on a near-term basis. This gives them ideas to work with and narrows their choices so they do not have to dig as deeply when they do their research.

Not only does it save them time, but it is also a direct path to the risk-controlled trading plans referenced at the onset of this chapter. The sentiment table is also tied to our individual stock reports. Figure 16.8 shows the 14 long-term neutral stocks from the image shown in Figure 16.7. This

FIGURE 16.8   Long-term neutral results.

Source: Stock Traders Daily

was generated by clicking on the number 14 in the table. Afterwards, if a user were to click on any one of the symbols in that list, the real-time trading report for that stock would appear accordingly. From there, the trading plans are revealed, and actionable strategies could follow seamlessly thereafter.

In turn, our sentiment table, like our stock filters, integrates directly with our focus list, and to the trading reports, which are integral to our tools section for seamless transition. This makes them both easy to use and immediately actionable. Being able to identify stocks that are strong relative to the market, or stocks that are weak at any point in time instead, can add tremendous value to the end user and save him or her time as well. However, I continue to prefer the contrarian indicator observable in the near-term row. In any case, the sentiment table is an added value that works with the click of a button. My clients can use it for varying reasons, but the integrated strategies help us reach our end goal. That means wealth preservation first, opportunity second, and the comfort zone eventually as well.

Fibonacci Calculator

This is where the title of this chapter comes from. Fibonacci was a scientist in the 1800s. He identified natural growth rates within our environment. His work produced a sequence of numbers that define each stage of the natural progression of growth over time. He called this sequence the *Golden Sequence*. Although his initial observations were somewhat different, the Golden Sequence applies to the stocks we follow and to the markets we observe to help us determine where those will stop falling and start turning higher, or vice versa. Sophisticated traders use this tool every day.

Many advanced charting programs also offer a derivative of Fibonacci calculations for their end users to apply to strategies. However, very few of those are as easy to use as the calculator I have produced. I have integrated the Golden Sequence into a *Fibonacci calculator* that I use regularly and offer to my clients as an associated market-timing tool. This is especially useful for long-term reversal triggers. The result of each calculation provides a sequence of numbers that act like support and resistance levels, and that gives us an understanding of how the market should naturally oscillate over time.

However, an important differentiation should be made before we move ahead. Although Fibonacci calculations are also identifiers of support and resistance levels, they are not the same as technical analysis. I use Fibonacci calculations to produce reversal triggers, not exact support or resistance. This is especially true when I conduct my longer-term analysis.

For example, if longer-term support was already established and if the market was already increasing toward resistance, we could review the longer-term charts to identify where the next resistance level exists. This would produce a longer-term resistance level and a clear upside target. However, at the same time, Fibonacci calculations can produce a slightly different measure, but an equally important one. Instead of pinpointing the exact resistance level, Fibonacci calculations would offer a confirmation level instead. More specifically, if the market increased to test resistance in line with this example, and if resistance held, then the market would reverse lower again. Confirmation would come after that pullback had begun.

Normally, the Fibonacci data point associated with this type of oscillation cycle would be slightly lower than the defined resistance level stemming from our technical analysis. Therefore, the Fibonacci result would act as our longer-term reversal confirmation. If the market pulled back from resistance and broke below that confirmation level, my downside risk assessment would increase measurably. On the other hand, if resistance was tested but a reversal confirmation did not occur, I would prepare for an eventual break above resistance again instead.

Although it does not pinpoint support or resistance levels on a longer-term basis, my Fibonacci calculator is a very valuable tool because of this confirmation quality. As I continue with this subsection, I will integrate this example into a real-life scenario to demonstrate its use.

The image in Figure 16.9 shows my Fibonacci calculator without any included data. Using it is as easy as using an old IBM calculator. For example, if we want to know where resistance levels exist, we type in the support level into the low box and click the calculate button. Appropriately, the resistance levels derived from that low are on the right-hand side of the calculator. Conversely, if we want to identify support levels after resistance is tested instead, we input the resistance level in the high box and click the calculate button. The results are on the left-hand side of the calculator. Afterwards, we simply input the current level of the market into the sequence to determine the confirmation level we are looking for. In fact, I will do that in the next part of this example (see Figure 16.9).

Accordingly, if we want to find resistance after support is tested, we type the low in the low box and look for the data to appear on the right side. In this example, I want to identify longer-term market-based resistance levels. In particular, if the market indeed rebounds in 2009 as my return to parity analysis suggests, I want to know where resistance will exist. Fibonacci tells me where to expect the market to stall. In order to find this, I must first identify the recent low of the market. Specific to this real-life example, in March 2009 the market established a low and began to bounce higher. Reasonably, the market could establish a lower low again at some point, but for the sake of this example, we will use the low from November to help us identify resistance. This, of course, already happened once.

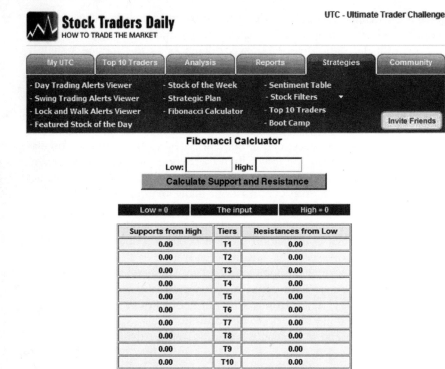

FIGURE 16.9 Fibonacci calculator.

Source: Stock Traders Daily

In Chapter 15 I provided an example with a word of warning, and it turned out to be a great one. Longer-term support was identified at 7441 in January 2009. However, that broke lower as the year progressed, and an update was needed. The references below include that update.

The low in March was 6440. We do not need to be exact when we integrate Fibonacci, just close to exact. Confidently, I type 6440 into the low box and click the calculate button to produce resistance data. The results on the right side of the calculator are the data we are looking for. Review the image depicted in Figure 16.10 for details.

In turn, this data allows us to identify my longer-term reversal confirmation level. However, in order to do this we must first have an understanding of the technical indicators associated with this oscillation cycle. We did that in the last chapter. Therefore, I am also going to bring in my technical

FIGURE 16.10   Resistance on the right.

Source: Stock Traders Daily

analysis of the market. In essence, this becomes a combined analysis of its own. In this case, we are combining the technical indicators with the Golden Sequence to identify the longer-term resistance level, which might be confirmed in 2009. By doing this, we are free to move ahead with a relative degree of confidence. Review our longer-term technical analysis of the Dow Jones industrial average in Figure 16.11 and then continue with the example.

Defined longer-term resistance is 10739. If we combine that with our Fibonacci calculations, we can also define a confirmation level that corresponds to that already identified technical indicator. Look at the results from the calculations once more, and this time pay careful attention to the T8 value specifically. T8 is relatively close to and slightly below 10739 at the same time, and therefore it is actionable. Fibonacci tells us that 10703 is an

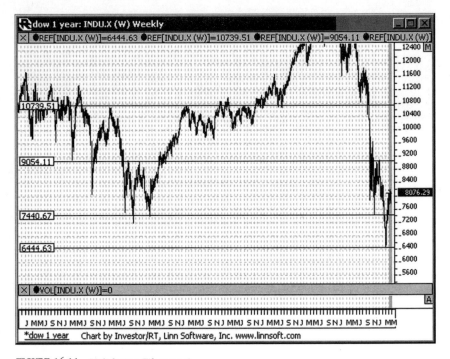

FIGURE 16.11   Validating Fibonacci.
Chart by Investor/RT, Linn Software, Inc. www.linnsoft.com

important data point based on natural growth trends, and our technical analysis tells us that 10739 is likely to be ultimate resistance. This combination fits right in line with what I was looking for.

Conclusively, in April 2009, I expected 10703 to break higher at some point, I expected an official test of 10739, and if that happens I will watch for confirmation. If the market breaks back below 10703 again, my Fibonacci calculator will have provided yet another reversal confirmation, and I will almost surely begin to warn brackish investors of downside market moves again, too.

Repeat warning: This is static look at a dynamic analysis. The analysis is subject to change as the market moves. Support and resistance levels adjust over time, and current updates are necessary.

If my return to parity analysis is true, and if the market is in for a good year in 2009, 10739 would fit. However, from there I also expect the Investment Rate to take over officially, and aggressive declines to follow. This could spell trouble for some, and it will almost surely cause another round of wealth destruction. However, we do not need to be run over by this freight train.

In every sense, with the tools I have already introduced and the actionable strategies that I will describe in the next chapter, I am making every effort to shelter everyone from the storm that lies ahead. Initially, and probably throughout the year, 2009 will give investors a head fake. Late in the year, economic numbers will improve, and investors will want to get back in at the top all over again. That is what small investors do. They buy at the top, and sell at the bottom all the time. I aim to change that for as many people as I can.

Rationally, my tools and strategies could protect real wealth ratios forever. That is why I continue to use real-world examples. The stock market is dynamic and we should be, too. The only way to do that is to learn in a dynamic environment, and this is my best effort to provide that textually. My examples and the tools we have used in this chapter do exactly that. However, the proactive strategies that I will disclose in the next chapter take my real-world examples to a whole new level. The actionable strategies are next.

Summary

Below is a summary of the most important topics in this chapter:

- The tools in this chapter support our strategies.
- The goal is to offer a correlated approach for stock investors.
- The stock reports provide actionable trading plans.
- The stock filters tell us which stocks are tradable now.
- The sentiment table helps narrow down our search.
- The Fibonacci calculator is a confirmation tool.

CHAPTER 17

Rule-Based Trading Strategies

This chapter details actionable trading strategies that can immediately control risk and provide opportunities. Until now, everything that we have done leads to this. Each step was important. I started with the Investment Rate because it is the foundation for all of my strategies. It proves that overall demand for investments in the United States declines every year from 2007 until 2023. If nothing more, the stock market and other associated asset classes will be volatile, and growth will be difficult as a result. However, the situation could also be much worse.

Without debating the propensity for a severe depression here, this provides ample warning. The Investment Rate and contemporary Darwinism tell us to start taking control of our wealth again immediately. From there, the emotional conditioning tools that I introduced eradicate some of the lingering fears and misplaced truths that the corporate structure of big brokers has imposed on the investing public. These golden handcuffs are widespread in the investment community today, but I have revealed them for what they really are. As a result, we can now embrace the responsibility of wealth management. Therefore, our eyes are now open to the environment around us, and we recognize the risks. We must be proactive, or we will continue to be subject to market-related forces and eventual deterioration. This provides the reasons we needed to move ahead.

Clearly, after laying the groundwork, the next step was to introduce the tools that make these proactive strategies work. The tools I defined in the previous chapters are a direct catalyst to the proactive trading strategies that allow us to both control our wealth and realize opportunity regardless of market direction. These strategies are the crux of this chapter, they are one of the most important parts of this book, and these proactive strategies are the best way to make money in any market environment. With these important tools in hand, all of the building blocks will be in place.

Therefore, without any further delay I will introduce six proactive trading strategies. Expect a detailed explanation of each strategy here and associate these strategies with your interests as you read them. I also offer support though our corporate website, www.stocktradersdaily.com, which helps investors identify the strategies best suited for their unique objectives.

Differentiating the Strategies

Some of these strategies will be more appropriate for active traders and others for investors with a longer-term objective. However, they all have a similar characteristic—they are all proactive strategies. That means risk controls are integral to each one of them. That also means that cash is a regular investment as well. In fact, cash provides a means to circulatory emotional conditioning, and that adds significant value to the process over time. Regular cash positions allow us to restart our minds from time to time, and that allows us to re-focus on our decision-making process objectively again. Ultimately, that is the underlying goal. We want to make proper decisions, reflexively, and cash helps us meet the requirements of that goal as we work with the strategies included in this chapter. Therefore, cash is both a wealth management tool and a conditioning tool all in one.

Of course, though, risk management is not the only quality inherent in these strategies. Opportunities for growth are also integral to our purpose. Reasonably, if we are able to control our risk, it will be easier to take advantage of opportunities when they surface. Because we remain in control, we do not need to make up ground the same way everybody else does. Instead, when opportunity comes, we will move forward while others just get back to even.

Most investors will embrace these strategies at the onset because times are tough, and initial integration is not complicated. Unfortunately, although these strategies are logical and easy to follow, some investors will also end up diverging from them.

In addition, over time some investors will not respect the risk controls integrated into these strategies either. Expectedly, there is a set of rules for each strategy. They are there to influence proper risk control. Initially, these rules may seem extensive, but they will become second nature soon after we implement them, and they will be easy to use eventually.

Even so, some investors will start incorporating the rules properly at first, and then diverge from strategy. This will be especially true if the market shows strength again. Instead of embracing strategies that work in both up and down markets, some investors will become arrogant or deterred and revert back to the misplaced traditional techniques that have already been the cause of widespread wealth deterioration. In that position, all they can do is hope for the best. That is where the mistakes start. Hope is a four-letter word, and an emotion investors should live without. Do not diverge from the strategy you select.

Immediately, when we neglect risk controls our corresponding ability to protect wealth spirals out of control as well. Clearly, this dissuasion is a byproduct of emotion. However, emotions have no place in this business nor do they have any place in our proactive strategies. Once we accept small losses as natural components of our strategies, we will welcome risk controls. Therefore, we should be willing to accept small losses from time to time. Still, some investors will undoubtedly forget this simple rule as economic cycles ebb and flow. That will be true of course, until the cycles force them to learn again.

Although I can repeat this point a dozen times in a row, some investors will still fail to engage appropriate risk controls, and losses will occur. That is Murphy's Law. My advice is: Do not let this happen to you. Without exception, every time we make a trade, risk controls need to be predetermined. This defines strategy, and this protects us from adverse market conditions over time. In addition, that allows us to transition with the market, up or down, and that keeps us on the right side of the curve. More important, this also allows us to realize the opportunities ahead of us. Therefore, consider risk controls as a natural gateway to growth over time, and embrace them always.

Other investors will have an apprehension to using these strategies from the beginning. Some of them will not be familiar with risk controls at all, but with experience that will change. Simulators can help with that, and so can paper trading. In fact, everyone should start slow, learn the strategies first, and build from there.

Reasonably, some investors will want to jump in with both feet when they should otherwise be taking baby steps instead. Paper trades help with this. I recommend that everyone start the process with paper trading, then use a very small number of shares to move forward. Paper trading will help us all understand the general process, and using small share amounts will allow us to become familiar with the nuances of trading these strategies in a live environment. Combined, these will act as building blocks to integration and allow us to eventually use meaningful dollar amounts to build wealth. Unquestionably, paper trading and trading with small shares at the beginning increases confidence, and that helps reduce the emotional burden associated with the direct application of these strategies over time. Eventually, that increases our reflexive prowess and points us toward our goal at all times.

Unfortunately, some investors will not want to take the time to manage their wealth at all. Instead, they will decide to stick with the brackish investment style that has gotten them in trouble in the first place. For those, I have a few general responses. Either we make a conscious decision to control our wealth now, or we allow the investment techniques of selfish big brokers to continue to expose our wealth to the risks of the market at all times instead. The choice is ours. Either we become independent and ascend to the strongest species of contemporary Darwinism, or we continue to accept the obvious pitfalls of the brackish investment techniques that big brokerage firms have imposed on the industry.

Although this sounds like an obvious choice, it is not. I am proposing a lifestyle change here, and that is a big deal. Regardless of the obvious nature of this transition, many investors have trouble with it. When moving from the traditional doctrine to an approach free from associated burdens, apprehension is a natural occurrence.

In spite of the initial apprehension everyone starts with, it only lasts until the learning curve is complete. Once investors realize the fluidity of these strategies, most of them embrace the strategies immediately.

The result is effective, but we cannot skip any of the building blocks I offered in this book. The outline I presented here was intentional. We need to start with a broad understanding of current and future economic conditions, we need to discount the noise and all misconceptions, and we need to approach the market with an open mind. Once we are there, we are free to move ahead with proactive strategies. From here, the comfort zone is around the corner, and the end is in sight.

The Six Proactive Strategies

Here are the six proactive strategies included in this chapter:

1. Featured Stock of the Day
2. Stock of the Week
3. Strategic Plan
4. Day Trading Strategy
5. Swing Trading Strategy
6. Lock and Walk Strategy

I have separated each strategy into a unique section, and I have divided each section into the following eight parts.

A. **Description of the strategy:** A summary of the section that reveals the face of the strategy appropriately.
B. **Objective of the discipline:** A detail of the strategy's purpose and underpinnings.
C. **Tools integral to positive results:** Explanation of which tools from prior chapters are incorporated in each strategy. Notably, though, the building blocks and the preliminary tools mentioned early in this book are not included. Instead, they are broad, sweeping, and integral to all of the strategies I offer. These additional tools are the Investment Rate,

contemporary Darwinism, Personal Balance Sheets, Personal Journal, and other emotional conditioning tools.

D. **Rules associated with the strategy:** This section is riddled with little things that might seem mundane, but are necessary to follow and understand. These rules cannot be broken, or the strategies will fail.

E. **Risk controls and assessments:** A description of the obvious risks and obscure hurdles associated with each strategy.

F. **Creating the strategy:** A description of how I create each strategy every day. I also provide a step-by-step review that will allow everyone to create and maintain these strategies independently. (This section is especially valuable to independent traders.)

G. **Real-world example:** Examples that will help you visualize the strategy and provide insight to real-world applications.

H. **Potential pitfalls:** A description of some prominent problems that people encounter from time to time.

Strategy 1: Featured Stock of the Day

Description of the Strategy

The Featured Stock of the Day is a proactive trading strategy designed to take advantage of the daily oscillation cycles in individual stocks. The strategy is used every day with integrated risk controls. This is a day trading strategy that focuses on one stock only. Every day, new trades happen, and associated market-timing tools identify the best ideas.

Objective of the Discipline

The objective of this strategy is to take advantage of small gains from a single stock every day, while remaining in control of our risk at the same time.

Tools Integral to Positive Results

- Day trading technical analysis for the market
- Day trading technical analysis for individual stocks
- Correlated filtering

Rules Associated with the Strategy

- Do not trade penny stocks.
- Do not trade stocks over $100.
- Do not select stocks that are illiquid, or hard to trade.
- Trade with the same number of shares every time.

- Define strategy using technical analysis.
- Define entry and exit levels for every trade.
- Limit sway to within $0.05 of the entry level.
- Incorporate a tight stop loss for every trade.
- Incorporate profit stops for every trade.
- Use trailing profit stops for every trade.
- Begin trading five minutes after the open.
- Conclude trading five minutes before the close.
- Do not diverge from predefined strategy.
- Be willing to repeat the trade up to five times.
- Day trading margin is acceptable.
- Use conditional market orders.
- End every day in cash.
- Avoid overnight risk at all times.

Risk Controls and Assessments

There are two important risk controls and assessments for the Featured Stock Strategy. First, stop losses are included in every trade. However, the integration of profit stops with stop losses could create a problem. Therefore, use this guideline to avoid slippage over time: ([Profit Stops − Trailing Profit Stops] should be greater than the Stop Loss by at least $0.10). This rule helps keep our margins positive and reduces our risk accordingly. Integrated in the strategies I use are $0.21 stop losses, $0.35 profit stops, and a $0.10 trailing profit stop for every trade.

For repeat trades, I recommend a maximum of three trades for every strategy. Some investors want a little more, so five is the limit, but three is a much more reasonable number in my opinion. In the event of stops, three is a limit we can all live with, where five stops would push the envelope beyond acceptability in many cases.

Creating the Strategy

The Featured Stock of the Day maintains an automated and correlated process. It combines both market timing and stock selection into an actionable strategy that anyone can use. To construct these plans, follow these steps:

- Conduct a technical analysis of the market for day trading purposes.
- Conduct a technical analysis of the stocks being considered.
- Define market strategy for day trading.
- Define day trading strategies for the stocks.
- Conduct these observations independently.
- Compare those strategies and identify correlations.

- Match the strategies of the stocks to already defined market analysis, not the other way around. Market analysis comes first.
- Select a stock and a plan based on evidenced parallels.
- Implement the plan for the stock that matches the plan for the market.

Real-World Example

The real-world example of the Featured Stock of the Day is an actual strategy made using the rules and structure outlined above. The trade was made in our simulator. That simulator assumes the use of a $30,000 portfolio with day trading margin. This is not set in stone, and individual investors can use varying dollar amounts as they see fit. However, the same number of shares should be used for every trade within this strategy. Otherwise, return ratios will skew considerably.

Margin was not required this time, but if the stock we selected was greater than $30 per share, we could have used it. We do not need to use all the money in our account all the time. In fact, I advise against it. Instead, use the same number of shares, and the process becomes much easier. In my example, and in the simulator, we use 1000 shares. The result of this strategy was a 4.45 percent return, given the objective portfolio. Of special note, each trade was closed via profit stop. In fact, this usually happens. Rarely does a trade follow through all the way to our target price. In total, there were six trades (see Table 17.1).

TABLE 17.1   WFC Trading Results: Trade History

#	Date/Time	Entry Price	Exit Price	Status	Trade #	Result
1	2009-01-23 09:35:38	15.0695	0	Open	1	
2	2009-01-23 09:36:58	15.0695	15.61	Close (Profit stop)	1	0.54
3	2009-01-23 09:45:43	15.085	0	Open	2	
4	2009-01-23 09:53:19	15.085	15.5	Close (Profit stop)	2	0.41
5	2009-01-23 10:43:00	15.08	0	Open	3	
6	2009-01-23 11:20:30	15.08	15.458	Close (Profit stop)	3	0.38

Trading Plan: Wells Fargo and Company (WFC). Buy WFC between 15.05 and 15.1. Target 19.45. If it is triggered, set a stop loss at 0.21 away from the entry price in case the stock moves against the trade to protect the position. If the stock triggers as indicated above and then moves into the money by $0.35, set a $0.1 trailing profit stop to secure a gain from the trade in case it reverses. This approach will maximize the value of the trade and protect the position, too. If it is stopped, re-enter the trade. Limit the number of trades to three, though. Do not trade it more than three times with both stops and profit stops included. No matter what, end the day in cash to avoid the risk of holding the position overnight.

Potential Pitfalls

The pitfalls of this strategy are usually associated with failed discipline. Those persons who execute trades manually often stop paying attention to the rules. Conditional and automated trades help solve that problem. In addition, though, if a stop occurs, new traders often want to win it back. On the other hand, if there have not been any trades, they want to force a trade. Neither of these is acceptable for this strategy, and each will usually result in avoidable losses. Investors should focus on strategy, adhere to the discipline associated with the rules, and execute trades like a machine. This process makes the strategy easy to follow. Any derivation will seriously complicate the potency of the system.

Strategy 2: Stock of the Week

Description of the Strategy

The Stock of the Week is a swing trading strategy focused on one stock and one plan for the entire week. These trades are held for more than one day, most of the time, but if certain conditions exist, they may not be. In this specific strategy, the trade is active for the entire week even if stops trigger in the middle of the week. The trade is not a static trade. There is a defined plan with price targets, stop losses, and re-entry strategies. This helps us control risk. Start this strategy on Monday and follow it until Friday. Every day, after market hours, we should make a new evaluation as well. Then, if necessary, we should update the plan. Any updates will affect the strategy for the next trading session, and possibly for the rest of the week as well. Regardless, this trade is closed on Friday before the market closes. Then we record the results and start the next week fresh, with a new stock and a new objective plan. As a result, we end the week in cash no matter what, and begin again objectively the following Monday every week.

Objective of the Discipline

The objective of this strategy is to realize gains from swing trading one stock every week. We are not looking for the stock poised to move aggressively from earnings or expected news releases, though. The outcome of these is often surprising, and we are not in the business of accepting avoidable risk. Instead, this strategy pinpoints the stocks that are likely to move in conjunction with our established market strategy instead. No news is therefore good news.

A secondary objective is emotional conditioning. Ending every week in cash is an excellent way to dampen the revolving burden the market may have over time.

Tools Integral to Positive Results

- Swing trading technical analysis for the market
- Swing trading technical analysis for individual stocks
- Correlated filtering

Rules Associated with the Strategy

- Begin every week in cash.
- End every week in cash.
- Define strategy outside of market hours.
- Execute strategy during market hours.
- Update the strategy overnight if needed.
- Do not update the strategy during market hours.
- Use conditional market orders to execute trades.
- Trade with the same number of shares every time.
- Use tight stop losses with every trade.
- If a trade is stopped, be willing to re-enter it.
- Re-entries are unlimited but overnight adjustments may be made.
- Do not diverge from strategy.
- Do not relinquish risk controls.
- Do not select penny stocks.
- Do not select stocks over $100.
- Do not select stocks that are illiquid or hard to trade.
- Do not select stocks scheduled to release earnings during the week.
- Do not select stocks that are slated to announce important news that could make the stock move aggressively in the week ahead.

Risk Controls and Assessments

Stop losses are integral to the Stock of the Week Strategy. They should be used for every trade, every week, in the same methodical manner. However, because this is a swing trading strategy, we are also subject to overnight risk. If a position is active, and overnight news causes the position to move against us, we may be stopped out with a larger than anticipated loss. If that happens, the larger loss should be stomached, the position should move to cash, and the strategy will be re-engaged the same way afterwards. Therefore, if a larger than expected stop occurs, and then the re-entry trigger hits again, the trade should also be re-entered according to rule. Otherwise, if no re-trigger comes, we never re-enter the trade.

Obviously, the risk increases if we select stocks scheduled to report earnings or release important news. Therefore, to control our risk we should not consider stocks that are scheduled to report earnings or expected to release news that could move the price significantly.

Creating the Strategy

The structure of the Stock of the Week Strategy is to maintain a correlated process that combines both market timing and stock selection into an actionable strategy that anyone can use. To construct the plans, follow these steps:

1. Conduct a technical analysis of the market for swing trading purposes.
2. Conduct a technical analysis of the stocks being considered.
3. Define market strategy for swing trading.
4. Define swing trading strategies for the stocks.
5. Conduct these observations independently.
6. Compare those strategies and identify correlations.
7. Match the strategies of the stocks to already defined market analysis, not the other way around. The strategy is based on market analysis.
8. Select a stock and a plan based on evidenced parallels.
9. Implement the plan for the stock that matches the plan for the market.

Real-World Example

The example below is an excellent example of the risk controls associated with this strategy. In this example, our correlated market analysis told us that the market had a strong probability of increasing during the week ending 1.23.09. This was a shortened week, by the way, and the same week Barack Obama was inaugurated. However, the market did not go up. Instead, it did exactly the opposite. In fact, the stock we chose, PRU, was under serious pressure all week as well.

To demonstrate the strategy, in Figure 17.1 I have also provided a chart of PRU during this timeframe. The stock triggered once, early on Tuesday, and then the position stopped by defined rule. Had we continued to hold it without that associated risk control, we would have been subject to significant losses. Instead we cut the ties fast, went to cash, and that is where we stayed all week. These risk controls are what allowed this strategy to return 60.8 percent in 2008, and they should never be relinquished. In fact, PRU was down by more than 17 percent during that week, as the chart shows. We are not in the business of assuming risks like this. Instead,

FIGURE 17.1 The trading pattern of PRU.

by limiting the downside we are able to realize gains the next time an opportunity surfaces instead. The Stock of the Week has a primary objective of risk control, and a secondary objective of opportunity.

I developed the original plan, which is depicted in Figure 17.1, on Sunday, and the bulleted entries represent the updates from the nightly analysis.

Potential Pitfalls

The main pitfall associated with this strategy is failed risk controls. Some investors might also let their emotions drive their decisions. This strategy is not for emotional investors. Instead, if emotions come into play, the strategy fails. More often than not, emotions and failed risk controls go hand in hand. For example, if we were suggesting a buy of a bellwether stock like GE, and the position stopped, some investors might choose not to respect those risk controls because of the perceived stalwart nature of GE. However, that dispels strategy altogether. We are not investing in companies; instead, we are engaging in trading strategies using the stocks as a vehicle. Those instruments are only a means to achieving our goal. We can never relinquish risk controls or we will end up holding big losses eventually. In the real-world example with PRU, we could have been sitting on 17 percent losses if we failed to nip the losses early. Losses are part of the business. They are integral to our continued success.

Strategy 3: Strategic Plan

Description of the Strategy

The Strategic Plan is an alternative to traditional buy and hold investment strategies. This is a proactive strategy focused on the Dow Jones Industrial Average, and it is not traded actively all the time. With predefined longer-term strategies in hand, the strategic plan is designed to guide investors through longer-term cycles by pinpointing major support and resistance levels in advance. That gives longer-term investors plenty of time to react appropriately.

This strategy is limited to two directly correlated market-based ETFs. Those are DDM and DXD. Cash is also an integral component. In fact, this strategy is often in cash. For example, in 2009, through April, this strategy had been in cash for 50 days, and returned 36 percent. We consider cash as an investment. It alleviates market strain over time, and it is important.

Although I expect this strategy to span one to three months normally, that is not always true. Volatile market conditions could make the duration much shorter. In any case, trading activity is usually limited to one or two days, and the rest of the time is either in DDM, DXD, or in cash. This is a long and short strategy, but because we use a short-based ETF for the down moves, we never actually short anything. This not only opens the door for use in IRAs, but it also helps eradicate the apprehension some longer-term investors have to shorting the market.

Objective of the Discipline

The objective of the Strategic Plan is to sidestep the pitfalls of buy and hold strategies while maintaining diversification at the same time. The ETFs we use are pre-diversified already. In addition, the Strategic Plan offers trading strategies that take advantage of one- to three-month market cycles. The direction can be up or down because it works both ways. The spreads are wider than our other strategies, too.

However, this strategy also requires a significant amount of patience and discipline, so it is not for everyone. The Strategic Plan is not an actively traded strategy. Our ultimate objective is wealth preservation, so cash plays an important role as well. This is an excellent strategy for business executives and retirees who are not interested in actively trading every day.

With that said, on occasion trading is required, as I will show, so do not misconstrue this for an idle process. It is not.

Tools Integral to Positive Results

- Longer-term technical analysis for the market
- General knowledge of current economic and market conditions

Rules Associated with the Strategy

- Use the Dow as a guide for this strategy.
- Limit entry levels to tests of long-term support or resistance levels.
- Tests are official when the Dow is within 25 points.
- Use conditional market orders.
- Always trade with the same dollar amount, i.e., $50K every time.
- DDM and DXD are the only two stocks traded in this strategy.
- Short either when resistance is tested or when support breaks lower.
- When we short, we buy DXD because that is a short-based ETF.
- Buy either when support is tested or when resistance breaks higher.
- When we buy, we buy DDM because that is a long market-based ETF.
- Stop losses should be 0.5 percent for every trade.
- Assuming a test of support has occurred, convert to DXD if support breaks lower as long as the market is still within 25 points of former support.
- Assuming a test of resistance, convert to DDM if resistance breaks higher as long as the market is still within 25 points of former resistance.
- Convert back again if the market moves the other way afterwards.
- Repeat this conversion process as many times as needed.
- Never initiate a trade in the middle of a channel.
- Use a 10 percent trailing profit stop.
- Expect to be in cash most of the time.

Risk Controls and Assessments

We use a stop loss of 0.5 percent for every trade in the Strategic Plan. This stop is tied to the 25-point requirement for tests of either support or resistance. For example, if we initiate a trade when the Dow is within 25 points of support, a break below that would correspond with the 0.5 percent stop we implement, because 25 Dow points equate to approximately a 0.5 percent stop in DDM and DXD.

Beware: This strategy may incur a series of 0.5 percent stops, all in a row. This could happen if the market begins to fluctuate around our predefined support or resistance levels. We can accept this as long as we also respect the trailing 10 percent profit stop associated with the plan. Over time, the gains are expected to outweigh the stops.

In addition, overnight risk also plays a role in this strategy. If we are in a position and the market moves against us, we may be faced with a larger than expected loss. If that happens, we should take the loss and move to cash. Then we should re-engage the strategy from a cash position again. If a trigger occurs, we should execute the trade according to plan. Otherwise, we should stay in cash.

Creating the Strategy

When creating the strategy for the Strategic Plan, we integrate longer-term market analysis with our conscious awareness to produce an actionable strategy. We already know that the brackish buy and hold techniques and the objectives of big brokerage firms present serious conflicts of interest. In turn, we also know that we must control our own wealth because no one will do it for us. This strategy plays an integral role in that process, and it helps us control wealth.

Follow these steps to create the Strategic Plan:

1. Conduct a technical analysis of the longer-term cycles of the market.
2. Define longer-term support and resistance levels accordingly.
3. Combine those data points into an actionable array.
4. Import the current level of the market into that array.
5. Define longer-term strategy based on the relationship of that data.
6. Remain in cash until a support or resistance level is tested.
7. When a test of either support or resistance occurs, follow the rules.

Real-World Example

The best example of the Strategic Plan came in the very beginning of 2009. We started the year in cash, but trading signals occurred in the first few days of the year. We had already identified a conversion strategy using DDM and DXD, so we were ready for tests of resistance accordingly. Those tests came early in the year. At the same time, though, we were also required to trade back and forth actively for two days, and then we sat on our hands. In the image that follows, I show the strategy before the tests of resistance occurred. This starts the explanation process.

Figure 17.2 represents our analysis prior to the beginning of 2009. Our longer-term trading array was as follows: 7400 – 9029 – 9707.

From there our actionable strategy was to trade DXD and DDM around 9029 until the market made up its mind on direction. Figure 17.3 illustrates the market action in the first few weeks of the year:

Although the market declines significantly, and our defined parameter was clearly a good one, 9029 did break higher a few times. If we assumed

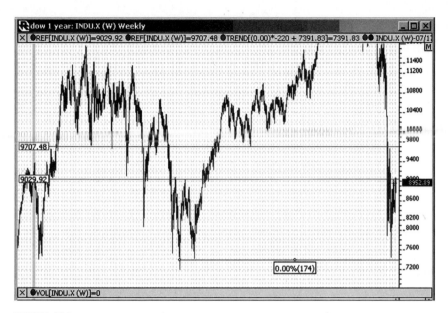

FIGURE 17.2   Dow one-year chart.

FIGURE 17.3   Dow in early 2009.

TABLE 17.2   A Typical Phase of the Strategic Plan

YTD Return: Strategic Plan = 14.08%

Enter date	ETF	Enter price	Exit price	Exit Date	Difference	% return
6-Jan	DXD	50.38	60.44	14-Jan	10.06	−19.97%
6-Jan	DDM	33.91	33.74	6-Jan	−0.17	−0.50%
6-Jan	DXD	50.4	50.1	6-Jan	−0.3	−0.60%
6-Jan	DDM	33.93	33.76	6-Jan	−0.17	−0.50%
6-Jan	DXD	50.44	50.16	6-Jan	−0.28	−0.56%
6-Jan	DDM	33.84	33.65	6-Jan	−0.19	−0.56%
5-Jan	DXD	50.55	50.23	6-Jan	−0.32	−0.63%
5-Jan	DDM	33.84	33.64	5-Jan	−0.2	−0.59%
5-Jan	DXD	50.55	50.24	5-Jan	−0.31	−0.61%
2-Jan	DDM	33.78	33.33	5-Jan	−0.45	−1.33%

that the market would increase, we would have been hurt seriously. However, we could have also been hurt if the market moved higher and we bet on the downside instead. Therefore, without hesitation we willingly converted back and forth between DDM and DXD according to our predefined rules. The results of this example are illustrated in Table 17.2.

This is a great example. In the first few days of the year, a number of trades were made. However, afterwards the position was idle and in cash after January 14. Specifically, we were active on the 5th and 6th of January, and then we held DXD (the short ETF) between January 6 and January 14. That was our money-making position, but it took a little work to achieve. This strategy is not actively traded all the time, but it does require occasional attention, as this example shows. As of February 2, 2009, this strategy was still in cash. Comparatively, though, the Dow was down 8.8 percent at that time, so this strategy had already outperformed the market by more than 23 percent in about a month. That is possible because this is a long-short strategy that allows us to produce positive results when the market declines. More important, though, the market was also erratic after January 14, but that did not matter to us at all. Anyone following this strategy was in cash and holding nice gains. Cash is critical to emotional control in this strategy. In fact, when the market is erratic, investors appreciate their cash positions and relax in the face of uncertain conditions. That is insight to the comfort zone.

As of April 17, 2009, the Strategic Plan was up 36 percent while the market was down 7.3 percent. Here are the 2009 YTD statistics:

- 30 trades
- 50 days in cash
- 36 percent YTD return

Potential Pitfalls

Because this strategy is an alternative to buy and hold strategies, many investors want to jump in and start using this with all their wealth. They do not see the pitfalls of putting it all on the line from the beginning. Because of this divergence, the emotional burdens are heavy. More often than not, investors stop adhering to the risk controls because those small stops make a difference to large sums of money. Therefore, I advise everyone to start small. This strategy is intended to be used with relatively large investments, but that can only be accomplished once an investor has confidence using the strategy with smaller dollar amounts first. The main pitfalls, therefore, are a combination of moving too fast and neglecting risk controls at the same time.

Strategy 4: Day Trading Strategy

Description of the Strategy

The Day Trading Strategy is an automated correlated market timing and stock selection tool that trades QID and QLD exclusively. This is a day trading strategy, so all trades are closed during the same trading session. Our current version focuses on two market-based ETFs instead of individual stocks. However, past versions have correlated our market timing signals with individual stock selection instead. The process of identifying correlated stocks worked just like our stock filters. Over time the disparities between the market and specific stocks made that process less effective than using these directly correlated ETFs. For market timing purposes, the choice to use the ETFs is obvious. Their correlation with the market is direct, and there is far less divergence as well.

Therefore, there are three possible positions in this strategy: cash, QID, or QLD. Using predefined Day Trading Strategy for the market and our associated rules, of course, the day trading alerts strategy is a process that reacts directly to intraday market action. We focus on the NASDAQ, but we can use the same process for the Dow or the S&P 500 if we want to, using ETFs related to those markets.

Although the strategy takes advantage of both up and down market cycles, the trades suggested in this strategy are never directly short anything. Instead, the QID position is already a short ETF by definition. Therefore, when we suggest a short position, we buy QID. That makes this risk-controlled strategy appropriate for IRAs, too. Unconsciously, this strategy also allows some of us to start appreciating the downside moves just as much as the upside moves by making the process virtually identical. Because every trade is virtually the same, shorting and buying are contiguous. That could be the most valuable part of this strategy, and it removes a built-in apprehension that many investors have to shorting stocks.

However, one more description is important. The layout of the strategy itself distills the noise that we hear every day. Therefore, the strategy allows us to revert to discipline and structure instead of intraday analysis as well.

Objective of the Discipline

The objective of this strategy is to take advantage of predefined market trend every day. We realize opportunities on the long and short side of the curve. The up moves and the down moves are virtually the same. In addition, this strategy weeds out all the noise surrounding current market conditions, and that allows traders to focus exclusively on strategy instead. By controlling risk and realizing small gains along the way, this strategy is both a wealth preservation tool and a means for opportunity. Every day ends in cash, and every day starts fresh as a result.

Tools Integral to Positive Results

- Day trading technical analysis for the market
- General knowledge of current economic and market conditions

Rules Associated with the Strategy

- Begin trading five minutes after the open.
- Stop trading five minutes before the close.
- Use the NASDAQ to guide all trading decisions.
- Trade QID and QLD exclusively.
- Use the same dollar amount for every trade, e.g., $50K per trade.
- Buy either when support is tested or when resistance breaks higher.
- Short either when resistance is tested or when support breaks lower.
- Buy signals tell us to buy QLD and to target the next level of resistance.
- Short signals tell us to buy QID and to target the next level of support.
- Use conditional market orders.
- Do not use stop losses. Instead, sell when support or resistance breaks.
- If support breaks after being tested, sell QLD immediately.
- If resistance breaks after being tested, sell QID immediately.
- Three-point rule: Tests are official when the market comes within three points of support or resistance respectively.
- Stop loss rule: If support or resistance levels break slightly after the three-point rule is satisfied, sell immediately; e.g., 0.001 is a break.

- Five-point rule: If the market moves five points above or below a parameter after balance, initiate a second trade in the direction of that break. If the direction is up, a long position is implemented (QLD). If the direction is down, a short position is implemented (QID).
- One-point rule: If the market reverses direction after establishing a second long or short according to the five-point rule, and the reversal causes the market to break that respective parameter again, close that position and revert to cash if the break is equal to or greater than one point.
- Limit stops to two stops per parameter. This would occur if a second stop occurs (one-point rule) after the five-point rule has been satisfied.
- Stop trading around that parameter after two stops occur. Refrain from trading around that parameter again until another parameter is tested first.
- Never initiate trades in the middle of a channel.
- Never hold a trade overnight.

Risk Controls and Assessments

The risk controls integrated into our alerts strategies are not traditional stop losses, but they do serve the same purpose. Instead of setting a stop loss, we know exactly where we will sell our position before we enter it. This is part of our predefined rules, and we base it on market levels. In addition, for every test of support or resistance, there are also two potential stops. The first is the stop from the initial test. Because we limit our entries to within three market points of support or resistance, our first stop should be equivalent to three market points as well. If a second stop occurs, the cause would be the five-point rule and the associated one-point break. Therefore, if we are stopped a second time, our loss should be about six market points accordingly. Therefore, because we limit the stops to two stops per test, we also limit our losses to approximately nine market points. Translated into percentage terms, a nine-point market loss is equivalent to a 1.5 percent loss in QID and QLD. This percentage may change with varying market levels. Therefore, because we use this defined strategy, we are also limiting our losses to about 1.5 percent every time two stops occur around a given parameter. That keeps losses small, and that gives us many opportunities to recover that small loss the next time tests of support or resistance levels occur.

In essence, if a stop occurs twice around a given parameter, we draw the line, and consider that parameter ineffective for the time being. We can use that parameter again, but only after another test of support or resistance has occurred first.

Given occasional volatility, our losses can fluctuate slightly, but the process is also unyielding. Therefore, we will revert to cash and control our risk no matter what, so we will always control our risk over time by rule.

Creating the Strategy

The Day Trading Strategy guides investors through structure and discipline every day. These are critical to successful investment strategy. The design is a mechanical process that allows the user to operate without questioning his or her decisions. The strategy is effective at both controlling risk and providing opportunities on a daily basis.

To create the strategy, follow these steps:

1. Conduct a technical analysis of the market to define Day Trading Strategy.
2. Define support and resistance levels accordingly.
3. Combine those data points into an actionable array.
4. Import the current level of the market into that array.
5. Define Day Trading Strategy by comparing current market levels to the data from the market analysis. That gives us current support and resistance levels and allows us to develop trading plans accordingly.
6. Remain in cash until a support or resistance level is tested.
7. When a test of either support or resistance occurs, follow the rules.

Real-World Example

In Chapter 14, I referenced a real-world example showing my actual analysis for January 20, 2009. Appropriately, I will use that same analysis again here. With follow-through, this continued example shows the results from that day. Table 17.3 reminds us of the data points first.

Figure 17.4 shows a graphical layout of the data. This graphical data helps us weed out the noise every day as well.

Figure 17.5 shows the corresponding market action on that day.

In Table 17.4 the trades that occurred and the performance that resulted from our observations are detailed. These figures came from our

TABLE 17.3   Trading Parameters

Initial intraday trading parameters for the NASDAQ exist between 1514–1530
If 1514 breaks lower, expect 1460
If 1530 breaks higher, expect 1574
Otherwise, expect 1514–1530 to hold

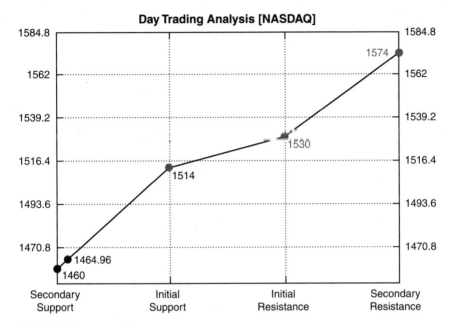

FIGURE 17.4 Actionable strategy.

FIGURE 17.5 Actual market action.

TABLE 17.4 Day Trading Strategy: Results

#	Symbol	Time	Entry Price	Time	Exit Price	% Return
4	QLD	2009-01-20 14:36:05	24.36	2009-01-20 14:47:18	24.08	−1.15
3	QLD	2009-01-20 14:18:29	24.24	2009-01-20 14:22:50	24.12	−0.50
2	QID	2009-01-20 09:44:55	58.82	2009-01-20 14:18:19	62.15	5.66
1	QLD	2009-01-20 09:35:23	26.1416	2009-01-20 09:38:24	25.88	−1.00

Automated QID—QLD [Day Trading]: Performance Records for 2009-01-20
We have already reduced these return figures by 10 percent to account for slippage.
Total (%) = 2.71
The net return was roughly 2.7 percent on four round-trip trades.

online simulator. They are in inverse chronological order. This is an actionable strategy, and these results were obtainable by following our rules on that day.

This is an excellent example of both risk controls and opportunities. More important, it also defines the structure of this strategy. In turn, that gives investors an opportunity to anticipate dynamic live trades if they integrate this strategy into their routine.

Appropriately, use the graph of market action and compare that to the data points associated with our predefined plan. Then, as we progress, observe the rules and continue to review the summary below.

The first trade hit approximately five minutes after the open. This happened when the market tested 1514. By rule, when the market is within three points of support we should buy QLD, so that is what happened. However, approximately 3 minutes later support broke, and the strategy sold QLD immediately. That was a balanced position by rule, and our first stop around support. From there we implemented the five-point rule and waited for the next leg of direction before we made our next trade. We were idle for about 6 minutes, and finally direction was determined. In this real-world example, the market turned down, as 1514 broke lower. When the market declined to 1509, a signal to short happened, and we bought QID according to the five-point rule. This was our second trade around that support parameter. Afterwards, and in line with our plan, the market continued to decline all the way to 1460. Then, when the market came within three points of 1460, we closed this first leg of the strategy and began the second.

The second leg of this strategy began when the next parameter was tested. In this case, the market tested 1460 perfectly, and a buy signal fired according to rule. When the market came within three points of 1460, we bought QLD in the same manner as we did in the first leg of the strategy. Although this was the third trade in this strategy, it was only the first trade around this parameter. Thereafter, the strategy sold QLD and went to balance because 1460 broke, too. Then, after that stop, we implemented the five-point rule as before. However, this time, instead of moving five points lower first, the market moved five points higher and threatened to head back toward 1514 again instead. That prompted a buy of QLD when the market was at 1465. Unfortunately, after struggling to move higher for 10 minutes, the market caved and turned lower. Eventually, the market broke back below 1460, and triggered the one-point rule at 1459. That was our second stop around 1460 and the strategy stopped trading around 1460 by rule.

The description above may seem complex, but it can be simplified with stacked conditional orders and automated systems.

Although the strategy is not perfect, the return of this strategy was excellent—even those stops were an integral component. The stops help us secure future gains by controlling our losses. However, stops are our integrated wealth preservation tool, too. Without them, this strategy would fall apart, even if the data points were exact. Interestingly, the data points are less important than the structure of the strategy, and the data points do not need to be exact. The data points should be close, but the driving force behind the success of this strategy is the structure, not the analysis. Therefore, respect the strategy more than the analysis and incorporate risk controls in every trade. In the end, although no one likes taking losses, this method should pay off for disciplined traders who have a combined interest of protecting wealth and realizing positive results in any market environment over time.

Potential Pitfalls

The pitfalls associated with this strategy are few, but they are critical. Most people fail because they do one of the following three things:

- Risk controls are neglected.
- Intraday analysis is conducted.
- Emotions begin to control decisions.

These are not only standalone potential hazards, but they can compound on each other as well. For example, an emotionally burdened investor might delay his prompt response to an alert. The reflexive nature of the strategy would be completely lost as a result. In turn, he might experience a larger loss, or his gains might be less than they should be.

In either case, this could cause him to stretch risk controls, or rework the strategy altogether.

Imagine taking a small loss, allowing emotions to settle in, and trying to recover that loss by changing the parameters intraday. Then imagine a second loss, and then a third. When emotions play a role, and when strategies are changed on the fly, we also relinquish risk controls and losses begin to escalate out of control. Secure that hazard now and bind it so it never affects the proactive approach we all should embrace.

We need to remain reflexive in order to make this work. That means we need to rid ourselves of the emotional burdens, limit analysis to after market hours, and respect risk controls every step of the way.

In summary, there are potential pitfalls with this strategy. However, with the use of the personal balance sheet and our other emotional conditioning tools, we all can take steps to sidestep these pitfalls and move forward proactively.

Strategy 5: Swing Trading Strategy

Description of the Strategy

The Swing Trading Strategy is an automated correlated market timing and stock selection tool that trades QID and QLD exclusively. This is a swing trading tool, so the trades are usually held for more than one day. However, they could also be closed the same day if the market moves all the way from support to resistance in one day, or vice versa.

There are three possible positions in this strategy: cash, QID, or QLD. Using a predefined swing trading strategy based on our combined market analysis, and our associated rules, the Swing Trading Strategy is a process that reacts directly to oscillating market cycles. We focus on the NASDAQ, but we could use either the Dow or the S&P 500 if we wanted to. Although the strategy takes advantage of both up and down market cycles, the trades suggested in this strategy never actually short anything. Instead, the QID position is already a short entity by definition. That makes this risk-controlled strategy appropriate for IRAs, too. Unconsciously, this strategy also allows some of us to start appreciating the downside moves just as much as the upside moves in the market. Thankfully, these opportunities are now virtually the same, with the exception of a simple symbol change, so everyone can do it.

Of equal importance, the swing trading alerts viewer also weeds out the noise surrounding the market every day. By distilling the noise, and by making every trade virtually the same, this strategy becomes one of the most effective swing trading strategies on the market. Those two qualities could be the most valuable parts of this strategy.

Objective of the Discipline

The objective of the Swing Trading Strategy is to take advantage of predefined market trends over the course of a few days. It also aims to separate the preconceived differences between long and short positions by treating them as equal opportunities. By controlling risk and realizing meaningful gains along the way, this strategy is both a wealth preservation tool and a means for opportunity. Cash is a regular investment and part of the overall objective. However, we often hold trades overnight, and that adds an additional degree of risk to this strategy. Usually, though, with added risk often comes added reward, and over time this has proven true in the swing trading strategies we offer. The final objective of this strategy is to weed out the noise that might otherwise detract from our proactive approach to the market, and it is very effective at doing that as well.

Tools Integral to Positive Results

- Swing trading technical analysis for the market
- General knowledge of current economic and market conditions

Rules Associated with the Strategy

- Begin trading five minutes after the open.
- Expect to hold all trades overnight.
- Use the NASDAQ to guide all trading decisions.
- Trade QID and QLD exclusively.
- Use the same dollar amount for every trade, e.g., $50K.
- Buy either when support is tested or when resistance breaks higher.
- Short either when resistance is tested or when support breaks lower.
- Buy signals tell us to buy QLD and target the next level of resistance.
- Short signals tell us to buy QID and target the next level of support.
- Use conditional market orders.
- Do not use stop losses. Instead, sell when support or resistance breaks.
- If support breaks after being tested, sell QLD immediately.
- If resistance breaks after being tested, sell QID immediately.
- Three-point rule: Tests are official when the market comes within three points of support or resistance respectively.
- Stop loss rule: If support or resistance levels break slightly after the three-point rule is satisfied, sell immediately; e.g., 0.001 is a break.
- Five-point rule: If the market moves five points above or below a parameter after balance, initiate a second trade in the direction of that break. If the direction is up, a long position is implemented (QLD). If the direction is down, a short position is implemented (QID).

- One-point rule: If the market reverses direction after establishing a second long or short according to the five-point rule, and the reversal causes the market to break that respective parameter again, close that position and revert to cash if the break is equal to or greater than one point.
- Limit stops to two stops per parameter. This would occur if a second stop occurs (one-point rule) after the five-point rule has been satisfied.
- Stop trading around that parameter after two stops occur. Refrain from trading around that parameter again until another parameter is tested first.
- Never initiate trades in the middle of a channel.
- If a position is open at the end of the day, hold it overnight.

Risk Controls and Assessments

The risk associated with the Swing Trading Strategy is greater than either the Day Trading or Lock and Walk Strategies because it includes overnight risk, where the other two do not. This same risk exists in the Stock of the Week Strategy as well. Although the strategies are similar, the overnight risk associated with the Swing Trading Strategy separates it from the other automated strategies mentioned here. However, at the same time, the spreads between support and resistance levels are usually wider, and that typically makes the associated reward greater over time as well.

In any case, given the added degree of risk associated with this strategy, an additional risk assessment is necessary. The possibility of a surprise overnight event could affect the results of this strategy. If that surprise has a negative impact on the overnight position, a greater than expected loss could occur. In the event that a surprise event causes the market to move aggressively in the opposite direction of our overnight trade, we should be willing to take a larger than expected loss immediately as well. We should then revert to cash and re-engage the strategy as if that stop never occurred. This is a machine-like approach and requires discipline. From there, we re-adopt the normal risk controls associated with this strategy and proceed to trade according to our already established plan.

Additionally, the risk controls integrated into our alerts strategies are not traditional stop losses, but they do serve the same purpose. Instead of setting a stop loss, we know exactly where we will sell our position before we enter it. This is part of our predefined rules. It is based on market levels, not stock prices.

Strictly, for every test of support or resistance, only two stops are allowed. The first is the stop from the initial test. Because we limit our entries to within three market points of support or resistance, our first stop should be equivalent to three market points as well. The second stop is based on the five-point rule and the associated one-point break. Therefore, if we are stopped a second time, our loss should be about six market points accordingly. Therefore, because we limit the stops to two stops per test, we also limit our losses to approximately nine market points. Translated into percentage terms, a nine-point market loss is equivalent to a 1.5 percent loss in QID and QLD. This percentage may fluctuate with varying market levels. Therefore, because we use this defined strategy, we are also limiting our losses to about 1.5 percent every time two stops occur around a given parameter. That keeps losses small, and that gives us many opportunities to recover that small loss the next time a test of support or resistance levels occurs.

In essence, if two stops occur around a given parameter, we draw the line and consider that parameter ineffective for the time being. That parameter can be used again, but only after another support or resistance level has been tested first. Given occasional volatility, our losses can fluctuate slightly, but the process is also unyielding. Therefore, we will revert to cash and control our risk no matter what, so we will always control our risk over time by rule.

Creating the Strategy

To create this strategy, follow these steps:

1. Do a technical analysis of the market to define swing trading strategy.
2. Define support and resistance levels accordingly.
3. Combine those data points into an actionable array.
4. Import the current level of the market into that array.
5. Define swing trading strategy by comparing current market levels to the data from the market analysis. That gives us current support and resistance levels and allows us to develop trading plans accordingly.
6. Remain in cash until a support or resistance level is tested.
7. When a test of either support or resistance occurs, follow the rules.

Real-World Example

We will continue to use the analysis of the example in Chapter 14 to review the results of the Swing Trading Strategy as well. In the prior chapter, we have already satisfied steps one and two. The next step is to create the array. By rule, the swing trading array is limited to the midterm and long-term data points only. With that, the array is shown in Figure 17.6.

Figure 17.7 shows the market during the trading session.

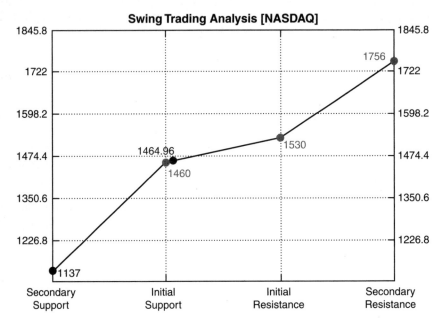

FIGURE 17.6   The actionable strategy: NASDAQ swing trading array: 1137 – 1460 – 1530 – 1756.

FIGURE 17.7   Market action.

TABLE 17.5   Results: Swing Trading

#	Symbol	Time	Entry Price	Time	Exit Price	% Return
2	QLD	2009-01-20 14:36:06	24.36	2009-01-20 14:47:19	24.08	−1.18
1	QLD	2009-01-20 14:18:30	24.24	2009-01-20 14:22:51	24.12	−0.50

Automated QID—QLD [Swing Trading]: Performance Records for 2009-01-20
These returns have been reduced by 10 [····· ·· ········ for slippage.
Total (%) = −1.85

Table 17.5 shows the actual trading results from our swing trading simulator on January 20, 2009. Compare the data points to market action to follow the records.

This is not a fabricated example. This was a losing phase of the strategy. Clearly, the market failed to test resistance at 1530, and declined all the way to test support instead. We remained in cash and waited for a test. Unfortunately, two stops occurred around support, and we reverted to cash again with a small loss in tow. From there, we waited for a new trading signal based on a test of predefined support or resistance levels. We did not adjust these parameters during the trading session. However, the parameters were adjusted slightly after market hours, and the same process continued through to the next trading session. Our process is unyielding.

Prudently, we accept small losses because they allow us to realize positive returns when our strategies perform well. In other words, we do not have to make up significant losses if we keep our losses small in the first place. Nothing will be perfect, and we all must realize that. This example is excellent, because it proves that the Swing Trading Strategy is not perfect either. Still, between January 1 and January 26 the Swing Trading Strategy had returned 12.24 percent already in 2009. For those investors who were willing to take the small losses and remain in control of their risk at all times, rewards were realized. Nevertheless, that required both patience and discipline, not one or the other.

Potential Pitfalls

The main pitfall associated with the Swing Trading Strategy is the misconception that the strategy allows investors more freedoms. Rightly observed, this strategy is less active than day trading strategies, but it also requires more attention. For example, if a position is open, we may be holding it for one or two days in a row. However, we must monitor that position at all times, because it is open. That is where the added attention comes in. Even though the position is static during that time, we still must monitor it for change. We can never walk away from an open trade. Otherwise, we relinquish our control. Swing trading strategies require us to watch closely, but most investors do not understand this, and instead think they do not need to pay attention when positions are open, when the opposite is true.

In addition, investors who understand the discipline might have an apprehension to stop losses. This might be especially true if individual evaluations of economic cycles and market conditions are part of the process. For example, if the Swing Trading strategy calls for a short and the economic conditions are poor, some traders might choose to avoid taking a stop with the expectation that the market will eventually turn down. That often results in serious losses. Because we are not smarter than the market, this is a losing proposition for a number of reasons, and none is more important than incurring larger losses. We should never relinquish our risk controls. In addition, though, over time our personal journals should help us free our minds from the clutter, which could cause this pitfall, too. Therefore, the personal journal plays an integral role in sidestepping this potential pitfall over time.

Finally, trading in the middle of a channel seems to be a major potential pitfall as well. Because the trading channels are wide, and because the strategy is in cash quite often, some traders become anxious. Instead, they should be patient. We do not trade in the middle of a channel. If we do, we completely lose control of our risk, and that is unacceptable. Instead of considering cash in the traditional sense, I encourage investors to treat cash as an investment instead. It is one of the three potential investment vehicles in this strategy, and it is important.

In summary, there are potential pitfalls with this strategy. However, with the use of the personal balance sheet and personal journal, we all can take steps to sidestep these pitfalls and engage proactive strategies appropriately.

Strategy 6: Lock and Walk Strategy

Description of the Strategy

The Lock and Walk Strategy is very similar to the Day Trading Strategy, but it is limited to one hour per day. I recommend the first hour of the day because that is usually the best hour to trade, but this strategy can be used to trade for one hour at any point during the trading session as well. This is excellent in conjunction with our automated system. If lock and walk is used in the first hour of the day, the results of the Day Trading Strategy and the Lock and Walk Strategy should be the same. In any case, after the hour is finished, the Lock and Walk Strategy reverts to cash. The Lock and Walk

Strategy will revert to cash if the strategy has earned 1 to 2 percent within the hour as well. The strategy "locks" when gains of 1 to 2 percent have been made, or when one hour of trading is complete. The percentage lock is at the discretion of the user.

The Lock and Walk Strategy is an automated correlated market timing and stock selection tool that trades QID and QLD exclusively. This is a day trading strategy, so all trades are closed during the same trading session. For market timing purposes, the choice to use ETFs is obvious. They are directly correlated with the market, and there is far less thought required to process the trade.

There are three positions in this strategy: cash, QID, or QLD. Using predefined market strategy and our associated rules, the Lock and Walk Strategy is a process that reacts directly to intraday market action. We focus on the NASDAQ, but the same process can be used for the Dow or the S&P 500 as well. Although the strategy takes advantage of both up and down market cycles, the trades suggested in this strategy are never actually short anything. Instead, the QID position is already a short by definition. Therefore, when we short, we actually buy QID. That makes this risk-controlled strategy appropriate for IRAs, too. Unconsciously, this strategy also allows some of us to start appreciating the downside moves just as much as the upside moves by distilling the noise we hear every day as well. Because every trade is virtually the same, shorting and buying are contiguous. That is a valuable part of this strategy, because it removes a built-in apprehension that many investors have about shorting stocks.

Objective of the Discipline

The objective of the Lock and Walk Strategy is to give everyone the opportunity to take advantage of proactive strategies every day without sacrificing time or lifestyle. Most people do not want to sit by a computer all day and trade, and this strategy gives everyone the opportunity to walk away. Typically, many people can address the market during the first hour of the day, or for an hour at certain times throughout the day. For those who can, the Lock and Walk Strategy is an excellent resource. Not only does this strategy incorporate all the risk controls of our proactive Day Trading Strategy, but it also gives us the freedom to control our wealth, realize opportunity, and still live a normal life.

Because activity is limited to one hour a day, we are also free from any emotional burden that might otherwise be associated with watching the market. This strategy is in cash usually. That is one of the main objectives. However, this is the epitome of a tortoise versus the hare investment strategy. It is slow and steady. The objective is to realize small gains regularly, with the expectation that those gains will build over time if we respect risk controls along the way. Reasonably, opportunities exist on both the long and short side of the curve so we must appreciate them both.

Tools Integral to Positive Results

- Day trading technical analysis for the market
- General knowledge of current economic and market conditions

Rules Associated with the Strategy (Assuming First Hour)

- Begin trading five minutes after the open.
- Do not trade for more than one hour.
- Use the NASDAQ to guide all trading decisions.
- Trade QID and QLD exclusively.
- Use the same dollar amount for every trade, e.g., $50K per trade.
- Buy either when support is tested or when resistance breaks higher.
- Short either when resistance is tested or when support breaks lower.
- Buy signals tell us to buy QLD and target the next levels of resistance.
- Short signals tell us to buy QID and target the next level of support.
- Use conditional market orders.
- Do not use stop losses. Instead, sell when support or resistance breaks.
- If support breaks after being tested, sell QLD immediately.
- If resistance breaks after being tested, sell QID immediately.
- Three-point rule: Tests are official when the market comes within three points of support or resistance respectively.
- Balance rule: If support or resistance levels break slightly after the three-point rule is satisfied, sell immediately; e.g., 0.001 is a break.
- Five-point rule: If the market moves five points above or below a parameter after balance, initiate a second trade in the direction of that break. If the direction is up, a long position is implemented (QLD). If the direction is down, a short position is implemented (QID).
- One-point rule: If the market reverses direction after establishing a second long or short according to the five-point rule, and the reversal causes the market to break that respective parameter again, close that position and revert to cash if the break is equal to or greater than one point.
- Limit stops to two stops per parameter. This would occur if a second stop occurs after the five-point rule has been satisfied.
- Stop trading around that parameter after two stops occur. Refrain from trading around that parameter again until another parameter is tested first.

- Never initiate trades in the middle of a channel.
- Never close trades in the middle of a channel.
- Only trade when support or resistance levels are tested.
- Lock in gains when they are between 1 and 2 percent.
- Never hold a trade overnight.
- Do not trade after one hour.
- Consider our automated system for this process.

Risk Controls and Assessments

The risk controls integrated into our alerts strategies are not traditional stop losses, but they do serve the same purpose. Instead of setting a stop loss, we know where we will sell our position before we enter it. This is part of our predefined rules, and it is based on the percentage gain from the trade. In addition, for every test of support or resistance, there are also two potential stops. The first is the stop from the initial test. Because we limit our entries to within three market points, our first stop should be equivalent to three market points as well. The second stop is based on the five-point rule and the associated one-point break. Therefore, if we are stopped a second time, our loss should be about six market points accordingly. Therefore, because we limit the stops to two stops per test, we also limit our losses to approximately nine market points each time. Translated into percentage terms, a nine-point market loss is equivalent to a 1.5 percent loss in QID and QLD. This percentage is subject to varying market levels. Therefore, because we use this defined strategy, we are also limiting our losses to about 1.5 percent every time two stops occur around a given parameter as well. That keeps our losses small, and that gives us many opportunities to recover that small loss the next time a test of support or resistance occurs again.

In essence, if a trade stops twice around a given parameter, we draw the line and consider that parameter ineffective for the time being. That parameter can be used again, but only after another support or resistance level has been tested first. Given occasional volatility, our losses can fluctuate slightly, but the process is also unyielding. Therefore, we will revert to cash and control our risk no matter what, and then we will begin again from a cash position.

Creating the Strategy

The Lock and Walk Strategy guides investors through structure and discipline every day. These are critical to successful proactive strategies. The design is a mechanical process, which allows the user to operate without questioning her decisions. The strategy is effective at both controlling risk and providing opportunities on a daily basis.

To create this strategy, follow these steps:

1. Conduct a technical analysis of the market to define day trading strategy.
2. Define support and resistance levels accordingly.
3. Combine those data points into an actionable array.
4. Import the current level of the market into that array.
5. Define day trading strategy by comparing current market levels to the data from the market analysis. That gives us current support and resistance levels and allows us to develop trading plans accordingly.
6. Remain in cash until a support or resistance level is tested.
7. When a test of either support or resistance occurs, follow the rules.

Real-World Example

In Chapter 14 I referenced a real-world example. That example showed my actual analysis for January 20, 2009. Appropriately, I will use that same analysis again here. With follow-through, this continued example shows the results of that analysis. Table 17.6 below reminds us of those data points.

Figure 17.8 shows the graphical layout of the strategy.

Figure 17.9 shows the market action on January 20, 2009.

Compare the data to the market action, and incorporate the one-hour lock and walk rule. Table 17.7 shows the results of this strategy taken directly from our automated simulation.

Because these trades were made in the first hour of the day, the results were exactly in line with the Day Trading Strategy in the first hour for the same day. By rule, the strategy began five minutes after the open, and the first trade was made when the market tested 1514. When the market is within three points of support, we should buy QLD, so that is what happened. However, approximately 3 minutes later support broke, and the strategy sold QLD immediately. That was a balanced position by rule, and our first stop around support. From there the five-point rule was implemented, and we waited for direction to be established before we made our next trade. We were idle for about 6 minutes, and finally direction was determined.

TABLE 17.6   The Parameters

Initial intraday trading parameters for the NASDAQ exist between 1514–1530
If 1514 breaks lower, expect 1460
If 1530 breaks higher, expect 1574
Otherwise, expect 1514–1530 to hold

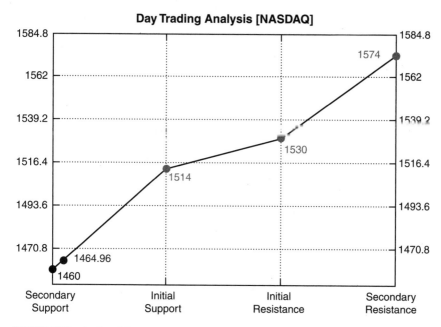

FIGURE 17.8 Actionable strategy.

FIGURE 17.9 Market action.

TABLE 17.7   Results

#	Symbol	Time	Entry Price	Time	Exit Price	% Return
1	QID	2009-01-20 09:44:56	58.82	2009-01-20 09:57:10	60.05	2.09
2	QLD	2009-01-20 09:35:23	26.1598	2009-01-20 09:38:25	25.882	−1.06

Automated QID—QLD [Lock and Walk Trading]: Performance Records for 2009-01-20
We have already reduced these returns by 10 percent to account for slippage.
Total (%) = 0.93

In this real-world example, the market turned down, as 1514 broke lower. When the market declined to 1509, a short was signaled, and we bought QID according to the five-point rule. This was our second trade around that support parameter. Afterwards, and in line with Lock and Walk Strategy, we waited for either a 1 to 2 percent gain, or the first hour to conclude.

Appropriately, this strategy closed the trade when the trade was in the money by 1 percent. Clearly, the trade returned slightly less than 1 percent, but it was close. We cannot expect it to be perfect, but we can expect it to be close to exact. The entire process took less than one-half hour. From there, the strategy was closed, and traders should have walked away from the market for the rest of the day with money in their pocket, and very little concern about market direction. This is what the comfort zone is all about.

Potential Pitfalls

Reasonably, the main pitfalls with this strategy surround the timing of the strategy. The first pitfall surfaces when the strategy closes well before the first hour is finished. Many traders think that they are free to trade after that because the first hour is not yet complete, but that is not what the Lock and Walk Strategy suggests. Instead, it tells us to lock in gains when we have them, and then walk away. The hour is simply a limitation, and it should not be considered anything else.

Next, because this strategy assumes both small gains and small losses over time, it does not move fast. Some investors want a faster-paced strategy. Lock and Walk does not provide that action. Instead, the Lock and Walk Strategy is a slow, monotonous, and disciplined strategy, and it is not exciting. Although some investors initially embrace this, it can become a serious pitfall. When investors start to want more, they start to relinquish risk controls and that causes them to lose more, too. With that understood, consider the following tortoise versus the hare analogy: Assume 0.5 percent returns per day on average, and assume 200 trading days per year. Who would win the race?

The Lock and Walk Strategy is my favorite, but it requires conditioning from the beginning, and all the way through. However, if investors are able to start on the right track, as I have outlined already, they are more able to embrace the patient strides that this forward strategy facilitates.

Pick a Strategy That Fits

In Chapter 14, I warned that challenges lie ahead. Before the simplicity of the system I use became clear, we needed to understand the derivation of my models. Those hurdles have now been overcome, and the tough part is behind us. We understand the purpose of conditioning, and we have learned the rules behind all of our proven strategies. One or more of these may be appropriate for everyone. Most readers probably know the ones that are best suited for their personal objectives already, so it is time to move forward. From here, the process becomes easy again. In the next chapter we will discuss the automated version of our rule-based trading system. With that, nothing could be easier.

Summary

Below is a summary of the most important topics in this chapter:

- The strategies should be understood.
- Objectives should be matched to strategy.
- Execution techniques should be considered.

CHAPTER 18

Automated Trading

Professional traders have probably been nodding their heads in agreement, as they worked through the last chapter, but normal investors may feel somewhat overwhelmed. Still, both have the same recurring hurdle to overcome. The strategies sound good on paper, but discipline is hard to maintain, and eventually all investors are prone to mistakes. This is human nature, and it was the focus of the building blocks outlined at the beginning. In this chapter, my objective is to offer a solution that all investors can use.

The actionable strategies detailed in the last chapter are sound, and they allow everyone to move toward the comfort zone. However, they are not easy to use without unyielding discipline. That is, unless investors incorporate the automated rule-based trading system we have developed. It incorporates the discipline for you, and that makes it easy. This tool not only allows professional traders to incorporate a mandate of structure and discipline into their efforts, but it allows normal investors to incorporate the same risk controls and realize the same opportunities that disciplined professional traders do, without sacrificing time or lifestyle. We call it Trend Tracker.

Trend Tracker

Trend Tracker watches the market, knows the rules, and executes trades automatically. Although it can be modified based on the end user's assessment of current market trends, Trend Tracker is designed to make sure everyone maintains structure and discipline at all times. We no longer need to place orders to buy or sell because Trend Tracker does the trading for us. We just need to define market channels and activate the strategy.

Without question, proactive strategies are the best way of managing wealth and realizing opportunity over time. Of course, they require structure, and yes, they require discipline. Reasonably, with a little effort

271

everyone can satisfy those without the use of an automated system. However, for anyone who moves forward with these strategies, I expect the discipline to be integral to the application of the strategy every time. This includes those people who do not think they have the time to use proper risk controls especially, because they are more prone to mistakes.

For those who do not think they have the time to follow the structure outlined in the last chapter, Trend Tracker is a resource. I began as a retail stockbroker, serving the investing public, so I am familiar with the objectives of working people. I was never on an institutional trading desk, I never managed billions of dollars, and I never left anyone out of my consideration because I was unbiased. From the beginning, I concentrated on the individual investor, and I remain that way today.

Obviously, disciplined professional traders and investors can adopt these strategies without using automated systems, but normal investors may not be able to. As a result, my primary concern lies with those people who believe that these strategies are unattainable. However, I am not discounting the need for structure and discipline for professionals at all. In fact, professional traders and investors need to adhere to these disciplines, too. The strategies are useful, they are effective, and they should be followed. Doing so will not only help keep everyone on the right side of the curve when the market moves, but it will also protect wealth if the market starts to move against us.

Therein lies my concern. For those people who believe that they are not capable of using these strategies because of associated time restrictions, a major problem presents itself. Almost surely, with this limitation investors will revert to the brackish investment strategies imposed by mutual funds, money managers, and large brokerage firms. If that is true, their monies will be at the mercy of the market again, and risks will remain uncontrolled just like they were in 2007, 2008, and probably for the early part of 2009. If the current environment were part of an upward-sloping cycle in the Investment Rate, I would have less concern with the buy and hold philosophy. However, it is not, and for now buy and hold is dead.

Because the Investment Rate is declining, buy and hold strategies will fail, as I have shown. Of course, there will be periods where position trades work, but those will be short lived, and the positions will need to be sold proactively. That is akin to our Strategic Plan. In fact, my return to parity analysis suggests that position trades will probably work after the first quarter of 2009. However, the Investment Rate tells us to expect that increase to be short lived, too, and to expect aggressive declines again afterwards. As of April 2009, I was expecting the downturn to become aggressive again early in 2010. That, in turn, tells us to expect buy and hold strategies to stay dead.

Therefore, the landscape has changed, and normal investors cannot sit idle anymore. For those investors who believe that they can allow themselves to be exposed to the market without risk controls, they have another think coming.

Although I realize my overall goal is impossible to achieve, I still shoot for the stars. Everything I do has the same underlying objective. I want to protect everyone from the weakness that lies ahead. Therefore, with normal people in mind, I produced Trend Tracker. I will discuss this with detail, but I must first discuss the strategies themselves and explain whom they are good for. In that way, we will all know how to proceed.

Integrating the Strategy

Reasonably, some people will be attracted to more than one of the strategies I offer. For example, an investor might like the Lock and Walk Strategy and the Strategic Plan at the same time. This is not only acceptable, but I encourage it. Clearly, no one can manage all six of the strategies at once, but using one or two of them at the same time is reasonable. However, when we do this, we must also separate the strategies to avoid confusion. In this example, a separate account should be open for the Lock and Walk Strategy and another for the Strategic Plan. Call your discount broker, and request new accounts. Rename one account the Lock and Walk Strategy, for example, and the other appropriately, too. Afterwards, you will have three accounts. One will be your original account, and the other two are separated for each strategy. From there, fund each of the strategy accounts with a reasonable amount and move forward with implementation. Reevaluate the performance of these accounts every quarter and reallocate funds then, if needed.

In addition, do not move money back and forth between the strategy accounts haphazardly. More important, do not begin to mix strategies either. These strategies are not effective if they are used sporadically. In fact, I have found that many users have failed because they have done exactly that. Some people move from one strategy to another because one of the strategies is performing better than another at a given time. However, like it is with annual mutual fund performance ratios, returns ebb and flow within these strategies, too. Specifically, and this is usually true, when one strategy significantly outperforms another, that strategy usually lags behind again for a short while afterwards. If investors try to follow the best performing strategy every time, losses could occur that otherwise should not exist. For example, if an investor moved from the Swing Trading Strategy to the Day Trading Strategy because the Day Trading Strategy seemed to be performing better, he or she may also miss a great run in the Swing Trading Strategy if it started to perform well. Not only that, if he or she took small losses in the

Swing Trading Strategy first, and then moved to the Day Trading Strategy in line with this example, he or she could incur additional losses there as well. Therefore, this investor could incur overall losses even though each of these strategies had positive returns over the same period. Therefore, I recommend that everyone stick to his or her chosen strategy, until at least he or she systematically re-evaluates those strategies every quarter.

When these accounts are established, do not commingle strategies. Separate accounts are required for a reason. However, this also presents one last hurdle before we can integrate any of them. We need to know which strategies are best suited for us.

For those investors and traders who have a significant amount of time on their hands, virtually any of these strategies are viable. However, I also have a general guideline that might prove meaningful over time. Specifically, for those investors who are able to watch their computers on a regular basis, but who do not want to trade multiple times every day, the Swing Trading Strategy may be the best choice. The Swing Trading Strategy requires everyone to monitor his or her computer, but it is not as active. This applies to the Stock of the Week, too. Other investors have some time to watch the market, but they do not have all day. Interestingly, retirees fit this demographic. They may also have quite a bit of time on their hands, but very few retirees I know are willing to sit by their computer all day and trade. Most of them want to live a life, and therefore the Lock and Walk Strategy is a logical alternative. This strategy can be used at any time during the day, but I recommend the first hour of trading because it is the best hour. Anyone on the West Coast may also embrace this strategy. The market opens at 6:30 AM on the West Coast, and therefore traders could take advantage of market cycles during the first hour and still make it to work on time. However, some investors want more action than that. That is where the day trading strategies come in. The day trading strategies trade the market actively all day long, but only at specific market levels. For those investors who have the time to watch the market, and who are interested in trading actively, the day trading strategies work wonderfully. While controlling risk along the way, they provide opportunities all day long. The day trading strategies include both the Featured Stock of the Day and the Day Trading Strategy itself. Interestingly, in the past, when we evaluated active trading strategies, we never thought about longer-term investments. That has changed. Our proactive Strategic Plan is an alternative to traditional buy and hold investment strategies. It is proactive, it includes risk controls, and it provides opportunities. Most often it is in cash, but sometimes active trades are needed. Therefore, longer-term positions that have been allocated to this alternative strategy also engage active policies on occasion. This is thinking outside of the box. Some of these strategies will be more attractive than others. Most of the time, these decisions will be based on time restrictions. In fact, time restrictions could negate the application of these strategies altogether and dissolve the wealth preservation attributes they incorporate. That is where Trend Tracker comes in.

Using Trend Tracker to Manage Wealth

Trend Tracker overcomes a few important hurdles, the most important of which is time constraints. These are essential to both professional traders and traditional investors, so the system is effective at managing risk and providing opportunities for all. In addition, it allows normal people, who might not otherwise have time, the opportunity to use risk-controlled rule-based trading strategies. This sets Trend Tracker apart from all other systems. It is a strategy tool, and it is automated, but it can also be controlled. The example provided in Figure 18.1 focuses on the Day Trading and Lock and Walk Strategies described in Chapter 17, and those are based on the NASDAQ. However, Trend Tracker can be used to trade the S&P, Dow, Russell, Oil, Gold, Copper, or individual stocks as well. This is a disciplined strategy, and it can work with all markets. When time constraints are present, or when discipline is lacking, Trend Tracker comes to the rescue.

Admittedly, Trend Tracker does not need to be used; it just makes the process much easier. Alternatively, the same result can be achieved using manual execution or stacked conditional orders. Consult your broker for details on how to program your trading platform for conditional orders. The rules in Chapter 17 describe how stacked conditional orders should be organized.

Benefits of Trend Tracker

Below is a list of the benefits of using Trend Tracker:

- Analysis is limited to market analysis—nothing else.
- Market-based support and resistance are all that matters.
- The rules are built into the application—it is intelligent.
- Discipline is unyielding. The system follows the rules.
- Execution is much faster because orders are electronic.
- Market makers never see the order until it is time to trade.
- It is automated, but it can be controlled.
- Users can deactivate, modify parameters, and reactivate the system at any time. This is especially useful for professional traders who want to adjust data points throughout the day.

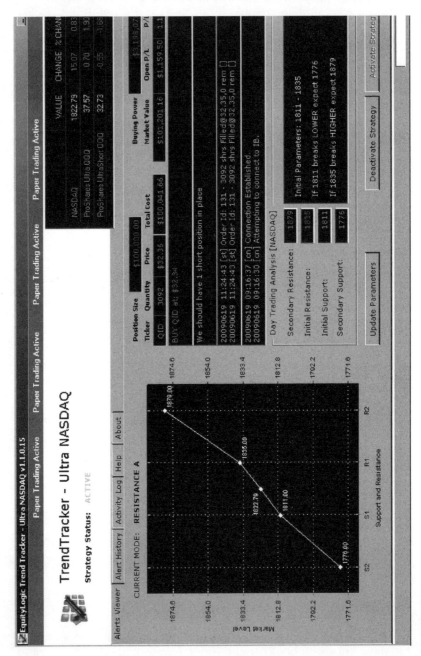

FIGURE 18.1 Trend Tracker.

- Never place an order again. Trend Tracker places all the orders for you, automatically, according to our proven and predefined rules.
- Emotions are controlled—you do not have the option of making avoidable mistakes because Trend Tracker will not let you.
- The business of rule-based trading has been simplified.
- Users can activate Trend Tracker and let the system run while they do other things.
- Users no longer have to watch the market all day to control risk and make money.
- The system provides opportunity regardless of market direction.
- Every day ends in cash.
- Although this is a day trading strategy, trades are few in number. On average, 3.8 trades occur every day.
- This is a tortoise versus hare strategy, and it does not swing for the fences. Instead, risk control is the first priority, and realizing opportunities comes naturally afterwards.

The Process of Using Trend Tracker

Below is the process needed to use Trend Tracker:

- Determine support and resistance levels for the market.
- Populate Trend Tracker with that data and activate the system.
- The program does it all from there.
- For Lock and Walk, deactivate when you have 1 to 2 percent in gains.
- Monitor the system from time to time.

Keep It Simple with Trend Tracker

With Trend Tracker, our responsibilities become focused and finite. All we need to do is pick support and resistance levels that are close to accurate. We do not need to be perfect; we just need to be close. Part of the service I provide is a daily analysis of market-based support and resistance levels, but my data does not need to be used to make Trend Tracker work. Trend Tracker will function with data derived by you or by third parties. For investors who want to control risk and realize opportunities regardless of market direction, and keep it simple at the same time, Trend Tracker is the logical option. Details can be found at www.stocktradersdaily.com

Summary

Below is a summary of the most important topics in this chapter:

- Discipline is always required.
- Most people have trouble following proven strategies over time.
- Rule-based strategies require adherence to discipline.
- Trend Tracker ensures that rules will be followed.
- It is automated, fully integrated, and results driven.
- Paper trading is available to test the system.

CHAPTER 19

A Greater Depression

When I began to discuss my opinion that buy and hold will be dead for a handful of years, and when I supported that with references to the Investment Rate, I was reserved. As of 2009, the third major down period in U.S. history had just begun, and the severity of the weakness that lies ahead will surprise many.

This chapter will be short, but not sweet. I am going to offer a forecast for the next handful of years, and that forecast will concern many people. Until now, my advice provided investors with tools used to embrace opportunities when they surfaced. Clearly, risk controls and wealth preservation play important roles. However, with this continued observation, I expect wealth preservation to take on a new meaning.

Clearly, this book is riddled with references to the Investment Rate. The reason is important. The Investment Rate is the most accurate leading longer-term stock market and economic indicator ever developed. It has been a leading indicator to all of the major economic cycles in U.S. history. That includes both the up cycles and the down cycles, respectively. Currently, the Investment Rate suggests that the market is in a down cycle, and risks are high as a result.

Even though I always look on the bright side, I cannot ignore risk. However, even in the face of risk, the cup can still be half full. Opportunities will always present themselves if we are in a position to take advantage of them. This will be true in both up and down markets. My job is to make sure we are in position accordingly. I have already done that with the strategies I have introduced. However, the proactive strategies I have offered in this book also bring with them subtle warnings.

Debt Is a Major Issue

In my opinion, based on the findings of the Investment Rate and the correlated policies enacted by the U.S. government, I believe that a Greater

Depression lies ahead. If nothing more, I am sure that demand ratios decline until 2023. That comes from the Investment Rate, as I have already shown. This has only occurred twice. Prolonged declines in the demand for investments have only happened during the Great Depression and the Stagflation period of the 1970s. Now, they are happening again.

Naturally, an oscillation cycle has already begun. Liquidity levels have already peaked, and risks are high. Clearly, this is not your everyday market decline. In fact, although I expect an interim bounce in 2009, such a move looked questionable as I wrote this in January. However, even if a bounceback occurs, as my Return to Parity analysis suggests, the significant weakness the Investment Rate warns us about will not go away. The duration of the Investment Rate is much longer than the interim period in my return to parity analysis, and it will prevail, in my opinion.

From there, we should draw another prudent observation. The current economic environment is similar to the Great Depression and the Stagflation period of the 1970s because, each time, correlated declining demand ratios existed. Uniquely, though, the current down period in the Investment Rate, which began in 2007, does not turn higher again until 2023. That makes this down period longer than the first two, and that is eye opening.

However, the length of the down period does not necessarily influence the severity of the associated declines. We can compare the Stagflation period of the 1970s to the Great Depression to see this more clearly. Although the market was volatile, and growth was nonexistent for 10 years, the declines during Stagflation were less than they were during the Great Depression. The recovery process was faster, too. When I introduced the Investment Rate in the first chapter and then detailed it in the second, I explained this relationship.

Unmistakably, government policy had a direct impact on the severity of these major down periods. The poor economic policies that were in place prior to the Great Depression made the associated declines severe. Conversely, the second major down period was tamer, as a direct result of better policies. Reasonably, the next step is to evaluate current policies to determine how they will play a role going forward.

When making evaluations like these, we should always look at debt levels first. Survival of the fittest often means the lean and nimble ones, so this evaluation is prudent in the face of contemporary Darwinism. Unfortunately, the U.S. government is anything but lean. In fact, if we added the debt from Social Security and Medicare to the balance sheet today, debt would be four to five times GDP. Not only is that excessive, but that is fiscally irresponsible. In addition, in the face of that massive burden, bailouts and spending packages have made this even worse. Unfortunately, those can do nothing to stop the declining demand ratios offered by the

Investment Rate. They will not prevent this natural cycle of economic weakness from coming.

Instead, the trillions of dollars spent by the U.S. government to stabilize the economy will only increase the burden on U.S. taxpayers. Eventually, the government will need to stop printing money, and taxpayers will have to pay the piper. Most likely, this will be the direct result of foreign pressures. As it is, I expect the value of the dollar to decline substantially in the years that immediately follow, and I expect foreign nations to begin to worry about the same thing very soon as well.

Eventually, the U.S. government will have two options. Either it will cut spending and start paying off the debt, or it will raise taxes to do the same. Reasonably, a combination of both could happen as well. In addition, we must consider a final option as well. Although I do not expect this to happen, the government could also continue to print money, continue to issue debt, and drive itself further toward a bankrupt state instead. Reasonably, I expect deficit spending to curtail and I expect prudent fiscal policies to prevail accordingly, but I always look at the risks, too.

However, as noble as prudent fiscal policies sound, they will have a negative effect on our economy. The third major down period has just begun, and it lasts for 16 years. Therefore, the decisions to raise taxes or cut spending, or both, will come while the economy continues to get weaker. That will stifle any attempt at recovery. In my opinion, there is no way around this. I already know that declining demand ratios are inevitable. With that, I am assuming that the government will also adopt sound fiscal policies soon. If that happens, the additional burden those policy decisions have on our economy will send it reeling, and that will create a circulatory depressionary environment that could trump anything we have seen before.

Interestingly, my debate does not even include the exodus of money that will result from retiring baby boomers. I referenced Medicare and Social Security earlier, which are byproducts of this, but the exodus of investment funds from the economy will also play a major role in its deterioration. Unfortunately, this is not a measurable event. The withdrawal of funds takes place over time, for sporadic reasons, and until age $70^1/_2$, it is not even required. Therefore, measuring withdrawal is almost impossible to do accurately. As a result, although we know it is coming, the withdrawal of funds by baby boomers can only be an added burden, and not a measured event.

In any regard, the best-case scenario, given past reference, is a stagflation-like economic environment. However, with the current situation at hand, the U.S. economy is not set up for the best case. In fact, not only do I expect the economic landscape to be similar to the Great Depression in the years that follow, but I also expect it to be worse.

What if I Am Wrong?

Admittedly, my outlook is both subjective and aggressive. However, it is not far out of line either. With that, I find an alternative discussion important. Specifically, what if I am wrong?

Reasonably, I have produced proactive trading strategies that can protect our wealth in the face of this major down period. These also provide opportunities when the market moves higher. Anyone who sees the associated risks offered by the Investment Rate can also see that a transition to proactive strategies is logical from a risk–reward standpoint. If the market goes down as I have suggested, the proactive strategies I have outlined will look good.

However, let us assume that I am wrong. As we did in the early chapters, let's play devil's advocate again for a minute. If I am wrong, and if demand ratios reverse higher for years instead, if government debt levels start coming in fast, and if the economy starts surging ahead again in the face of higher taxes, what should we do then? If that happens, some people may think that the steps to protect wealth in the face of the third major down period in U.S. history might seem futile if it never actually happened. I will save the arguments made in the brackish investor chapter for individual reference, but I have a simple answer. Nothing changes. The strategies should be implemented anyway, because they protect wealth now and work in both up and down markets over time. Our strategies work when the market goes up, too, so the arguments from advocates of buy and hold, who usually have an interest in generating fees, become moot.

I encounter these doubts every day, and I should. Although the Investment Rate is a proven theory, it is not widely accepted yet. Only with repetition do investors truly understand it. However, it also does not immediately influence our proactive trading decisions. Instead, it encourages people to consider proactive trading strategies to manage risk, and that is critical.

Therefore, because our proactive strategies work in both up and down markets, they can work if I am wrong about the next handful of years, too. Our proactive strategies will have the ability to perform even if the Greater Depression I foresee never happens. That negates the argument completely. These strategies will work either way, so start using them now. If the economy crumbles in the next four to five years as I expect, I want to be able to buy the extreme trough when it comes, and the only way to do that is to protect ourselves at all times right now.

Although my outlook may be the gloomiest outlook imaginable, the cup is still half full. When Erin Burnett called me the Grim Reaper on CNBC in the middle of 2007, I told her the same thing. The cup is always half full.

Even though the slope is down, we can embrace this opportunity and use it to secure our wealth and incorporate proactive strategies. That simple resolution could make all the difference. I stand firm in my outlook, but I also know the market surprises us on occasion. The strategies I have offered here will allow us to take advantage of those surprises and go with the flow of the market regardless of direction. That makes right or wrong, in relation to a Greater Depression, an irrelevant point. With structure and discipline, we can make money in any market environment, during depressions and boom periods, while preserving our wealth every step of the way. My proactive strategies make this possible. Then, my automated systems make it easy, too. When it comes to the risks associated with the market, it just does not matter to us anymore. The market could move up, or down, and it would be all the same to us.

Although this is profound even in normal environments, if you can embrace opportunity now, in the face of a Greater Depression, you are also ready to enter the comfort zone. You have stared risk in the face, and you have beaten it back with a stick. You have jumped hurdles, you have implemented risk controls, and volatility is now your friend. If that is you, then you are ready to move forward.

In fact, you are probably already there.

Summary

Below is a summary of the most important topics in this chapter:

- A Greater Depression is possible.
- The Investment Rate proves this.
- Managing risk is required.
- Proactive strategies are the best approach.
- Proactive strategies work in up or down markets.
- If the market goes up instead, our tools will still be effective.
- Either way, we remain in control.

Welcome to the Comfort Zone

This is the place where our investments are no longer heavy burdens on our lifestyle. Economic news no longer matters. Corporate scandals do not affect us, and the pundits who vocalize their opinions every day do not have the opportunity to influence our decisions. This is a place free from market-related stress, without emotional restraint or heavy ties. We are not dependent on the economy, the market, money managers, or financial institutions to secure our wealth.

Instead, we are independent, confident, and sure. Our direction is clear, but it is never one-sided. We are nimble, we have competitive advantages, and other people might consider us aggressive. However, we control our risk at all times, so if aggressive means risk control, that is what we are. We have conditioning models, building blocks, tools, and strategies we use every day, and we use them well. These further our objective. This is a lifestyle.

The comfort zone allows us to walk down the street with a smile on our face where others might not be able to. The burdens levied on the world are not a concern of ours anymore. Objectively, we can pursue the things in life that are truly important to us again, without worry.

The dynamic nature of the comfort zone welcomes everyone. We can all hope for the best, hope for recovery, and hope that a Greater Depression will never happen, but we are not affected by the outcome. Cash is an integral component. With restraint, we stare risk in the eyes, and beat it back with confidence. Because we are always in control, the market no longer controls us.

This is a beautiful place, yet something many people believe is unachievable, but it is. The tools and strategies outlined in this book allow this to become a reality for everyone. The risk controls and opportunities of proactive strategies are no longer limited to disciplined professional traders. Everyone can use them, with unyielding structure and discipline.

This is only possible because we Keep It Simple all the time. From ending every day in cash, to only trading two market-based ETFs in our automated system, the comfort zone is a reality because our models work.

Welcome to the Comfort Zone.

A Real-Life Example

Although the comfort zone includes specific benefits for unique individuals, it also contains global significance for everyone. Every day I come across people from various walks of life. Some are professional traders, hedge fund managers, and advisors. I have explained theory to partners from Goldman Sachs, I've offered strategy to the Senate Joint Economic Committee, I've sent economic forecasts to Dianne Feinstein, and I have approached Governor Arnold Schwarzenegger with a simple policy that could potentially save the state of California from related economic disaster during the credit crisis of 2008. However, more often than not, my clients are individual investors who are directly influenced by the decisions of these institutions instead.

Although institutional clients and governments are important, doctors, lawyers, business owners, and executives from all industries and all walks of life are the heart and soul of my business. I believe I have touched many of them by showing them the path to the comfort zone. For some, I have changed their lives forever, and I hope to be able to offer my strategies to like individuals eternally. My strategies are timeless, and they apply to everyone, regardless of age or net worth. They can be used in any market environment, regardless of economic conditions, to protect wealth and provide opportunity at all times. For corporations and governments, these same tools apply to policy decisions and forecasting models. However, resoundingly, individual investors are much more nimble, and they are able to embrace my efforts with comparative ease.

This is a real-life example.

Tom was a logistical engineer for Anheuser-Busch. His company had recently received a buyout offer from InBev, and his stock options were going through the roof. Tom had worked as a financial advisor in the past, so he was aware that his situation was unique. In June 2008, as the global economy was reeling on the heels of one of the worst financial disasters of all time, most people were more concerned with declining stock prices than with skyrocketing vested options.

Initially, this would appear to be the one of the best-case scenarios for anyone subject to economic or market-related risk during a recession. However, in the face of his financial windfall came additional challenges. Job security was a major concern. Tom wondered if he could find a position anywhere in the world like the one he had with Anheuser-Busch. Anheuser-Busch is renowned for being an extremely good company to work for. The company was and still is a model for U.S. business practices. It treats its employees well, and it rewards hard work. Unfortunately, those important fundamental principles have arguably been replaced by an earnings-driven approach to rewarding employees instead. In our modern economy, employees can't just work hard and remain productive; they need to be better than the next guy or they may be overlooked by management when promotions are being considered. Competition is healthy, but so is employee loyalty, and that comes from recognizing hard work. Assuming attrition, finding another company as good as BUD would be tough, if not impossible.

Given the economic conditions in 2008, Tom began to branch out. Tom started to reconsider his past career for opportunities. He had wealth now, something he did not have before, and maybe, he thought, the financial industry was a good place for him to secure that wealth. In turn, he believed he could leverage the tools available through big brokerage firms and make his money work for him, too. He began to search the Internet for answers to his developing questions, and his research led him to me. We immediately began to discuss his goals, his objectives, and his concerns.

Having been a financial advisor in the past, and an educated investor, Tom recognized that major financial institutions had an underlying incentive that kept them from making proactive decisions to protect the wealth of their clients. I presented this reality at the onset of our relationship, and he agreed resoundingly. Arguably, big brokerage firms are focused first on making money for themselves. Corporate reactions to shifts in the economy and the market were prehistoric in 2008 anyway, and because client accounts came second to company accounts, investors were becoming concerned as they watched their accounts decline with the market. At the same time, as concerns escalated, brokers continued to recommend that investors stay the course, just like they had been for years. This time, though, it wasn't working. These troubles were becoming more and more obvious every day. Tom was witnessing these tribulations firsthand, and he was concerned just like everyone else. Soon he realized that his initial interest in the financial industry may be a little off track, and he began to reconsider his approach.

Most brokerage firms, mutual funds, and money managers get paid to have their clients invested at all times. In upward-sloping market cycles that is an acceptable strategy for passive investors, given the right money manager, of course. However, in downward-sloping market cycles these strategies don't work at all. Buy and hold strategies fail during major down periods. These failed strategies cause significant declines in client portfolios as a result, and the recovery process is usually extensive. Absolutely, the underlying incentives that exist within all major brokerage firms will eventually cause significant declines in customer accounts because they do not move to cash in down markets, and they do not protect client wealth.

But this also assumes the performance of those accounts remains in relative parity to the market, too. Interestingly, most managed accounts don't keep pace with the market anyway. More often than not, managed accounts underperform the market over time, so direct investments in the market are more prudent almost always. Statistically, 95 percent of all mutual funds underperform the market over 10 years. This data is readily available through various research reports online, and I encourage everyone to research the subject independently. Specific to 2008, according to Morningstar, the average diversified stock fund was down 40 percent, while the S&P 500 was down 38 percent and the Dow Jones Industrial Average was down 34 percent. Clearly, the average fund underperformed the market in 2008, and that was typical of relative underperformance.

But this disparity does not need to have limited assessment. We can also prove this with current examples at any point in time, and that might be more meaningful to new investments. The next time anyone evaluates the performance of a money manager or a mutual fund, compare the performance of that fund to the market itself, not to the peer group of the fund, or its Lipper Average. Instead, compare the return of the fund, net of fees, to the S&P 500 or the Dow. The results will almost surely be enlightening for a number of reasons. First, managers and fund families often tout strong relative performance ratios but fail to compare those to market returns. They do this to entice investments into the fund; with a little study, that itself should be enlightening.

Next, the subtraction of management fees from a portfolio's return plays a very important role in compound performance ratios of those investments over time. This is true even though they may seem to have relatively small influences on current year statistics. For example, in 2008 the 2 percent differential didn't seem like much, but over a 10-year timeframe that disparity becomes significant. Indeed, management fees impact long-term performance returns in a meaningful way, and the brackish nature of the portfolios does as well. Each of these, and other factors, detract from performance ratios over time. Please take the time to research these important facts; everyone will find the revelation surprising. Most managers don't keep pace with the market itself, and they fail to protect wealth at the same time.

With that understood, if historical relative performance remains constant and the market declines, most managed accounts will experience a greater decline than the decline of the market. Where's the risk control? Where are the proactive steps to protect client wealth?

Risk controls don't exist because brokerage firms only get paid when assets are invested. Corporate profits come first, so the firm needs to collect fees no matter what happens to the market or client accounts. Brokerage firms keep everyone invested in spite of the risks that lie ahead in the economy; they do this so they continue to make money. Sure, clients are important, but corporate policy ensures that the firm makes money no matter what happens to individual accounts or the market, and that's a red flag for individual investors who trust large brokerage firms to protect their wealth.

Most people have accepted this, but they don't do anything about it. Other people don't recognize it at all. But some, a select few, have identified this hazard and have taken proactive steps to shelter themselves from the resulting pitfalls that are bound to arise. Tom was one of the select few.

After realizing this drawback, Tom and I discussed the current state of the economy, and I introduced him to the Investment Rate. This helped me enlighten him about the future direction of the market and the future health of the economy. That was more important than current conditions, of course. The Investment Rate is a proprietary Longer-Term Economic and Stock Market Analysis that I created to help my clients understand future economic and stock market cycles in advance. This is one of the tools provided through Reuters to its institutional clients, and it is included in this book. The Investment Rate warned him that additional market declines were likely in the years ahead, and that influenced his decision.

The Investment Rate, in my opinion, is the most accurate leading longer-term stock market and economic indicator ever developed. It proves longer-term economic and market-related cycles, and it tells us what to expect from both the economy and the stock market well into the future. The Investment Rate has already accurately predicted major market cycles since 1900, and it predicts those cycles going forward as well. This allows us to prepare for the conditions that lie ahead in advance. 2007 was a great example; the Investment Rate identified the peak in liquidity years before it happened, and that is what inspired our early warning signs. Reuters offers this to its institutional clients for a hefty fee, but I gave Tom a copy to help him make his potentially life-changing decision with confidence.

After Tom read the information, the Investment Rate changed his thinking, and it helped him realize just how out of touch major brokerage firms are from time to time. 2008 was one of those times. With his new-found knowledge, his decision to look for something else was clear. He realized that the brackish investing strategies advised by big brokers were rife with losing probability, and his choice to adopt a proactive approach based on the findings of the Investment Rate helped him achieve a 40 percent return for himself and the accounts he managed through the third quarter of 2008. The market was down approximately 23 percent from its highs during this same time. Any other managed accounts that were keeping up with the market during that decline were down significantly, too, as we would expect. Clearly, a more constructive path was chosen, proactive strategies were adopted, and it resulted in a positive return when the market was in free fall. I am happy to say, his decision was influenced by the Investment Rate.

The Investment Rate has already changed the lives of countless individuals by helping them protect their wealth from pitfalls like the one mentioned above, and I expect it will continue to do so forever. It can have a sweeping influence on personal wealth ratios over time, and it can be used by everyone. The Investment Rate can help formulate sound economic policy on a government level, and it can help corporate America plan effectively for the future as well.

More important to me, though, it can also help individual investors secure their wealth regardless of the sometimes selfish decisions made within the capitalistic structure of our economy. The Investment Rate will play an integral part in this book, and I believe it will change the way we approach our investments from this point forward.

About the Author

Thomas H. Kee, Jr., is president and CEO of Stock Traders Daily. He is the founder of the Investment Rate, which is the most accurate leading longer-term economic and stock market indicator ever developed. He is also the architect of the ATAP Program and Trend Tracker, which are automated trading systems that allow everyday people to manage risk. He is a specialist in technical analysis and an advocate of proactive trading. Rule-based trading is not an option; it is a requirement, in his opinion. This opinion comes from the findings of the Investment Rate, and what it tells us about the future. He has developed automated trading programs designed for both professional and nonprofessional traders. These risk-controlled programs help normal people, who do not have the time to manage risk, control their risk, and realize opportunities regardless of market direction. This provides structure in an environment prone to pitfalls. That is required given the economic environment that lies ahead. His research can be found through Reuters and Yahoo Finance, he writes a monthly column for MarketWatch, and he is regularly featured in *Barron's* and other financial media channels.

In 2007, Mr. Kee was nicknamed the Grim Reaper by Erin Burnett on CNBC. His prediction of a Greater Depression in July 2007 brought chuckles to an audience who believed the economy would never stop accelerating. At the time, his warnings fell on deaf ears. Now, people are listening. *Buy and Hold Is Dead* says it all . . .

Index